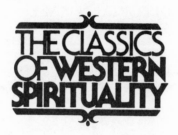

Early
Anabaptist Spirituality
SELECTED WRITINGS

TRANSLATED, EDITED AND WITH AN INTRODUCTION BY
DANIEL LIECHTY

PREFACE BY
HANS J. HILLERBRAND

PAULIST PRESS
NEW YORK • MAHWAH

Cover art: The two cover portraits were painted by Oliver Wendell Schenk, who is also referred to as Tom Schenk. The more prominent portrait is that of Menno Simons, who, as Dr. Liechty points out, "assumed leadership among Dutch Anabaptists at a crisis point in their history, following the Münsterite debacle." The Simons portrait is used courtesy of Eastern Mennonite Seminary. The less prominent portrait is that of Felix Mantz, a Swiss Anabaptist, who was the movement's first martyr. The Mantz portrait is used courtesy of Laurelville Mennonite Church Center. It is one of a number of paintings commissioned by Laurelville to communicate an image and the spirit of the church's founding fathers.

BX
4931.2
.E37
1994

Library of Congress Cataloging-in-Publication Data

Early Anabaptist spirituality: selected writings/translated,
    edited, and introduced by Daniel Liechty.
        p.   cm.—(Classics of Western spirituality)
    Translation of writing from their original Dutch and German.
    Includes bibliographical references and index.
    ISBN 0-8091-0466-0 (cloth)—ISBN 0-8091-3475-6 (pbk.)
        1. Spiritual life—Anabaptists.   2. Anabaptists—Doctrines.
    I. Liechty, Daniel, 1954-   . II. Series.
    BX4931.2.E37   1994
    284′.3—dc20   94-8478
                                                                                    CIP

Published by Paulist Press
997 Macarthur Boulevard
Mahwah, New Jersey 07430

Printed and bound in the
United States of America

Contents

Foreword xi

Preface xv

Introduction 1

PART I: SWISS ANABAPTISM

Felix Mantz
"Letter from Prison"(1527) 18

Balthasar Hubmaier
"Concerning Freedom of the Will" (1527) 21
"A Short Meditation on the Lord's Prayer" (1526) 38

Ausbund
"Six Anabaptist Hymns" (1526–1529) 41

PART II: SOUTH GERMAN
AND AUSTRIAN ANABAPTISM

Hans Hut
"On the Mystery of Baptism" (1526) 64

Leonhard Schiemer
"Three Kinds of Grace" (1527) 83
"Three Kinds of Baptism" (1527) 95

CONTENTS

Hans Schlaffer
"Instruction on Beginning a True Christian Life" (1527) 99
"Two Prayers" (1527) 109

Hans Denck
"Concerning True Love" (1527) 112
"Divine Order" (1527) 121

PART III: HUTTERIAN ANABAPTISM

Peter Walpot
"True Yieldedness and the Christian Community of Goods"
(1577) 138

PART IV: DUTCH ANABAPTISM

Dirk Philips
"Concerning the New Birth and the New Creature" (1556) .. 200
"Concerning Spiritual Restitution" (1559) 218

Menno Simons
"A Meditation on the Twenty-fifth Psalm" (1537) 248

Appendix 273

Notes 280

Select Bibliography 296

Index 301

Editor and Translator of this Volume
DANIEL LIECHTY studied philosophy at the University of Budapest and received a Dr.theol. degree from the University of Vienna, specializing in religious radicalism in the sixteenth century. He also holds a D.Min. degree in Pastoral Counseling from the Graduate Theological Foundation in Donaldson, IN. His books include *Andreas Fischer and the Sabbatarian Anabaptists* (Herald Press, 1988), *Theology in Postliberal Perspective* (Trinity/SCM, 1990) and *Sabbatarianism in the Sixteenth Century* (Andrews University Press, 1993). He is presently an independent scholar living in Philadelphia and is a member of the Germantown Mennonite Church.

Author of the Preface
HANS J. HILLERBRAND holds a Ph.D. from Erlangen University in Germany. He has taught at various universities, including Union Theological Seminary, City University of New York, Southern Methodist University and Duke, where since 1988 he has chaired the Department of Religion. His scholarly publications include *Bibliography of Anabaptism* (1992), *The World of the Reformation* (1976) and numerous articles on facets of the radical Reformation of the sixteenth century. He is currently serving as editor-in-chief of the *Encyclopedia of the Reformation*.

Foreword

Anabaptism began in the third decade of the sixteenth century as part of the events which established Protestantism, along with the Eastern and Roman confessions, as the third force in European Christianity. Beside the Lutheran, Reformed and, later, the Anglican aspects of Protestantism, historians also recognize what has been called the "Radical Reformation."[1] This Radical Reformation consisted of such diverse elements that it can be misleading to place them all under one unified heading. Yet very basic features of commonality can be discerned. The most distinguishing characteristic of the Radical Reformation was the fact that, whether by conscious design or by turn of circumstance, the radical reformers attempted to carry out their program without the aid of secular power and authority.

For more than a millennium, all people in Christian Europe were assumed to be Christians by right of birth. This was symbolized by the practice of the baptism of infants. Although during the centuries of medieval history there was a continuing struggle between sacred and secular authorities for ascendancy and dominion, the basic legitimacy of the synthesis of church and state was firmly established.

The unity of Western Christendom as an international entity was challenged during the sixteenth century by the rise of Protestantism. Although originally stemming from a religious urge to reform the Christian Church as a whole, Protestant leaders very soon attached their reforming efforts to the rising independent territorial princes, who offered support and protection within their territorial realms. This led to a situation in which Lutheran, Reformed and Roman Catholics alike, whenever they could control it, tried to use all the apparatus of secular government to enforce confessional monopoly within a given region.[2] The constant fighting received only a temporary lull when it was decided at the Peace of Augsburg (1555) that each prince or prince-bishop would decide the confession which would be practiced within his domain (*cuius regio, eius religio*—whose region, his religion.) But even this decision did not quell the ideal of a total, Christian Europe united under one religious confession. It took the devastation of the Thirty Years War in the seventeenth century and the emergence of the Enlightenment in the eighteenth century before the ideal of freedom of religion and conscience could be planted in the European mind.[3]

In our time we speak of Europe and North America as moving into a "post-Christian" era, an era in which Christianity takes its place as one among many of the world's religions and tolerance of people who have chosen other options has become both a religious and civic ideal. Yet the formative roots of the major Christian confessions were established during the time when the coextension of citizenship and church membership was simply assumed, and this is reflected to one degree or another in the theology and ethics of the major confessions.[4] It is in this situation that a renewed interest in and appreciation of the witness and testimony of the Radical Reformation is growing far beyond the boundaries of those few sects and denominations, principally the Mennonites and Amish, Hutterians, Unitarians and Schwenkfelders, which are the direct historical descendants of that movement. For we find in this testimony the struggle to articulate and foster a Christian spirituality which was independent of the political establishment. In many ways, the spirituality of the Reformation radicals must strike us as alien and foreign, for they lived in a time and a society quite different from our own.[5] Yet if the same Spirit speaks its voice in each generation, acquaintance with the genius of their spirituality may offer a deeper perception of the life of the spirit to those in the post-Christian era.

The Radical Reformation, as has been said, consisted of very diverse elements among which the differences are at times more pronounced than the similarities. Harvard historian George Huntston Williams has produced the most synoptic view of the Radical Reformation.[6] On the basis of the history and theology of the many leaders and groups within the Radical Reformation, Williams perceived three major streams, distinct yet interrelated. These he labeled as Anabaptists, Spiritualists and Evangelical Rationalists. Williams remained very aware that these groupings overlapped at the edges, and that certain individuals may have moved from one category to another during their lifetime; still, these basic designations continue to have interpretive value.[7]

FOREWORD

This collection of writings focuses on early Anabaptist spirituality. It is limited to the writings of those people who are recognized leaders in Anabaptist groups. Therefore, it is not intended to be a comprehensive representation of the spirituality of the Radical Reformation. It is further limited to the early period of Anabaptism, which, with one exception, is taken to mean the first generation. The exception is the inclusion of a writing by Peter Walpot, representing the Hutterian current.[8] But even though Walpot wrote during the second generation of Anabaptism, the treatise selected is thought to capture the unique Hutterian spirituality of the earlier years.

Following the lead of recent scholarship, the selections have been grouped around the three "fountainheads" of Anabaptism—the Swiss, South German/Austrian and Dutch movements.[9] The Hutterites grew out of South German/Austrian Anabaptism and share the unique spiritual characteristics of that movement. But because the Hutterians continued the economic communalism of that movement into a full-fledged form of Christian communism in which private property was specifically eschewed, and thus pronouncedly distinguished themselves among that movement, a special section was reserved for a writing illustrative of their unique spiritual character.

Anabaptism was, for the most part, a lay movement and did not stress the development of lengthy theological writings.[10] The writings which have survived are, for the most part, letters from prison, hymns, and short, ad hoc writings of immediate and practical concerns. In the selection process, I tried to choose those writings which give clear expression to Anabaptist spirituality and which are of sufficient length to avoid a feeling of choppiness for the modern reader. I further tried to select those writings which have not yet been translated into English so that the selections are weighted toward the South German/Austrian materials; this is a reflection of the above concerns and the fact that my own scholarly work has been in that area of Anabaptism and these are the materials with which I am most acquainted.

In translating these documents, I have been unabashedly guided by the concerns of the modern reader. While remaining true to the sources, I have attempted to render these texts in the most easily comprehensible language possible. This has meant many value judgments on my part concerning the places a sentence might be broken, the choice of adjectives, the rendering of set phrases, and so on. Sensitivity to modern concerns has also led me, wherever possible, to use inclusive language, which at times could only be accomplished by changing the singular into plural and repeating a noun where a pronoun appears in the text.[11] Modern readers are asked to read these selections in the inclusive spirit in which they were written as there was no way to mute this language completely in the text. Another area of concern was to eliminate as much as possible any elements of antijudaism, which, to the great misfortune of humankind, was implicit if not explicit in the Christian consciousness of the sixteenth century.[12] In summary, I have labored to produce a readable text, a text which addresses the modern person in his or her spiritual quest, rather than the definitive scholarly edition.

I would like to thank the German Verein für Reformationsgeschichte for permission to use its source publications in the series *Quellen zur Geschichte der Täufer* as the basis for the translation of many of these selections. A special word of thanks is due to Mr. Lloyd Zieger, curator of the Mennonite Archives in Lancaster, Pennsylvania, and to Mr. Joseph Springer, curator of the Mennonite Historical Library in Goshen, Indiana, for providing photocopies of rare Dutch editions of the writings of Menno Simons and Dirk Philips, respectively. I would like also to thank the Zondervan Publishing Company for my use of the New International Version for most of the biblical quotations. Finally, I would like to thank the series editor, Prof. Bernard McGinn as well as Paulist Press, for their continued efforts in publishing *The Classics of Western Spirituality* series.

Preface

The Anabaptists were the major fringe group of the Protestant Reformation of the sixteenth century.[1] And since history tends not only to be made but also written by the winners, the fact that the Anabaptists proved to be the losers in that momentous turbulence (nowhere did they gain formal recognition) has meant that their history and thought have been ignored, if not derided. The achievements of the theological giants of the age, the likes of Martin Luther and John Calvin, understandably overshadowed everything else. Every epithet from the arsenal of centuries of theological polemic was thrown against the Anabaptists—Donatists; heretics; seditionists; blasphemers; rebaptizers. The Anabaptists of the Reformation, in short, had a bad press, not only in their own time, but in subsequent centuries as well, including much of our own. A little over a generation ago a distinguished American Reformation scholar called the Anabaptists the "Bolsheviks" of the Reformation, at the time the worst epithet imaginable.[2] Of course, the Anabaptists also had their supporters who were deeply attracted to the Anabaptist vision of the Christian faith, but they were few and far between. The historical legacy is thus a bit depressing, especially since the Anabaptists assuredly were a vital expression of religious reform and theological insight in the spectrum of the Reformation. Indeed, theirs was an abiding legacy—the formulation of a distinctive expression of Christian thought and spirituality, often called "the free church" ideal.

Anabaptist conventicles made their appearance in the mid–1520s in Switzerland and a number of theses have been advanced in Reformation scholarship as to the rationale for their emergence. Earlier in this century the forceful argument was made by the Mennonite scholar Harold S. Bender (an argument since then echoed by John H. Yoder) that the rise of Anabaptism must be understood as the effort to bring the work of religious and theological reform begun by Martin Luther and Huldrych Zwingli to its consistent biblical conclusion—which is very much the way the early Anabaptists themselves saw it.[3] Martin Luther had broken the pope's pitcher, observed one Anabaptist, but had kept the pieces in his hands. More recently the thesis of a convergence of social concerns and theological issues has been advanced, specifically the import of the social and political compromises of Zwingli over the tithe and the anticlericalism of Conrad Grebel and his Zürich circle.[4] So understood, the beginnings of Anabaptism must be placed into the matrix of that broad understanding of the nature of reform which sought to encompass not merely religion but also society, and which culminated in the German Peasants War of 1524/25.

Whatever the insight of these recent analyses, there is something to be said for locating the emergence of Anabaptist sentiment simply in the ambiguities of theological reform as it related to the issue of baptism. None other than Martin Luther had posited, in his 1520 tract *On the Babylonian Captivity of the Church*, that a sacrament needed the recipient's faith to be effective. His focus had been on the eucharist, and he had coyly slid over the tricky question how, with this new definition of a sacrament, the traditional affirmation of the baptism of infants could be retained. Luther's pronouncement had put the matter on the agenda, albeit not in an urgent way, since there was no dispute between the reformers and the Catholic Church over baptism. It is easy to see, however, that it was going to be only a matter of time before this unresolved theological issue was going to be pursued. This is precisely what happened, when the so-called Zwickau Prophets appeared in Wittenberg late in 1521, and Andreas Carlstadt and Thomas Müntzer took to the pen a short while later. Luther had raised questions which needed to be explored.

This issue of infant baptism was a hornet's nest or, to say it differently, the implications went far beyond the theological matter of baptizing or not baptizing infants. Surrendering the centuries-old tradition in Europe of baptizing every infant entailed the possibility that some, upon growing to adulthood, might not wish so to be baptized. While the sources are not altogether clear if the Zürich Anabaptists early on entertained this possibility, or merely envisioned the continuation of the status quo with the baptismal age simply delayed by a dozen or so years, it soon became an obvious consequence. Thereby, the identity of civic and religious community, as it had prevailed since the Emperor Constantine in the fourth century, was disrupted. The intense hostility of both the ecclesiastical and the political establishment against the Anabaptists finds its explanation right here. They were unable to envision society in any different way.

Since Anabaptism did not enjoy the support of any political authority, it turned into an underground movement, officially not merely not recognized, but in fact persecuted. In a time when book censorship was writ large, the Anabaptists could not use established printers who were so conveniently at the disposal of the mainstream reformers. To be sure, there were exceptions, such as the Augsburg printer Philip Ulhart whose publishing program included not only mainstream Reformation materials but also a number of "radical" tracts, including those of Hans Hut. But most of the Anabaptist writings were printed clandestinely, by underground printers whose identity in many instances remains uncertain to this day.

The fact that Anabaptism was an underground movement also meant something else: it possessed no cohesive organizational structure. Anabaptist congregations came into being in a clandestine fashion: a peripatetic preacher made converts in a town or village and then moved on, leaving the fledgling throng of believers with the barest of outlines of the faith to which they had committed themselves, constantly under the threat of governmental suppression. Under those circumstances, the lack of theological sophistication as well as organizational cohesiveness becomes understandable.[5]

Two generations ago, when the sixteenth-century Anabaptists first began to be rehabilitated, scholars emphasized that the founding group—Georg Blaurock, Conrad Grebel, Felix Mantz and others in Zürich—was comprised of singularly well-educated men, Erasmian humanists most of them. While this was true, the Anabaptist movement as a whole was singularly bereft of theological expertise. In fact, even among the early Anabaptists, only Balthasar Hubmaier can be said to have been a trained theologian, conversant with the broad range of the scholastic theological tradition. The others, including the authors of the present anthology, were laymen, even though some had been priests (the best example is Menno Simons), while others, such as Dirk Philips and Hans Schiemer, had been Franciscan monks. There are numerous sophisticated Anabaptist theological writings, for example, those of the leader of second generation South German Anabaptism, Pilgram Marpeck, not to mention Menno Simons who consolidated the disparate North German and Dutch Anabaptist groupings after the debacle of the Anabaptist "Kingdom" in Münster in 1534/35.

This observation is not meant to denigrate the theological substance of the Anabaptist movement. After all, neither John Calvin nor Philipp Melanchthon qualified as trained theologians in that sense either. The significance of the observation is that this Anabaptist leadership formed a piety and theology that drew on sources other than those relevant for most Protestant theologians. Anabaptist spirituality, certainly that of the rank and file, was oriented by the Bible with directness and immediacy.

A word must be said about the special sources that enrich our understanding of Anabaptist theology and spirituality. In addition to theological tracts and devotional writings, there is an abundance of source materials of a quite different sort—letters, court records and proceedings, interrogation records. Some of these sources come from the Anabaptists themselves, some from their opponents. Collectively, they offer a rich picture of the spirituality of the rank and file of the movement, not merely of the theologians' sense of it. Most of these sources are oral sources, that is, they had their origin in the spoken word, and thus they convey an immediacy and a rhetoric which make them especially valuable for the appropriation of Anabaptist spirituality. While one must be careful not to use these sources all-too-freely for delineating Anabaptist thought, except in its basic outline, one encounters a spontaneous, immediate expression of the meaning of the Christian faith from the lips of the rank and file of the movement. In other words, these distinctively Anabaptist sources provide insight into the piety of the entire movement, something that is far more difficult to obtain in any of the mainstream Reformation movements. The court records of Anabaptists interrogated by theologians frequently depict the theologian easily (and condescendingly) out-arguing the Anabaptist. Many such telling instances are recorded in *The Martyrs Mirror*. For example, an inquisitorial interrogator arrogantly asked an Anabaptist prisoner: "What do you understand about St. John's Apocalypse? At what university did you study? At the loom, I suppose. For I understand that you were nothing but a poor weaver and chandler before you went about preaching and rebaptizing. . . . I have attended the university at Louvain, and studied divinity so long, yet I do not understand anything at all about St. John's Apocalypse."[6] The point here made by *The Martyrs Mirror* is important for understanding Anabaptist spirituality. That it is given to the poor in spirit as well as in body, and not to the learned and famous, to understand the mysteries of God's kingdom is a constant theme in Anabaptist writings. Perhaps the Anabaptists made virtue out of vice since they themselves were precisely the ones they so described, but they also spoke to a rich historical tradition which long preceded them, which the major reformers had initially appropriated, but then dismissed. The authors of numerous testimonials in *The Martyrs Mirror* are simple women and men, housewives, blacksmiths—all claiming the power to interpret scripture.

Anabaptism emerged as a conscious and explicit challenge to the understanding of Christianity, and therefore of reform, on the part of the reformers, notably Martin Luther and Huldrych Zwingli. The charge was that these reformers had not fully returned the church to its apostolic origins and faith; too much popery had remained, and it was only among the Anabaptists that the true apostolic faith was restored. The Anabaptists charged that the mainstream reformers were thieves and murderers, shepherds who led their sheep astray, wolves who attacked the flock.[7] The indictments levied by the Anabaptists were severe and categorical, though occasionally a modest semblance of appreciation for the courage of the likes of Luther and Zwingli remained.

The bill of particulars against Zwingli and Luther (no less than against the Catholic Church) was the important point of departure for Anabaptist spirituality: the Christian faith was utterly serious business. Thus the first (and perhaps foremost) characteristic of the Anabaptist understanding of the Christian faith lies in the categorical opposition to the notion that the civic community and the Christian church were identical and that all people were in fact "Christians." The Anabaptists argued that not all people were serious about their religion, even as not all were fully committed to the way of Christ. The Anabaptists pursued a serious Christianity, uncompromising, categorical, earnest.

To the reformers' rejoinder that they, too, saw the Christian faith as serious, the Anabaptists responded that there was no visible evidence among them to substantiate their contention. For the Anabaptists commitment entailed an externally visible change of life. An "amendment of life" had to take place.

The Anabaptists agreed with the mainstream Reformation emphasis on justification by grace alone (although among the rank and file of the Anabaptists that notion was not always clearly expressed).[8] Hans Schlaffer, one of the early Anabaptist theologians, wrote "we are all by nature an evil tree and are incapable of doing good." The Anabaptists were well aware of Protestant soteriology, and yet tried to find a way—as did John Calvin in mainstream sixteenth-century Protestantism—for the truly sanctified, both public and private. Wrote Hans Denck: "To the chosen one there is no temptation so high that resistance and victory would not be still stronger." Their main concern was on something else. It was the "Christian life," and most of their doctrinal and devotional writings focused on that. What that meant was the conviction that divine forgiveness entailed a radical transformation of one's whole being from which followed personal holiness "without spot or wrinkles." Indeed, some Anabaptists, such as Melchior Hoffman, held that the true believer no longer sinned and attained, therefore, a state of perfection.

This vision of the sanctified life of the individual believer had its corollary in the vision of the community of believers. The church was also to be "without spot or wrinkles." Menno Simons wrote that the church was to be pure now and not a mixture of true and false believers until the day of judgment when God would separate them.

The Anabaptists took Jesus' hard sayings, essentially those found in his Sermon on the Mount, as the touchstone for his true disciples. Anabaptist spirituality was thus a spirituality of doing. Aside from the mandate of personal holiness, the Anabaptists were also greatly concerned about the relationship of the true believer to the social and political order. Following the mandates of the Sermon on the Mount, the Anabaptists refused to swear oaths, refused to occupy governmental offices, and refused military service. It is not that the Anabaptists sought to impose their point of view on to society at large—so as to make pacifism the public policy of a realm. They were quite content to be passive in this respect: much as centuries before Francis of Assisi had not sought to impose his vision of the moral precepts of Jesus on the Catholic Church at large, but was content to be allowed by the church to live his life according to his understanding of the precepts of the gospel.

Anabaptist baptism became the outward sign of the commitment to an amendment of life. The person baptized voluntarily chose to make a confession of his or her Christian commitment and thereupon received baptism.

The Anabaptists experienced immense suffering at the hands of the governmental and ecclesiastical authorities. Their story—well into the seventeenth century—was a story of suffering and martyrdom, and both the foremost Anabaptist hymnal, the *Ausbund*, and the several Anabaptist martyrologies, depict the Christian life as one of suffering and persecution. Indeed, the reality was gruesome. According to one estimate some 2500 Anabaptist were executed in the Low Countries in the sixteenth century.[9] The most famous Anabaptist martyrology, Tieleman Jansz van Braght's *The Martyrs Mirror*, which alongside the writings of Menno Simons was the most frequently reprinted Anabaptist book over the past four centuries, lists some 803 Anabaptist martyrs, mainly from North Germany and Holland. There can be no doubt but that the sixteenth-century Anabaptists supplied victims of the executioner's sword in greater numbers than any other ecclesiastical faction of the time.

This ubiquitous experience, where the Anabaptists lived constantly under the threat of being called upon to suffer for the sake of their faith, had a profound bearing on the formation of Anabaptist spirituality. For the Anabaptists found that their experiences were presaged in scripture, that both scripture and history showed that the true witnesses to God had always been persecuted. As far as the Anabaptists were concerned, their suffering was not accidental, even as the persecution which they endured was anything but a serendipitous happenstance. "The history of the world has been from the very beginning a conflict between God and Satan, the children of light and the children of darkness." There have been, so *The Martyrs Mirror* noted, "two different peoples, two different congregations and churches, the one from God and from heaven, the other of Satan and the earth." What emerges from this picture is that in this conflict suffering is the inevitable fate of the children of light. Wrote Hans Schlaffer: "The whole Scripture speaks only of suffering," and then again: "Whoever does not suffer with Christ will not share the inheritance." In this regard, too, Jesus became the exemplar to be followed. He "testified to us of a model with his life that we also should love and act as he."

Anabaptist spirituality is thus a spirituality of suffering, of a quiet acceptance of the vicissitudes of life. This theme is first sounded in the letter of Conrad Grebel to Thomas Müntzer in which Müntzer's espousal of force to realize the gospel was rejected. It was also vividly expressed in the genre of Anabaptist writings which soon made its appearance—the records of Anabaptist martyrdom. Beginning with the record of the trial of Michael Sattler in 1527 and ending in the middle of the seventeenth century with *The Martyrs Mirror*, an endless stream of such testimonies issued forth. These testimonies had in common the notion that Christian commitment is unthinkable without suffering, indeed, the highest sacrifice of one's life. Aptly, the genius of Anabaptism has been identified as the vision of discipleship or the theology of martyrdom.[10]

Theology and experience undoubtedly intertwined. In other words, the Anabaptists' experience was such that they were forced to relate to the suffering motifs in scripture. By the middle of the seventeenth century (and the time of *The Martyrs Mirror*) this theology of martyrdom had reached its nadir—and this, of course, precisely at a time when external persecution was beginning to cease and the Mennonites (as they were now called) were on the verge of attaining civic respectability.

And what about the lasting legacy? A generation ago Robert Friedmann, then an indefatigable scholar of Anabaptism, propounded the thesis of the connection between Reformation Anabaptism and seventeenth-century German Pietism.[11] As in all instances where causalities between broad historical movements are posited, the case for the connection between Anabaptists and Pietism is not easy to sustain. But there are discernible connections. Anabaptist writings from the early part of the sixteenth century—including two from the present collection—were reprinted in the seventeenth century to accommodate Pietistic sentiment. Even if one acknowledges that the German Pietists appropriated widely from the rich devotional literature of early modern Christianity, the spiritual kinship between the two movements is unmistakable. Both shared a common spirituality. Both were concerned to gather those who wanted to be serious Christians; both defined the church as the gathering of those who were so minded; both talked about an externally visible amendment of life. That there was no external break in the late seventeenth century between the Pietists and their church, as had been the case in the early Reformation as regards the Anabaptists, surely speaks to the serendipities of the early Reformation. It also testifies that the rich tapestry of sixteenth-century Anabaptist spirituality has had a long and meaningful history even without its name.

Notes

1) The best overall introduction continues to be in George H. Williams' magisterial *The Radical Reformation*. 3rd ed., Kirksville, MO, 1992.

2) There are a number of insightful historiographical surveys of Anabaptist research, beginning with my own essay, "Die neuere Tauferforschung: Fotschritt oder Dilemma?" *Lebendiger Geist. Festschrift für Hans Joachim Schoeps*, Köln, 1960, and, most recently, Werner O. Packull, "Between Paradigms: Anabaptist Studies at the Crossroads," in *Conrad Grebel Review* 8:1–22, Winter 1990.

3) Peter I. Kaufman, "Social History, Psychohistory, and the Prehistory of Swiss Anabaptism," in: *Journal of Religion* 68:527–544, 1988.

4) See the essay "The Rise of the Baptism of Adult Believers in Swiss Anabaptism," W. Klaassen, ed., *Anabaptism Revisited*. Scottdale, PA, 1992, pp. 85–97.

5) The Hutterite Brethren, named after Jakob Hutter, the great organizer of this branch of Anabaptism in Moravia, may be seen as an exception. All the same, the reasons at once take us back to the observations made above: the Hutterites enjoyed a measure of benign toleration by the local nobility, lived geographically in a fairly circumscribed area. See L. Gross, *The Golden Years of the Hutterites*. Scottdale, PA, 1980.

6) *The Martyrs Mirror*. Scottdale, PA, 1951, p. 775.

7) Täuferakten Zürich, 125; 67; 75.

8) John W. Friesen, "Free and Perfect: Justification and Sanctification in Anabaptist Perspective," in *Conrad Grebel Review* 6:74–76, Winter 1988.

9) N. van der Zijpp, *Gesschiedenis der Doopsdezinden in Nederland*, Arnhem, 1952. p. 77.

10) E. Stauffer, "Anabaptist Theology of Martyrdom," *Mennonite Quarterly Review* 19(1945), 179–214.

11) Robert Friedmann, *Mennonite Piety through the Centuries*. Goshen, IN, 1949.

Introduction

A. The Historical Origins of Anabaptism

Early Anabaptism consisted of three major streams, that of the Swiss, the South German/Austrian and the Dutch. Interaction and some cross-fertilization of ideas did occur between these streams, especially as refugees from persecution crossed paths in their search for sanctuary. All existed in a general intellectual milieu which has been characterized in current scholarship as a widespread "anticlericalism," which the Anabaptists shared with other types of religious and political radicals of the time.[1] Yet it is clear that in the earliest period, the differences among the three streams of Anabaptism are as important as the similarities, for these differences resulted in marked dissimilarities in emphases, in style of communications, in modes of leadership and in other areas of general spirituality.

Although the "radical" nature of Anabaptism is usually stressed by friends and foes alike, it should be noted that this generalization is somewhat a distortion. The Anabaptists came to believe in the separate nature of the church from the world. This idea was the seed of what we in our time call the "separation of church and state," and was a major innovation in the sixteenth century. Therefore, in terms of their understanding of church and politics, the Anabaptists were radicals indeed. However, Anabaptist theology, as will be seen in the texts presented here, was very different from both Lutheran and Reformed Protestantism. The major strains of Protestantism stressed the absolute helplessness of the human individual before God to in any way affect salvation. Only God could bring about individual salvation. Anabaptists, on the other hand, stressed both the corporate character of salvation and the ability of the individual to cooperate with God's grace in the course of salvation. Therefore, in terms of theology and anthropology (that is, their understanding of human free will to cooperate or resist God's grace) the Anabaptists were much closer to medieval theol-

1

ogy. Compared to Luther, Zwingli and Calvin, the Anabaptists were the theological "conservatives" of the Reformation.

Priority has often been given to the *Swiss Anabaptist* movement, since chronologically Anabaptism first appeared there. But a more careful reading of the sources leads us to date the beginnings of Anabaptism as 1525 for the Swiss, 1526 for the South German and 1530 for the Dutch movements.[2]

The Reformation in Switzerland was led by Ulrich Zwingli, a professor and preacher in Zurich. He was supported enthusiastically by his students, who participated with him in a series of Bible studies. But some of his students were more willing than Zwingli to institute changes in church polity and practice. Whereas Zwingli conceived of the changes to be made as taking place in an orderly fashion, suggesting alterations to the city council and then following their advice as to a timetable for instituting these changes and thus maintaining the Christian character of the city, the young radicals wanted to move more quickly than the council was willing to go.[3] This finally led to a split between Zwingli and the radicals, his former students, a split which marked the beginning of Anabaptism in Switzerland.

A contemporary chronicle of Anabaptist bias gave this account of the first adult, believer's baptism in Switzerland:

> It so happened that Ulrich Zwingli and Conrad Grebel, of noble background, and Felix Mantz, all three of whom were educated men in German, Latin, Greek and Hebrew, came together to dispute with one another concerning matters of faith. They all acknowledged that infant baptism was unnecessary and was, in fact, no baptism at all. But two of them, Conrad and Felix, believed and acknowledged in the Lord that a person should be and must be baptized correctly, according to the order and institution given by the Lord, Christ, who said, "Whoever believes and is baptized will be saved." But Ulrich Zwingli, who shrunk from the cross of Christ, from being held in low esteem and from persecution, did not want to do this and insisted that it would lead to disorder. But the other two, Conrad and Felix, continued to insist that this was no reason to forsake what was very clearly a commandment and charge of God.

> Now it happened that a man from Chur came to them, a priest by the name of George of the house of Jacob, also called "Blaurock" because during one of the public disputations on the faith, when this George spoke out concerning his views, someone asked who it was that had

spoken. And someone answered that it was that one there in the blue coat (blaurock) who had spoken. So that is why he got that name, because he was wearing a blue coat. This George was a man of particular zeal and everyone thought of him as a rather inferior and simple-minded preacher. But in terms of matters of faith and divine zeal for the grace of God which was given to him, he handled himself in a marvelous and courageous manner in the work of the truth. He first came to Zwingli and had much discussion with him concerning matters of faith, but they came to no agreement. Then he was told that there were others who were more zealous than Zwingli. He inquired concerning these men and finally came to them, that is, to Conrad Grebel and Felix Mantz, and discussed matters of the faith with them. These men found themselves in agreement and found and acknowledged among themselves a true fear of God. They agreed that the divine word and preaching must result in a true faith shown in deeds of love; that this faith should be confessed and acknowledged in a true Christian baptism, a covenant with God for a pure conscience, to serve God in all matters through a holy and Christian life; and to this one must remain steadfast, through all suffering, even to the end.

And it so happened that when they had come together, an anxiety came over them and they felt it heavy upon their hearts. They fell to their knees and called upon the most high God in heaven. They called upon God as the one who knows all hearts and prayed for mercy and that God would show them his divine will. They were not urged forward in this by flesh and blood or human desire, for they knew that it would lead them into suffering. When the prayer was ended, George of the house of Jacob stood up and asked Conrad Grebel, for the sake of God's will, to baptize him with a true Christian baptism on his own faith and confession. With that request and desire, he knelt down again, and Conrad baptized him, since there was no ordained minister there to do it for him. And then the others asked George to baptize them in the same way, which he did according to their request. And so in the highest fear of God, they gave themselves to the name of the Lord, each authenticating the other in the service of the Gospel, to learn and to keep the faith. And that was the beginning of the separation from the world and its evil works. And soon others were doing the same thing, such as Balthasar Hubmaier of Freiburg, Ludwig Hetzer and others, men educated in German, Latin, Greek and Hebrew languages, who ably preached the Bible. Also other preachers and other people, who soon were to give witness with their own blood.[4]

The meeting described in the text above took place in late January of 1525 in the home of Felix Mantz. During the following weeks and months, as the text indicates, more baptisms were administered and the movement grew in the German cantons, to Basel and Bern in the west, and to St. Gall in the east. Most of the time, the preaching and baptisms took place in small groups. However, some of the more ardent leaders also used very public and confrontational tactics to spread their message. George Blaurock, as one example, stood up in the Zollikon church and challenged the minister there concerning his right to preach. Basing himself on charismatic authority, Blaurock proclaimed, "You were not sent to preach—I am!"[5]

Swiss Anabaptism became a mass movement in St. Gall, where the authorities had a tolerant attitude toward the new movement. A powerful political leader there, Vadian, was the brother-in-law of Conrad Grebel, and he at first even sympathized with their rejection of infant baptism. By April of 1525, Conrad Grebel, who had come to St. Gall on a visit, had baptized a large number of people there. Anabaptist preachers held open meetings and it was said that these meetings were much better attended than the officially sanctioned Reformed preaching services. The leadership of the Anabaptists centered on Balthasar Hubmaier, and the popular nature of the movement drew Ulrich Zwingli himself into the fray, for Zwingli saw in the movement a threat to the theocratic unity of the Swiss Confederation. Legal sanctions against the Anabaptists only strengthened their resolve and made the cause more popular with the common people. However, as the movement grew, it suffered from the sort of excesses which have accompanied more recent mass revivals and charismatic movements, including people experiencing comatose states and glossolalia. Although these types of excess happened mainly on the fringes of the movement and were not characteristic of Swiss Anabaptism as a whole, Vadian and other leaders finally sided with Zwingli and the mass character of the Anabaptist movement died down. With this and the increase in persecution in all of the Swiss territories, Swiss Anabaptism became decidedly sectarian.

The original Swiss Anabaptist leaders were highly educated young men, students at the universities or sometimes priests. The influence of humanist learning was strong among them, as was seen especially among the circle of Conrad Grebel in Zurich. Like Erasmus, they taught freedom of the will and were relatively optimistic about the possibilities of human betterment. Their movement was characterized by an inner-worldly asceticism which, when coupled with a political

4

INTRODUCTION

theology of the two kingdoms, soon developed into pacifist and religious sectarianism. This sectarianism was crystallized in the fourth article of the Schleitheim Confession of 1527, which reads in part,

> We have been united concerning the separation that shall take place from the evil and the wickedness which the devil has planted in the world. . . . We have no fellowship with them and do not run with them in the confusion of their abominations. . . . Now there is nothing else in the world and all creation than good or evil, believing and unbelieving, darkness and light, the world and those who are come out of the world, God's temple and idols, Christ and Belial, and none will have part with the other.[6] *Either—or—*

As citizens of the Kingdom of God rather than the worldly state, these Anabaptists rejected the civil loyalty oath and military service, along with the "religious" practice of infant baptism. They enforced church discipline by use of the "ban," which often extended to severing social relations with the erring brother or sister. Their goal was to restore the apostolic church, organized according to the explicit precepts of the New Testament.

South German and Austrian Anabaptism had much in common with the Swiss. But there, the influence of medieval mysticism, rather than humanistic learning, formed the core of spiritual life. Two major sources of the mysticism which informed South German and Austrian Anabaptism were the "cross mysticism" of Thomas Müntzer and the medieval book which inspired the young Martin Luther, the *Theologia Deutsch*. Müntzer's ideas entered the Anabaptist movement through Hans Hut, while the influence of the "German Theology" entered through Hans Denck. These two men, Hut and Denck, were the central figures of this stream of Anabaptism in its formative years.

Although there is no record of a dramatic beginning of South German Anabaptism comparable to the story of George Blaurock and the Swiss movement, it is clear that by about May of 1526 an Anabaptist congregation had formed in Augsburg under the leadership of Hans Denck. Denck had been expelled from Nuremberg already in January of 1525 for expressing views which appear in hindsight to be very close to those of the Swiss Anabaptists.[7] It is possible that he was baptized by Balthasar Hubmaier, who was on his way from Switzerland to Moravia. Denck was less concerned than were the Swiss about the explicit organization of the church. His emphasis was on Christ's teaching that love was the sum of all the commandments, and it was this that he tried to implement as the basis for polity in the Anabaptist assembly.

The influence of the "German Theology" on Denck is found in his teaching concerning freedom of the will, a general atonement for all of humankind and his insistence on betterment of life as a result of Christian faithfulness. Although Martin Luther had earlier approved of the *Theologia Deutsch*, had seen to its publication and written an appreciative foreword, by the latter part of the decade he had changed his mind about this mystical theology. By 1528, when an edition of the book was printed in Worms, it carried Denck's foreword and not Luther's.

Hans Denck baptized Hans Hut in the summer of 1526. However, it could hardly be said that Hut was a disciple or follower of Denck. Hans Hut, a self-educated bookseller, had only recently been involved with Thomas Müntzer at Frankenhausen, where he took some obscure part in the peasant uprising there. Hut was convinced that God would soon slay the rich and the powerful in preparation for the final triumph of the Kingdom of Christ. If, like Müntzer, Hut had erred in thinking that the German peasant wars were the prelude to this battle, he found in Anabaptism a new outlet for his apocalyptic speculations. Müntzer had taught the bitterness and pain of the inward struggle of the cross. Hut now extended this theology of suffering to include the outward persecution which the Anabaptists had to endure.

Hut was a fiery preacher and missionary, who carried the Anabaptist message throughout Austria, founding Anabaptist congregations all along the Danube River up into Southern Germany. After preaching and baptizing, Hut would immediately appoint the most able among the new converts to be missionaries themselves. Two of these were Hans Schlaffer and Leonhard Schiemer, whose writings are also represented in this collection. Hut's gospel of suffering, which he called "The Gospel of All Creatures," was taught by the missionaries he sent out. It is not clear, however, that Hut's political apocalypticism was passed on to these converts. It may well have been a kind of "secret doctrine" which Hut revealed only to his most inner circle. Like all groups in the sixteenth century, the Hutian Anabaptists had great doubts about the salvation of anyone not a part of their circle. But the spirit of vengeance which can be detected in Hut is not present among his followers such as Schlaffer and Schiemer, or in Hans Bünderlin, Oswaldt Glaidt or the later Hutterians.

INTRODUCTION

Of the Germanic cities in the sixteenth century, Strassburg, under the leadership of Martin Bucer and Wolfgang Capito, was the most tolerant of religious diversity. Many Anabaptists, as well as Spiritualists such as Caspar Schwenckfeld, found their way to Strassburg at one or another point in their careers. Among those Anabaptists who resided in Strassburg in the earliest years of the movement were Michael Sattler, Pilgram Marpeck, Hans Bünderlin and Hans Denck. Most significant for *Dutch Anabaptism* was the arrival in Strassburg, in June of 1529, of the fiery Livonian "Lutheran" named Melchior Hofmann. Hofmann had spread the Lutheran reform in the north all the way into Sweden. But when he accepted the iconoclastic views of Andreas Bodenstein von Karlstadt concerning the nature of the sacraments, he found himself in strong opposition to Lutheranism. He was even personally denounced by Luther himself. Befriended by Karlstadt, Hofmann arrived in Strassburg with a recommendation to Bucer written by Karlstadt. But he broke with Karlstadt by 1530, for by then Hofmann had come into contact with Anabaptists and was moving in that direction himself. He accepted baptism and moved into the Netherlands to preach his new message. The beginnings of Dutch Anabaptism can be dated, in 1530, with the arrival of Melchior Hofmann in the Low Countries.

Hofmann's message received mass support almost immediately. The ground had been prepared there by decades of sacramentarian teaching, which rejected the Roman view of the transubstantiation of the sacramental elements. Also, the Netherlands was the place of a fourteenth-century movement of Catholic piety known as the *Modern Devotion*.[8] This reform movement stressed the importance of the Bible and fought against the immorality of much of the clergy. The spirit of reform was still present in the sixteenth century through the Brethren of the Common Life. Although no organic connections can be established between the Brethren of the Common Life and the Dutch Anabaptists, it remains clear that the roots of a reforming spirit were planted deep in the mindset of the people in the Low Countries. Yet a third preparation for Hofmann's message, to which social historians have pointed, was the economic hardship which the Low Countries suffered in the years just prior to Hofmann's arrival there. Natural disasters such as repeated crop failures, plus political calamities such as embargoes in shipping, caused hunger, inflation and unemployment, creating a general apocalyptic mood among the masses.

Melchior Hofmann had long been attracted by charismatic and

visionary speculations concerning the end times, and he claimed for himself the ability to interpret the Bible in allegorical and prophetic fashion. He quickly assimilated to his own purposes the Anabaptist notion of freedom of the will and a universal grace which illuminated all people, which he learned in Strassburg from Hans Denck. Although he was baptized in Strassburg, he appealed to his own authority to baptize others. Many of his followers in the Low Countries saw him as a Second Elijah. In the end, he was undone by his own attraction to prophecy. It was prophesied by one of his group that he would be arrested in Strassburg and this would precipitate the Second Coming of Christ. He joyfully went to Strassburg and turned himself in to the authorities there. He died some ten years later, a broken man.

Hofmann was himself a teacher of peaceful Anabaptism. However, his visionary apocalypticism, carried into the social and political context of the Low Countries, was easily co-opted by Anabaptist revolutionary leaders. The Melchiorite Anabaptists soon divided into peaceful and revolutionary factions. The revolutionaries carried out a number of attacks on churches and monasteries, smashing images and stealing anything valuable. Their actions culminated in the tragedy of Münster (1534–1535), where Anabaptists took over the city and tried to establish the Kingdom of God there. Placed under siege and embargo, this Anabaptist "Kingdom" degenerated into cannibalism before the city finally fell.

The Münsterite debacle fully discredited the revolutionaries. But it left the peaceful Anabaptists in crisis as well. Many of them, including one of their most able leaders, Obbe Philips, left the movement entirely. It was left mainly to Obbe's brother, Dirk, as well as to Menno Simons, to gather the confused and dispersed remnants together, furthering among them a pacifist Anabaptism aimed at creating a church "without spot or wrinkle." Although the peaceful Anabaptism had considerable numerical strength in the Northern Netherlands (some 25 percent of the population were considered to be Anabaptists), the movement took on a quietist and sectarian character in reaction to the Münsterite tragedy and was eclipsed, from about 1550, by the Calvinistic Reformed Church.

B. The Spirituality of Early Anabaptism

From the sketch of the historical origins of early Anabaptism, it is already clear that this was a diverse movement about which it is difficult to generalize. There are, however, certain basic themes of spirituality which are common to each of the historical streams of Anabaptism.

Anabaptists all stressed *the immediacy of the human relationship with God*. The experience of the immediacy of God led Anabaptists to reject any notion that special places, persons or objects brought one closer to God. The relationship of the human being with God was not dependent on clerical or sacramental mediation. In the Anabaptist view, religious institutions were human inventions, at best, and downright detrimental to spiritual well being at worst. Although different Protestant theologians held to some notion of the "priesthood of all believers," Anabaptism abolished the clerical office altogether.

The spiritual experience of the immediate relationship between God and human beings had the consequence of elevating the common person to a position equal to that of the clergy and nobility. This leveling of all people in relationship to God was one way in which the social program of the peasants was carried on in the spiritual plane, even after they had been defeated on the battlefield.

It was this spiritual experience which led Anabaptists to a scathing criticism of the clergy. Many Anabaptist leaders had themselves been monks and priests. They knew from the inside what went on in the monasteries and parish houses. In their view, the clergy kept themselves in positions of power by convincing the common people that they were a necessary institution for the salvation of the populace. But once it was seen that each person could approach God directly, the transfer of wealth to the clergy was viewed as little more than robbery. Anabaptists declared that the clergy should find useful employment. Typical of the Anabaptist attitude, Michael Sattler, on leaving the monastery, learned a trade to support himself. Furthermore, the personal lives of many of the clergy exhibited behavior which was far below the moral standards demanded of the common people. Anabaptists demanded that the same moral standards apply to all Christians. Therefore, although it is undoubtedly true that a general mood of anticlericalism prevailed in the Germanic lands during the sixteenth century, and Anabaptist pronouncements against the clergy reflect this mood, it is also true that for Anabaptists, their pronouncements against the clergy also reflect their own spiritual experience of an immediate relationship with God.

A second feature central to the Anabaptist spiritual understanding was that of *a life of discipleship*. Anabaptists did not dwell on the question, "What must I do to be saved?" Rather, they were concerned with the question, "How should a Christian live?" They did not agonize over and question their salvation. Their experience of salvation, what they called the "new birth," was for them a beginning point. To become a "follower of Christ" in daily life, exhibited in active love, was at the very heart of their understanding of spiritual salvation. It was for them the highest meaning of human existence.[9]

The Anabaptists conceived of themselves as living "outside" of the order of worldly citizenship. With a few noted exceptions of revolutionary excess, they tried to be good citizens and to accommodate themselves to the demands of political authorities. But they placed their first loyalty in Christ and refused to follow the demands of their political leaders when this contradicted the clear teachings of Christ. This was integral to their understanding of Christian discipleship. The follower of Christ could not have divided loyalties. Those actions which placed them most at odds with the society in general—their refusal to defend the political state with violence, and their refusal to take the loyalty oath—were rooted in their spiritual understanding of the meaning of a life of discipleship.

Repeatedly, the criticism Anabaptists made of Protestant reforms was that these reforms were "external" reforms only. They brought no internal, spiritual renewal of the people and did not lead to any noticeable moral improvement in the behavior of the people. This distinction between the "inner" and the "outer" word was not an esoteric hermeneutic. It was rather their attempt to comprehend how it could be that the Protestant Reformation had essentially failed in the area of improving moral conduct. That persecution and charismatic excesses also led some Anabaptists into isolated incidents of immoral conduct did not change the fact that in the Anabaptist view, no spiritual experience of God or Christ could take place without it resulting in a marked betterment of life. A deepening spirituality meant a moral change in living habits. There was no other way for them to conceive of it.

It was for this reason that the Anabaptists rejected the Protestant doctrine of the bondage of the will. Teaching people that their will is not free to choose good over debauchery was for the Anabaptists a simple license for sinful living. Anabaptists, therefore, also rejected the Protestant formulation of the doctrine of original sin. Some Anabaptists taught the view of the medieval mystics, that there were elements of the divine nature in human beings which could respond to God. Other Anabaptists taught the spiritualist view, that the gulf between

10

human beings and the divine was bridged in Christ. But in both teachings, the will and ability to respond to Christ and his teachings were an accomplished fact and were not hindered by the sin of Adam.

Anabaptists also rejected the Protestant distinction between justification and sanctification. For the Anabaptists, justification and sanctification were an inseparable continuum, an ongoing experience of conformity to the will and character of Christ. Although Anabaptists did not claim perfection as an accomplished state, they did view the Christian life as a life "on the way" to perfect unity with Christ. The notion of being simultaneously justified and a sinner simply made no sense to them. No life which was not on the way to more perfect unity with Christ could be considered a Christian life.

The Anabaptists were optimistic about human potential to respond to the divine will. Their experience taught them that God's power and Spirit were granted to those who desired them, and that this Spirit led the person into a real and genuine change, conformed to the image of God in Christ. Any person who willed to respond could respond. However, they were not optimistic about human prospects on the whole. They knew that the large majority of human beings would not respond to the divine will. Furthermore, those who did not respond would hate those among them who did so respond because it would be taken as an implicit judgment of their refusal. Therefore, the optimistic anthropology of the Anabaptists was offset by their realization that discipleship would all but inevitably include suffering and even martyrdom. And indeed, as many as five thousand Anabaptists were put to death for their faith in the first generation.

In Anabaptist spirituality, martyrdom was raised to a spiritual level unequalled by any other experience. In its view, God's people always were called upon to suffer. From the Hebrew prophets to the apostles and the early Christian martyrs, the path of persecution and martyrdom was clear, and they placed their own suffering and martyrdom in this context. The cross of Christ had a special role in this history of martyrdom, and it was a common Anabaptist teaching that the suffering of the "head" would also be visited upon the "members," those of the body. The cross of Christ was a guide to God's people through all of human history. They saw themselves as heirs to this entire tradition of Hebrew and Christian martyrs. For the Anabaptists, depth of spiritual experience led directly to the acceptance of persecution, suffering and martyrdom.

A third feature of Anabaptist spirituality was its distinct teaching

concerning *the corporate nature of the Christian life*. The Pauline metaphor of the church as the body of Christ was common to all Christian
groups. None would have denied it. But in Anabaptism, this metaphor
takes on an almost literal form. Christ was actually experienced in
an incarnate form through the gathered assembly of believers. This
gathered assembly was the actual body of Christ in the world and to
participate in this assembly was to participate in the body of Christ.
Therefore, for the Anabaptists, the *unio mystica*, the mystical union of
the believer with Christ, was found in participation in the gathering
together of the believers.

The place of the gathered community in the spirituality of Anabaptism was recognized by their contemporaries. Writing in 1531
(before the rise of the revolutionary Melchiorites in the Low Countries) Sebastian Franck wrote the following in his *Chronica*:

> The Anabaptists spread so rapidly that their teaching soon covered, as
> it were, the land. They soon gained a large following, and baptized
> many thousands, drawing to themselves many sincere souls who had a
> zeal for God. For they taught nothing but love, faith and the need of
> bearing the cross. They showed themselves humble, patient under
> much suffering; they break the bread with one another as an evidence
> of unity and love. They helped each other faithfully, called each other
> brothers, etc. They increased so rapidly that the world feared an upris-
> ing by them, though I have learned that this fear had no justification
> whatsoever. They were persecuted with great tyranny, being impris-
> oned, branded, tortured and executed by fire, water and the sword. In
> a few years very many were put to death. Some have estimated the
> number of those who were killed to be far above two thousand. They
> died as martyrs, patiently, and humbly endured all persecution.[10]

For some Anabaptists, this mystical union with Christ in the gathered group was first experienced in the solidarity of revolutionary
action, from which it was carried into their conversion to Anabaptism.
For other Anabaptists, this mystical union with Christ in the gathered
group was first experienced in the small meetings for Bible study and
discussion, from which it was carried into their conversion to Anabaptism. For others still, this mystical union with Christ in the gathered
group was first experienced in the Anabaptist conventicle itself.[11] For
all, however, it represented an erotic and powerful desire for social
connection and confirmation and was the root spiritual experience
behind the Anabaptist claim, in the face of the majesty and tradition

of the Roman Church, and the learning and political power of the Protestant Churches, that their small bands had found God's own truth. This truth had such a grip on them that they gladly faced the suffering and persecution which their dissenting position brought upon them.

The experience of community was so strong among Anabaptists that they were persuaded that it was only in community that one could be a Christian. For it was within the community that the process of discipleship, of disciplining life, took place. This disciplining could at times lapse into legalism. But at its best, it was a manifestation of genuine love among the gathered assembly, a recognition of the mutual needs and the interdependency of human beings.

The love and disciplining of the community had direct application in the area of economics. In the case of the Hutterites, this took the form of a full-blown communism which rejected private property as evil in itself. Not all Anabaptists accepted this practice. But in all Anabaptist groups, personal or private property was placed at the disposal of the group for meeting the needs of those within the assembly.

Anabaptist communities, at their best, were communities of real liberation in which the people involved set themselves to the task of restructuring their religious and social world together in ways which fostered the creative abilities of each person. They were communities in which each person was valued as a member of the body. This is why the body metaphor took on such a central location in Anabaptist ideology. The love for each other experienced in their gatherings was understood as the very love of God, heightened by the real knowledge that each person could face arrest and persecution for participation in the gathered assembly. The loss of each person was experienced as a loss of a member of the body.

This experience of community, of genuine love and sharing between people, claims a place of deep longing in our lives today.[12] An entire history of our civilization could be centered around the quest for, partial achievement of, and subversion and loss of, this kind of human community. This quest for communities of meaning and value, in the face of the atomizing forces of technology and capitalist individualism, is one of the forces which attract us to the mystical traditions and spiritual disciplines of the past. The early Anabaptists of the sixteenth century are an example of people who were able to achieve this type of community, if only temporarily and on a very limited scale. The later history of the religious sects and denominations which survived from the Anabaptist movement demonstrate the need for ongoing reform and renewal of this vision of human community.

While it is impossible simply to copy the Anabaptist model, their witness does assure us that at least partial achievement of true human community is possible. The experience of the divine in the gathered group is there for us. If we have become more sophisticated in our psychological, sociological and historical understanding of the dynamics behind this quest, this ought not to lead us into simple cynicism concerning the quest itself. The enduring witness of the Anabaptist spiritual experience is that human community is possible, as a gift of the Spirit of God, as a response to that spirit which is deepest within each human being.

Part I:
Swiss Anabaptism

Felix Mantz

Felix Mantz was the first martyr of the Anabaptists. Born in 1498 in Zurich, he was schooled in Greek, Hebrew and Latin. Mantz became an enthusiastic student of Swiss Reformer Ulrich Zwingli and regularly attended Zwingli's Bible lectures. It was from among this circle of students that the first Anabaptists emerged. A public disputation was held in January of 1525 in which Mantz, along with Conrad Grebel, representing those opposed to infant baptism, took issue with the Zwinglians. The city council decided against the young radicals. It was at a meeting at Mantz's house on January 21, 1525, just days after this disputation, that George Blaurock asked to be baptized as a believing adult. It is from this act that many scholars have dated the beginning of the Anabaptist movement.

Mantz soon became an outspoken advocate of the new baptizers' movement. He took part in further public debates and his preaching helped to spread the new faith in the area surrounding Zurich. He was arrested and jailed numerous times during the next year. Each time he was released, he picked up his agitation where he had left it. The sentencing became increasingly severe, and by January of 1527, he was sentenced to death. He was taken out in a boat on Lake Zurich, where, bound with ropes, he was thrown overboard and drowned. He was not yet thirty years old.

The writing presented here is a letter written from prison in 1526. It is document 201 in the source collection Quellen zur Geschichte der Täufer in der Schweiz, Band I, ed. Muralt/Schmid (Zürich: S. Hirzel Verlag, 1952). It was written to the Anabaptist congregation in Basel about one year before his execution. This letter was the source of a poetic rendering which made its way into the Swiss Anabaptist hymnody, as song number 5 in the Ausbund. Although there had not yet been any executions for the crime of Anabaptism in Switzerland at the time Mantz wrote this letter, it is clear that he was already having intimations of what was to come.

"Letter from Prison" (1527)
Felix Mantz

My heart rejoices in God. He has given me much knowledge and wisdom, whereby I can escape the eternal and unending death. Therefore, I praise you, Lord Christ in heaven! For you have taken away my distress and unhappiness. You my savior have been sent by God as a model and light. You have called me before my final days into your heavenly kingdom so that I may have eternal joy with God and love him and his righteousness which remains both here and in eternity. Without this righteousness, nothing can help or endure. That is why so many people who do not have this are deceived by various empty opinions. Unfortunately, we find many people these days who exult in the gospel and teach, speak and preach much about it, yet are full of hatred and envy. They do not have the love of God in them, and their deceptions are known to everyone. For as we have experienced in these last days, there are those who have come to us in sheep's clothing, yet are ravaging wolves who hate the pious ones of this world and thwart their way to life and the true fold. This is what the false prophets and hypocrites of this world do. These are the ones who both curse and pray with the same mouth and live unruly lives. These are the ones who call upon the government leaders to murder us, destroying the very substance of Christ.[1] But I will praise Christ the Lord for his great patience with us. He teaches us with divine grace and shows love to all people, which is the nature of God his heavenly Father. No false prophet could do this.

Let us take special note of this difference. The sheep of Christ seek the honor of God. They choose this and allow neither property nor temporal goods to hinder them in it, for they stand under the protection of Christ. Christ the Lord does not force anyone to his glory. It is obtained only by those who want it and ready themselves for it through true faith and baptism.[2] When a person works authentic fruits of repentance, the heaven of eternal joy, which comes by graces through Christ, is secured for that person and obtained through Christ's innocent blood, which was willingly shed. For with his blood he demonstrated his love for us and gave us part in the power of his Spirit. Whoever receives and exercises this gift will grow and become

18

complete in God. Only the love of God through Christ is meaningful and enduring—not boasts, threats or denunciations. Love alone is pleasing to God. Anyone who does not have love has no place with God. The genuine love of Christ will scatter the enemy. Whoever would be an heir with Christ is also expected to be merciful, just as the heavenly Father is merciful. Christ never brought legal proceedings against anyone as the false teachers of our time do. They show by this that they do not have the love of Christ and do not understand his word. Yet they want to be shepherds and teachers! They will one day despair, if they do not mend their ways, when they realize that they have earned by this eternal anguish. Christ never showed hatred toward anyone. Therefore, following Christ in the true way which he himself showed us, his true servants should also hate no one.[3] We have before us this light of life and we rejoice to walk in that way. But whoever is full of hatred and envy, whoever villainously betrays, accuses, beats and quarrels, cannot be a Christian. These are the ones who run after Christ like thieves and murderers and use any pretense to shed innocent blood. Anyone can see from this that they do not belong to Christ. They are children of Belial, for out of envy they work to destroy the order of Jesus Christ, doing just as Cain did when he murdered his brother Abel when God found Abel's offerings acceptable.

Here I will finish my reflections. I admonish all of the pious to consider the fall of Adam. When he accepted the advice of the serpent and was disobedient to God, he was cursed with the punishment of death. This will also happen to those who do not accept Christ, those who resist him, those who love the world and do not love God. So I close with this statement, that I will remain steadfast in Christ, trust in him who knows my every need and can deliver me from it. Amen.

Balthasar Hubmaier

Balthasar Hubmaier (1480–1528) was the most important Ana-
baptist leader in Moravia during the years 1526–1528. There, in and
around Nikolsburg, he led a cluster of congregations of about twelve
thousand people. He grew up in Friedberg, near Augsburg, in South
Germany. Hubmaier studied theology at the University of Freiburg
and was a favored student of Johannes Eck. Ordained a priest in 1510,
he later studied at Ingolstadt, where he received a doctorate in theol-
ogy. He became the pastor of the cathedral in Regensburg and later
in Waldshut. By 1522, Hubmaier began to show signs of accepting
the new theology of the Reformation, favoring the Zwinglian over the
Lutheran doctrine. He married, and was asked to leave Waldshut in
1524. But he soon returned there and brought the city to the Protestant
side. It was during this period that Hubmaier became involved in
aiding the armed resistance of the peasants near Waldshut, the crime
which led to his execution some four years later.

By 1525, Hubmaier had become a leader and the most able writer
among the Swiss Anabaptists. He came to Nikolsburg a committed
Anabaptist in the summer of 1526. He began to build his congregation
there under the approval and protection of the local lords. There
Hubmaier wrote and published his many theological tracts, many of
which were dedicated to various princes, lords and noblemen whose
favor he courted. While enjoying relative freedom in Moravia, he
remained a hunted man in all Austrian lands.

The details of Hubmaier's capture are not known. It is thought
that his extradition to Vienna was not because of his religious views
but because of his earlier political activity in Waldshut. He is known
to have been held in the dungeon of the Kreuzenstein castle in early
1528. Concerted effort was made to have Hubmaier recant but he
refused to do so. By February, he was back in Vienna facing heresy

charges. He was tortured, but refused to retract his teachings. He was burned at the stake on March 10, 1528.

The two writings presented here are Hubmaier's defense of freedom of the will and a short meditation on the Lord's Prayer. These are documents 22 and 11, respectively, from his collected writings, Quellen zur Geschichte der Täufer IX: Balthasar Hubmaier Schriften, ed. Westin/Bergsten (Gütersloh: Güterloher Verlaghaus Gerd Mohn, 1962). In his writing on the freedom of the will (1527), Hubmaier takes issue with the Protestant doctrine of bondage of the will. He insists that if we teach that we are saved by faith alone, and at the same time teach that we have no free will, this becomes nothing more than an excuse to continue in sinful living. It removes all incentives to improve one's life and thus does more harm than good. While Hubmaier does not doubt that human will is fallen, he has a stronger belief in the power of regeneration than the mainline Protestant reformers. Therefore, for the believing Christian, freedom of the will is restored and that person becomes responsible for the decision to sin or not to sin. Hubmaier considers it blasphemy to place the responsibility for one's sin back onto God under the guise of bondage of the will. Similar themes are sounded in his exposition on the Lord's Prayer of 1526.

"Concerning Freedom of the Will, Offered by God to All People Through the Sending of His Word; For in This God Has Given Power to All His Children to Choose What is Good. Or They May Remain, According to Their Nature, Children of Wrath." (1527) Balthasar Hubmaier

To the most noble and highborn prince and lord George, Margrave of Brandenburg, Stetin and Pomerania, Duke of Kashubes and Wends, Burgrave of Nuremberg and Prince of Ruegen, and my merciful lord. Grace, joy and the peace of God to you.

Although for some years now the gospel has been earnestly preached to all creatures, I find many people who have learned or grasped only two concepts from all the preaching. On the one hand it is said, "We believe. We are saved by faith." On the other hand it is said, "We can do no good works. God must work in us the will and fulfillment. We have no free will."

21

Now such ideas are only half truths. And from such half truths one only may come to incomplete conclusions. But when we take an incomplete conclusion as a final conclusion, ignoring those scriptures which counter it just as strongly, a half truth is actually more detrimental than a whole lie.[4] When a half truth is believed and spread as a whole truth, we end up with all kinds of sects, disunity and heresies. This is only dealing with scripture as a patchwork. One must look at the counter scriptures and try to unite both ideas into a complete conclusion. Whoever is unable to understand scripture in this way eats of unclean animals who do not divide the hoof (Leviticus 11).

Under cover of such half truths, all kinds of evil, dishonesty and injustice have taken the upper hand. There wantonness and presumption have full sway. Dishonesty and falsehood sit on the throne, ruling and mightily exulting in all things. Christian works no longer shine forth from the people. Brotherly love is snuffed out in people's hearts. Indeed, it is as the prophet said, "Truth has stumbled in the streets, honesty cannot enter" (Isaiah 59:14). Wisdom calls aloud, but nobody will listen (Proverbs 1).

The fact of the matter is (which God truly laments) the world is an even more evil place now than it was a thousand years ago. This is what our history books show. This has taken place, it hurts to say, under the cover of the gospel. For as soon as you say, it is written, "Turn from evil and do good" (Psalm 37:27) the answer comes back, "We cannot do good works. All things happen according to the plan of God, by necessity." They think that this is an excuse for sin. And if you go further and say, "It is written, Whoever does evil will be cast into the fire" (John 5; Matthew 25), they quickly find some fig leaf to cover their shame and replay, "Faith alone saves us, not our works." Yes, I have heard of many people who for years have not prayed, fasted or given to the poor because their priests have told them that their works are worthless in the eyes of God. So they simply don't do these things. These are the half truths under which we, like little angels, cover over all sorts of fleshly laxity. And then, as Adam did to Eve and as Eve did to the serpent (Genesis 3), we blame God for our sin and guilt. Why yes! God must be responsible for our sins! This is the greatest blasphemy on earth.

To root out such weeds as these, I have put together this small book in which I have summarized briefly what a person is capable of inside and outside the grace of God. I ask in all humility that you accept this booklet from me graciously. Nikolsburg, April 1, 1527.

22

The human being is a physical and rational creature, made by God as a unity of body, soul and spirit (Genesis 2).[5] These three aspects are essential to the human being and found in different degrees in each person, as the scriptures clearly state.

As God made the human being from the dust of the earth, God blew into him the breath of life, making the human a living soul. Moses here uses three distinct words to make a point. First of all, the body or flesh is made of the earth—namely, the dirt or clay. The Hebrew words here are *aphar* and *eretz*, which can best be translated as dust, ashes or loam taken from the earth. Secondly, look at this living breath. The Hebrew here is *neshamah*, which can be translated as blowing upon, breathing upon, exhaling, or as spirit. Thirdly, the soul, which is the life of the body, is designated separately and is called *nephesh*.

The apostle Paul, in writing to the Thessalonians, also used three distinct Greek terms to refer to these three essential substances. He wrote of *pneuma*, *psyche* and *soma*. In Latin these are *spiritus*, *anima* and *corpus*. In our language these are spirit, soul and body. So it says, "May God himself, the God of peace, sanctify you through and through. May your whole spirit, soul and body be kept blameless at the coming of our Lord Jesus Christ" (1 Thessalonians 5:23).

Likewise, in Hebrews we read of this difference between the soul and spirit. "For the word of God is living and active. Sharper than any two-edged sword, it penetrates even to dividing soul and spirit, joints and marrow. It judges the thoughts and attitudes of the heart" (Hebrews 4:12). Also Mary, the pure and virtuous virgin, referred clearly to this difference between soul and spirit when she said to Elizabeth, "My soul glorifies the Lord and my spirit rejoices in God my savior. For God has been mindful of the humble state of his servant" (Luke 1:47–48).

So here it is said precisely—soul, spirit and misery. *Misery* means the body, or in Greek, *Tapeinosis*, which means misery or the humble state of humanity. *Tapeinophrosyne* means humbleness of spirit. Christ also made this distinction very plain when he said, speaking to his disciples on the Mount of Olives, "My soul is overwhelmed with sorrow to the point of death. . . . The spirit is willing but the body is weak" (Matthew 26:38 and 41). That is why the troubled soul of Christ cried out, in accord with the weakness of the body, "My Father! If it is possible, take this cup from me!" But then according to the spirit he added, "May your will and not my will be done." Therefore, Christian reader, you can see obviously and clearly that these three particular and essential substances, the soul, spirit and body, are united in every person as a likeness to the Holy Trinity.

Based on scriptural authority, nobody can deny these three essential things or substances. It follows, therefore, that one must also confess three corresponding kinds of will in the human being. There is the will of the flesh, the will of the soul and the will of the spirit. I will be able to draw these obvious distinctions with clear scriptures. So the Spirit of God spoke through John, speaking of the will of the flesh (which does not want to suffer), the will of the soul (which is willing to suffer but under the influence of the flesh does not seek it) and the will of the spirit (which is willing to suffer.)

I want to clarify these three kinds of will with certain scriptures, such as the teaching of the Spirit of God through that apostle whom Christ loved. This is the word of the true and eternal light which came among his own as a human being. But his own did not accept him. But to as many as did accept him, he gave the power to become children of God. Yes, those who believe in his name are not born of blood and the will of the flesh, or by human will, which the scriptures call the soul. They are born of God (John 1; 1 Samuel 10).

Now, as Paul said in his letters to the Romans and Ephesians, we are born once in original sin and wrath. This is said also by David, Job and Jeremiah. Because of this, we must be born again. Otherwise, we can neither see nor enter into the kingdom of God. We must be born of the water and spirit. That is, we must be born through the word of God. This is the water for all those who thirst for salvation and it will be made a living water in us through the Spirit of God. For without the working of the Spirit it is a deadening letter.

This Spirit of God aids our spirit, giving it witness and strength in the battle and struggle against the flesh, sin, the world, death, the devil and hell.[6] Every word from the mouth of God aids the spirit so that the flesh, with its will to evil and lust, can find nowhere to hide or be concealed. It finds no external rest or recess from the preaching of the word of God, which resounds throughout the whole world. Internally also it is everywhere convicted by the Spirit. For so long as the witness remains in the mouths of even two or three, the conscience will be like a worm gnawing on the minds of people.

This is the true rebirth which Christ speaks about in John 3. Through this rebirth our Adam, who had become a woman and an Eve in the fall, regains his manhood, and the soul, which had become as flesh, regains its spiritual nature. Saint Peter wrote clearly of this new birth, saying, "Now that you have purified yourselves by obeying the truth so that you have sincere love for your brothers, love one another deeply, from the heart. For you have been born again, not of perishable seed, but of imperishable, through the living and enduring word of God. For all men are like grass, and all their glory is like the flowers of the field; the grass withers and the flowers fall, but the word of the Lord stands forever" (1 Peter 1:22–25).

Now note this, pious Christians! Through the disobedience of Adam, the soul has become flesh and must be reborn as spirit through the Spirit of God and the living word.[7] For what is born of Spirit is spirit (John 3). I cannot say here why Peter speaks only of the soul, saying, "Make your soul pure," and did not go further and say also "your spirit and flesh." But he knew well that from the beginning the spirit is wholly a divine creation and does not need to be born again as spirit. That is why he said, "through obedience to the truth in the spirit." Likewise, the rebirth does not pertain to the flesh, for God has already judged the flesh and through his power decreed that it must wither like grass and ashes. Otherwise, one can never enter into the kingdom of God (1 Corinthians 15; Matthew 16).

It is also worth noting that the human being should be seen as having three natures or forms. The first is before the fall of Adam. The second is as Adam after the fall. And the third is as the human being is after redemption.

Human Beings Before the Fall of Adam

Before the transgression of Adam, the three of the human substances—flesh, soul and spirit—were good (Genesis 1). For God looked at all things he had created and saw that they were good. In fact, human beings were especially good, for they were made in God's likeness. The three substances were also wholly free to choose good or evil, life or death, heaven or hell. They were originally made by God good and free to recognize, will and act for good or evil. The scripture witnesses to this when it says, "God made the human being good from the beginning and then left him free to make his own decisions" (Ecclesiasticus 15). God gave commandments and laws and said, "If you will keep these laws, they will preserve you." Note here, God said, "you, human beings, will"—so it is possible to keep these laws! It then continues, "He has set fire and water before you (note!

25

before you!) and you may stretch out your hand to whichever you choose. For humans have before them life and death, good and evil. And whichever they prefer (yes! they prefer) will be given to them." Here the scripture demonstrates clearly and without question that originally the human being was free in body, soul and spirit to will, choose and act upon either good or evil. But after Adam's transgression all of that changed.

Human Beings After the Fall of Adam

A. CONCERNING THE FLESH

After our first father, Adam, transgressed the Law of God by his disobedience, he lost his freedom, both for himself and for all who came after him. If a nobleman receives a grant from the king, but then uses it against the king, the king will take the grant back from the nobleman and his entire line. For they also must bear the guilt of their ancestor. Likewise, the flesh entirely lost its goodness and freedom through Adam's fall and became totally worthless and without merit right up to the time of death. It can do nothing other than sin, strive against God and be at enmity against God's commandments. That is why Paul, writing to the Romans, expressed his terrible complaint against his miserable and cursed flesh. And therefore, according to the curse of God, the flesh must return to the very earth from which it came. Otherwise, one can never possess the kingdom of God. For as Christ said to Peter, "Blessed are you, Simon son of Jonah, for this was not revealed to you by man, but by my Father in heaven" (Matthew 16:17).

When Eve, who is a symbol of the flesh, wanted to eat and did eat of the forbidden fruit, she lost the knowledge of good and evil. Indeed, she lost the ability to will and act upon the good. And for this she had to pay with death. So now as soon as a person is conceived and born, he is conceived and born in sin. He is from the very first moment buried in sin up to his ears. And from that first hour onward, he begins to die and return to the earth. For as God said, "You must not eat from the tree of the knowledge of good and evil, for when you eat of it you will surely die" (Genesis 2:17). That is why both Job and Jeremiah cursed the day they were born. Likewise, King David fervently bewailed the day of his birth, complaining to God that he was conceived in evil and that his mother gave birth to him in sin (Job 3;

26

Jeremiah 20; Psalm 51). This is what Paul meant by his short saying that we all died in Adam. God calls it returning to earth and ashes.

B. CONCERNING THE SPIRIT

The human spirit remained honest, whole and good before, during and after the fall. For the spirit was not in any way involved in the disobedience of the flesh in eating of the forbidden fruit—neither in suggesting it be done nor in the act itself, neither in terms of will nor deed. The spirit partook of the fruit only as a prisoner of the body. But the guilt of this act is not that of the spirit, but only of the body and the soul, which acted with the flesh. Saint Paul clearly witnessed to the wholeness and honorable nature of the spirit when writing to the Thessalonians. "May your whole spirit, soul and body be kept blameless at the coming of our Lord Jesus Christ" (1 Thessalonians 5). He said, "your whole spirit," and not your whole soul or your whole body. For what is fallen and broken is no longer whole.

King David also bewailed the fall and cried out to God, "I have become like broken pottery" (Psalm 31:12). Likewise, Paul, in the power of our Lord Jesus Christ, gave the fornicator over to the devil for the destruction of the flesh—that is, he urged the bride of Christ, the Christian Church, to exercise the power of the keys to bind and loose on earth, so that the man's spirit might be saved (1 Corinthians 5). In effect then, Paul was saying, "If the flesh wants to be rotten and of the devil, then let the devil have it. But the spirit remains blessed and whole on the day of the Lord. Then God can deal with it as God sees fit. It is unnecessary for us to know more."

C. CONCERNING THE SOUL

The third part of the human being, the soul, was wounded as to its will through the disobedience of Adam. It has become deathly ill and on its own cannot choose to do the good. Nor can it overcome evil, for it has lost knowledge of good and evil. It can do nothing other than sin and die. Indeed, in terms of accomplishing good, the soul has become totally powerless and ineffective. The flesh is the tool of the soul—only the flesh can act. Without it, the soul can do nothing. But because the tool can do nothing, how can anything good come from it, even if that were what the soul truly wanted and strived for? And yet the fall of the soul can be made good again through the word of God. This word of God teaches what it means to will good or evil. And after this life, through the resurrection of the flesh, the body will

27

again become heavenly, eternal, glorious and spiritual, able to act and bring to fulfillment. This is the body of those who have been born again of the water and the spirit. For the first Adam was created in the natural life and the last Adam in the spiritual life. The first Adam is earthly, of the earth. But the last Adam is heavenly, of the heavens.

That the fall of the soul is reparable and harmless on earth, while the fall of the flesh is irreparable and deadly is because of the following. Adam, who is a figure of the soul (as Eve is of the flesh) did not want to eat of the forbidden tree.[8] Adam was not deceived by the serpent. Eve was deceived. Adam knew that the words of the serpent were contrary to the word of God. But he ate of the fruit against his own conscience so as not to betray or anger Eve, his rib and flesh. He did not want to do it. But he lost knowledge of good and evil because he was obedient to Eve rather than to God. He could then no longer choose between good and evil. Nor could he refuse or flee from evil, for he no longer knew what, before God, good and evil were. His tastes were nothing other than what Eve, his flesh, wanted and which seemed good. He lost his true tastes.

Think of it this way. A wounded and feverish person will want or like nothing good and healthy to eat or drink. Only cold water and unhealthy food tastes good to him.[9] That is because his healthy nature and true complexion are turned around by the sickness. He has lost his right and healthy taste for knowledge. His bitter tongue judges as good that which is harmful to him, and as bad that which would do him good. That is just how it is with our soul after the transgression of Adam. From the very hour that he ate of the tree of knowledge of good and evil, he lost his taste for knowledge of good and evil. He no more knew or was able to judge what, before God, was truly good or evil, what kind of actions were adequate before God or what works were pleasing to God.

It does not matter that he would truly want to do what is right according to the spirit. For this desire is present even today in all people, as Paul wrote to the Romans.

Of course the blind want to see. The lame want to be well. One who has fallen among murderers and left wounded and half dead would of course want to be healthy. But all who are not taught by the word of God err as to the right way, truth and means for coming to this health of the soul. And from this flows all sorts of errors, false teachings, idolatry and heresy.

Also excluded are all those people who have sinned against the

28

Holy Spirit.[10] For in such people all things, the will and desire, have been perverted. The judgment of God is just against them because they will to be judged according to their own desire and stubborn wickedness. They strive against the very truth they know and acknowledge. They have turned their backs on God and then say that God will not let himself be seen. They stuff their ears against the voice of God. They think that to heed the voice of God would be to die, even though it is the way of life. They avert their eyes from God and then blame God for not wanting them to know him. They shut the door of their hearts from God and then complain that God neither knocks nor seeks them. But actually, when God knocks, they do not answer, and when God seeks them, they do not allow themselves to be found. What they have they deny. So God gives them what they do not want. That is the fate of those who deny that an infant has free will. The time comes when they would seek God, but then cannot find him.

Even if they flee from God, they run right into God's hand. For just as they demonstrate their trust in God, that is how they will be met by God, exactly according to their faith. For if their sin is never forgiven, the Spirit of God will be taken from them—without which the human spirit is totally helpless. That is why, with David, we must earnestly pray that God not remove his Spirit from us.

But let this also be said here of all people who hunger and thirst after righteousness and who truly desire to do what is right, who seek and ask this of the God who created heaven and earth—those who recognize God's invisible essence, God's eternal power and divinity, in the work of the creation of the world. God will not leave them idle and empty, but will fill them with goodness and send messengers and writings to lead them along the right path, just as was done by Philip for the treasurer of Queen Candace of Egypt and for Cornelius by Peter (Acts 8 and 10). Yes, before God would forsake such a spiritually hungry person, God would send down all the angels of heaven through which to proclaim God's glory. God on high wills from us true peace on earth and good will to all people, just as was announced and shown to the shepherds of the field on the night of Christ's birth. That is why the scriptures often refer to God's word as bread, water, drink and meat or blood. For God wants to nourish all who so hunger and thirst, leaving none to suffer from want.

Now, is there such a power in us to want what is right and good? It is not in us in the sense of being from us. For its origin is in God and the image of God in which we were created. That old snake almost extinguished and darkened this by sin. Even so, this breath of God was not extinguished in us entirely. That cannot be done, for God allows no person to be tempted beyond that person's ability to resist. But as a punishment, God can indeed extinguish it. Then a person may have eyes, ears and heart and yet be unable to see, hear or understand.

So it is clear that after the fall, the flesh can do absolutely nothing. In terms of doing good it is useless and dead. In all its power it is unable to do good. It is powerless, an enemy of the Law, to which it will not submit even unto death. That is why King David cried out and lamented so strongly that there was no health in his flesh. Paul said the same thing. "I know that nothing good lives in me, that is, in my flesh" (Romans 7). And the spirit, though it wants to do what is right, is imprisoned by the flesh and can do nothing other than bear inward witness of purity against what is evil, crying out to God without end as a captive, with unutterable groaning.

The soul is as one fallen among murderers, mortally wounded and half dead. It no longer has the taste or knowledge of good and evil. That is why Paul said concerning it, "The man without the Spirit does not accept the things that come from the Spirit of God, for they are foolishness to him and he cannot understand them, because they are spiritually discerned. The spiritual man makes judgments about all things, but he himself is not subject to any man's judgment" (1 Corinthians 2:14–15). And here you see once again, dear Christian, the wholeness of the human spirit which rightly judges all things—and the maimed soul which is useless in discerning anything. Both the flesh and soul are crippled and seriously injured. Only the spirit preserves that original righteousness in which it was created. This is the picture of the three substances of human beings before and after the transgression of Adam, our first father. Forget what the high-minded scholastics say about the higher and lower portions of human beings. That heathen Aristotle has led them astray because he knew and described the human being only in terms of the soul and body.[11] The spirit was too heavenly for him to know. He was unable to comprehend through his natural and pagan mind this breath of the Living God.

Human Beings After the Restoration

Looking at the human being after the restoration from the fall through Christ, one sees that the flesh is useless and wholly destroyed. This is lamented throughout the scriptures. The spirit, on the other hand, is joyful, ready and willing to do all good things. The soul is sorrowful and troubled, standing between the spirit and flesh. The soul on its own natural power is blind to the things of heaven and does not know where to turn. It is awakened, however, by the word of the heavenly Father—by words of comfort, warning, promise, goodness, punishment and other such prompting. Through this the soul is admonished and drawn and is restored to health by God's beloved Son and enlightenment of the Holy Spirit. This is shown by the three central tenets of our Christian faith—that God is Father, Son and Holy Spirit. And so the soul again comes to knowledge of good and evil. The soul's lost freedom is now regained and it can freely and willingly become obedient to the spirit, choosing and willing the good, shunning and fleeing from evil, just as it could before the fall.[12]

This is the work in the soul of the sent word of God. As David said, "He sent forth his word and healed them" (Psalm 107:20). And Christ also said, "If you hold to my teaching, you are really my disciples. Then you will know the truth and the truth will set you free" (John 8:31–32). If the Son has made you free, then you are free indeed.

Now note this well—who has ears, hear! We have been set free again through the sent word and truth of God, through God's only begotten Son Jesus Christ. Therefore, there is certainly true health and freedom again in people after the restoration from the fall. For God always works in our willing and doing according to a good conscience. And although the flesh does not want this, it must act according to the united will of the soul and spirit. That is why David cried out to God, "I am laid low in the dust (that is, the flesh). Preserve my life according to your word" (Psalm 119:25). Now from this basis it must be concluded that a true health and freedom are in humanity after the restoration from the fall. Otherwise these scriptures could not stand, and that is far from God.

Both Christ and Paul assign this freedom to humanity, saying, "If you want to enter life, obey the commandments" (Matthew 19:17). "For if you live according to the sinful nature, you will die. But if by the Spirit you put to death the misdeeds of the body, you will live" (Romans 8:13). This is contained also in that old saying, "Man, help yourself! Then I will help you." Yes, God speaks and gives power through his word. So now it is given to a person to help himself through the power of the word, or to willfully neglect to do so. That is why it is said, "God created you without your help. But God will not save you without your help!" God first created the light. Whoever accepts it will do so according to the promise of God. But whoever shuns the light is rightly judged by God to fall in darkness. The talent which that person has but will not use, hiding it under a handkerchief, will simply be taken away.

The soul stands between the spirit and the flesh. It is as Adam, who stood between God—who told him not to eat of the tree of knowledge of good and evil, and his Eve—who told him to eat of that tree. The soul is again free and may follow either the spirit or the flesh. If it follows the flesh it becomes as the flesh. But if it is obedient to the spirit, it becomes as the spirit. But the soul should be warned not to remain too long at that tree of human decision. It should decide which to follow, the flesh or the spirit. For it must not become as Absalom, who hung between heaven and earth (2 Samuel 18). Otherwise it may be stabbed by that slave of sin, the flesh, receiving three wounds of will, word and deed. That is why David said, "Lord, I have hurried and not tarried in keeping your commandment" (Psalm 119:32). And elsewhere, "Today, if you hear his voice, do not harden your hearts!" (Psalm 95:8). He said "today!" and not "Cras, Cras" (tomorrow) as the ravens cry!

Therefore, through the sent word, the soul is again made healthy and truly free from the fall. It may then choose to will and do the good. Much is expected of it, for it can command the flesh, tame and master it, so that, contrary to the nature of the flesh, it must go into the fire along with the spirit and soul for Christ's name. And although there remains in us, unworthy servants that we are, a measure of imperfection, weakness and defect both of commission and omission, this is not on account of the soul, but rather that evil and useless instrument, the flesh.

Here is an illustration. A craftsman wants to make a clean and smooth table. But his plane is crooked and full of nicks. With such a tool the craftsman cannot make what he wants to make. But the plane is to blame, not the craftsman. Likewise, such a defect does not damn the soul, although it suffers from it and confesses its unworthiness before God. But for the flesh it is a disgrace and it must therefore pay the punishment, which is to suffer and return to the earth. But even after the restoration, the soul is free to choose evil and bring about evil. For in doing evil the soul has a sure and suitable instrument— namely, the flesh, which by nature is quick and inclined to do evil.

That is why it is often said that sin is done willingly—if it were not done willingly, it would not be sin. It is this willfulness to sin

32

which all the scriptures point toward and for which God reproves us for the fact that we will not hear, know or accept what is good. As Christ said, "O Jerusalem, Jerusalem, how often I have longed to gather you as a hen gathers her chicks under her wing, but you were not willing!" (Matthew 23:37). And he also spoke to the young man who asked him what he should do to inherit eternal life. He answered, "If you want to enter into life, obey the commandments" (Matthew 19:17). Now willing and keeping the commandments must have been within the power of the young man, for he said, "I have kept them from my youth." Without a doubt, he spoke the truth, for Jesus looked upon him with love and Jesus would not have loved a liar. Yet Christ pointed toward his inborn imperfection, which is in every person. Christ told him to sell all that he had and give to the poor. And this moved the man to sorrow. But this sorrow was not harmful to him, for it is fulfilled through Christ, who is the Alpha and Omega, the beginning and end of the fulfillment of all God's commandments. Our perfection is in Christ. As Augustine said, if the commandments of God are fulfilled, those things in which we fall short are forgiven us. John also wrote very clearly concerning this power, saying that God has given us the power to become children of God.

Here you see clearly, Christian reader, that it belongs to us to whom the word is sent to will the good. But we do not find it in ourselves to fulfill it. That is because of our pitiful body, in which nothing but sin can be found.

In summary, the spirit remains whole after the restoration from the fall. The flesh is anything but whole. The soul may either sin or not sin. But the soul which sins will die. Therefore, such a soul must surely say, "It was my own doing. The flesh has received its judgment. The spirit remains whole. Therefore, if I will it, I can be saved by the grace of God. But if I do not will it, I will be damned. And that condemnation will be because of my own guilt and head-strong obstinacy." Therefore, God's Spirit spoke through Hosea saying, "The condemnation is yours, Israel! Only in me is your salvation!" (Hosea 13:4).

From what is said here it is easy to note that the Law operates in different ways. For the flesh, it brings recognition of sin. For the spirit it is an aid and witness against sin. And for the soul it is a light to show and teach the way of righteousness and to flee from sin and evil. So when the flesh hears the Law, it is frightened and its hair stands up in terror. The spirit leaps up in joy. The believing soul thanks and praises God for this lamp and light for the pathway. For as the devil neither wills nor can do the good, so it is with the flesh, which, having seen that the forbidden fruit was pleasing to the eye and good to eat, sinned willingly. But the soul did not sin by its own will. It sinned only because of its weakness and the urging of the flesh. For Adam did not want to anger Eve, who was his flesh. He then made excuses and said, "The woman you put with me—she gave me some fruit from the tree, and I ate it" (Genesis 3:12). Only the spirit remained aright in this fall. Therefore, it will return to the Lord who created it.

In short, here you see, dear reader, that God created human beings free. It would have been possible for humans to remain in their created state of innocence and righteousness without an infusion of new grace, right on into eternal life. But it was also possible to forfeit this grace through disobedience. And that is what happened. And because of this fall, grace and freedom were darkened and lost to such an extent that, without an infusion of new and particular grace of God, humans would not be able to know the difference between good and evil. So how could humans will the good and avoid evil? We cannot will the good unless we are shown it beforehand. But after the restoration from the fall, through the service of our Lord Jesus Christ, humans are again given such grace, health and freedom that we can will and do the good, even though that is contrary to the nature and will of the flesh, in which nothing good is contained.

Free will in human beings is nothing more than a power, force or ability of the soul to will or not to will, to choose or to flee, to accept or reject good and evil, according either to the will of God or the flesh. So actually this fleshly will or ability might well be regarded as feebleness rather than as power or might.[13] For the soul lost the knowledge of good and evil in the sight of God by eating of the forbidden tree. It had this knowledge before the fall—at least in as much as it was necessary and right for a human creature to know. That is why this tree was called the tree of knowledge of good and evil, from which God forbid Adam to eat. That is, it was a desire to know and experience more than is necessary for a human being. But Eve desired, after the promise of that crafty snake, to know all that God knows. "For God knows that when you eat of it your eyes will be opened, and you will be like God, knowing good and evil" (Genesis 3:5). Therefore, they were rightly terrified of God because of this knowledge of good and evil. And they became as horses or mules, lacking in all understanding.

If a person does not accept a gift of God with thanksgiving, or does not even want it, then even that which he has will be taken away. And that is what happened to humanity in the fall. As a result, a person can neither will that good nor flee from evil unless shown first what, in the eyes of God, is good or evil. Therefore, the recognition or power of knowledge, will and work must be attained through a new grace and attraction of the heavenly Father. The Father now looks upon humanity in a new way because of the service of our Lord Jesus Christ. He blesses and draws us toward him through his living word, which speaks to the human heart. This attraction and bidding is like an invitation to a wedding feast or banquet. God gives power and might to all people to come. Inasmuch as they want to come (and it is a free choice) they can become born anew, as creations in the beginning, just as people were in paradise (except for the flesh) and become true children of God.

But whoever does not want to come, like Jerusalem and those who have bought oxen and houses and have taken wives, he leaves behind as unworthy of this celebration. He wants only uncoerced, willing and happy guests and givers. These he loves. For God forces no one—God works only through the sending and calling of his word.[14] It is like the two disciples at Emmaus. They did not force Christ to remain with them. They only asked and employed kind words. The same with Lot and the two angels in Sodom. God's word is so mighty, powerful and strong in the believer that the person (but not the godless one) wills to do everything the word wills and commands. For the gospel is a power of God for the salvation of all believers.

When the man who lay sick for thirty-eight years in front of the pool at Bethesda heard the word of Jesus, saying, "Stand up, take your bed and go" (John 5), in the power of these words of Christ he freely stood up, took his bed and went. He certainly could have done otherwise, saying in unbelief to the Lord, "That is impossible!" or "I would rather just lay here!" Just so, Christ could not do many signs and wonders in his homeland because of their unbelief. But as soon as this sick man heard the word and believed, he was made healthy, stood up and walked. In the same way, when Christ says to someone, "Keep my commandments, forsake evil and do what is right," from that hour on the person receives in faith the power and ability to will and do it.

Indeed, all things are possible for the believer in that one who gives strength, that is, Christ Jesus. Here we could cite scripture after scripture which witness to the power and working of God's word.

We surely know that God originally created all things good, and in particular, human beings, in spirit, soul and body. And it is only because of the disobedience of Adam that this goodness in us has been wounded in the soul, darkened in the body which holds the spirit captive, and totally destroyed in the flesh. If we are again to be free in spirit and healed in the soul, and even in the body not be harmed by this fall, then it absolutely and unequivocally must happened through the new birth. This is as Christ said. We can never otherwise enter into the kingdom of God. As James wrote, God willingly gives us this new birth in the power of his word, "so that we might be a kind of firstfruits of all he created" (James 1:18).

In this word (which Peter calls an indestructible seed) we become again free and healthy, so that absolutely nothing damnable remains in us. As Christ said, "The truth will make you free" (John 8:32). Also David said, "He sent his word and healed them" (Psalm 107:20). And elsewhere also, "Lord, make me alive according to your word" (Psalm 119:25). So it follows without doubt that in the believer there must be true freedom, health and real life, through the power of God's word. Otherwise, we would have to simply toss out half the Bible! And we certainly cannot do that.

From what has been said, it is noted clearly and surely that humanity received two wounds in the fall of Adam. One is internal, an ignorance of good and evil, because Adam was more obedient to the voice of his flesh than to the voice of God. The other wound is external, in action and fulfilling. Because of this we are unable completely to hold and fulfill the commandments of God, because of the inborn evil of the flesh. In all our works we are as useless servants. And this breach or defect springs from the fact that Adam had not truly mastered his rib, Eve, according to the commandments of God. Contrary to God's command, he ate of the tree which was forbidden on pain of death.

The first wound is healed by the outpouring of wine by the Samaritan, Christ—that is, through the Law in which, by a new grace, the human being is taught once again what is truly good and evil before God. The second wound is healed with oil, that is, with the gospel. Thus this sin or breach is no longer poisonous or damning if we do not willingly walk in it. Therefore, in the New Testament, Christ the true physician mixed together both oil and wine, Law and gospel, and made from it a healing balm for our soul. And by this our soul is made righteous and healthy once again.

Here one grasps with both hands how Christ has neutralized the fall of Adam, how the head of that old serpent is crushed by the seed of woman, how the thorn was removed and its poison made harmless for us. Therefore, no one may now cry over Adam and Eve and excuse or cover up his own sin by pointing to the fall of Adam. For now all that was lost, wounded and killed in Adam has been sufficiently restored, healed and made healthy again. For the Spirit of Christ has obtained for our spirit from the heavenly Father the assurance that our spiritual imprisonment will not harm us. And through his Spirit our spirit is again taught and enlightened as to what is good or evil. Indeed, through his flesh our flesh has earned assurance that after it has become ashes it will again be resurrected in honor and immortality.[15] From then on, every soul bears its own sin. For it is willfully responsible for its own sin and not Adam, not Eve, not the flesh, sin, death or the devil. For these all are already captured, bound and overcome in Christ. So with Paul we give him praise, honor and thanks in eternity.

And finally, we now see here most clearly what sort of gross error has been introduced and brought into Christianity by those who deny human freedom of will and say that this freedom is an empty and idle concept, without substance. By this our God is shamed and blasphemed, likened to a tyrant who would condemn and punish humans for something they could do nothing about. This also throws out the just charge Christ will make on judgment day, when he will say, "For I was hungry and you gave me nothing to eat" (Matthew 25:42). For then they could easily excuse themselves and answer, "It was impossible, for because of Adam you robbed us of our ability to will and do the good." For in your unchanging wisdom you foresaw and predestined in eternity that we would not feed you! The same for Judas Iscariot, who betrayed you. And Pilate, who sentenced you in your innocence. So how can you blame us now? We are not guilty. You yourself are guilty. For you made us a vessel of dishonor. And now, just so that your eternal wisdom and foreknowledge remain true and just, we must be condemned to eternal fire with the devil!"

By denying free will, much cause is given to evil people to lay all of their sin and evil on God, saying, "It must be God's will that I be an adulterer and run after harlots. Well, God's will be done! After all, who can thwart the will of God? If it was not God's will, I would not sin. When God wills it, I will stop sinning!"

I do not even speak here of the fact that, because of this error or opinion, many people are led into sloth and great despair, thinking, "Well, since I can neither will nor do anything good, and all things happen by necessity, I might as well relax. If God wants me, God will draw me to himself. If God does not want me, then my efforts are useless and fruitless." Yes, such people wait for a wondrous, unusual and miraculous drawing of God, for proof that God has use of them, as if the sending of his holy word to draw and call them were not enough.

All of this is the work of an evil, sly and blasphemous devil! I do not see how a more harmful Satan could arise among Christians to hinder righteousness and godliness on earth. For through this falsehood the greatest part of the holy scriptures are thrown out and made powerless. May the almighty, good and merciful God help us against this gross error and crush it by the breath of his mouth through Jesus Christ our Lord. Amen.

"A Short Meditation on the Lord's Prayer" (1526)
Balthasar Hubmaier

Our Father. Gracious Father, I am not worthy to be called a child of yours or that I should be able to call you my Father. I have not always done your will. I have often done the will of the Father of Lies. Forgive me, merciful Father, and make me a child of yours in the faith.

Who Art In Heaven. Father of goodness, look upon us, we who live in this miserable state of woe. We know that children cannot find a better condition than to be with their loving father, who feeds them, gives them drink, clothes them, protects them and shields them from all needs. Gracious Father, take us, your miserable children, to be with you in heaven.

Holy Is Your Name. Merciful Father, we know that we are guilty of continually dishonoring your name with our words and actions. The suffering of Christ, which for us is medicament for eternal life, we make into an eternal reproach by our cursing and rebuking. Forgive us, Father, and give us grace so that your name will never come from our mouths unprofitably. Help us to cease all blasphemy and swearing so that your holy name will eternally be glorified, enhanced and praised.

Your Kingdom Come. Gracious Father, we know that we are captives to sin, the devil, hell and eternal death. But Father, we cry out and call to you as our loving Father to come quickly with your kingdom of grace, peace, joy and eternal salvation. Come to our aid, gracious Father, for without you we are totally miserable, afflicted and lost.

Your Will Be Done On Earth As In Heaven. Good Father, we confess publicly that your fatherly will does not suit us earthly people. Our will is completely and totally hostile to your divine will. We ask you to send your Holy Spirit to work in us authentic faith, steadfast hope and ardent love, so that our will is conformed to your divine will in all things.

Give Us Today Our Daily Bread. Compassionate Father, we live not by bread alone, but by every word that comes from your holy mouth. Therefore, we humbly pray that you will feed us with the bread of your holy word. This is the bread of heaven, and whoever eats it will be eternally filled. Make it a living presence in our souls. Make it grow and bring forth fruits of eternal life. Give us diligent Christian workers who will spread this bread among us in pure, clear and untarnished manner so that your Fatherly will, which is known only from your word, will be fulfilled.

Forgive Us Our Debts As We Forgive Our Debtors. Kind Father, we know that we are guilty of having sinned in words, deeds and evil thoughts. We do not even know the number, portion or extent of our sins. Father, forgive us and give us power to better our way of living, even as we forgive those who have caused our suffering. Father, forgive them too, for they do not know what they are doing. Enlighten all those who misunderstand your holy word, who abuse and persecute us, so that they might come to the true way that leads to eternal life.

Lead Us Not Into Temptation. Heavenly Father! Look on the fear, barrenness, misery, persecution and hardship which we must endure here on earth, and ponder also our human weakness. For this reason, sweet Father, we ask of you, through your Fatherly love, that you do not forsake us in our anguish and suffering, that we not be defeated nor fall away from your holy word. Do not allow us to be tempted beyond that which we can endure. We are weak and frail, while our enemies are strong, powerful and heartless. You know these things, merciful Father.

Deliver Us From Evil. Deliver us from evil, from sin, from the devil, from our own lust, which is our greatest enemy. Deliver us from all that keeps us far from you. Moreover, give us all that brings us closer to you. *For dominion, power and glory are yours forever in eternity.*

Eternal Father, as we have prayed to you here, bring it to fulfillment according to your Fatherly good will. These things we pray through your mercy and through your gracious promises which you have given to us consistently through Moses, the prophets and the apostles. But we pray this especially, pleading with you, through your most beloved son, our Lord Jesus Christ. He has surely promised us, and proved it through his bitter death, that whatever we pray for in your name you will give us. Father, we place our bodies, lives, honor, possessions, soul and spirit into your hands. All that we have received from you we offer back to you, for you give and your take away. Praise be to your name. Amen and amen.

"Six Anabaptist Hymns" (1526–1529) from the *Ausbund*

The Ausbund *is the oldest hymnal of the Swiss Anabaptists and is still used by the Amish in North America today. It is a collection of hymns of praise, supplication and stories of martyrdom suffered by the early Anabaptists. The* Ausbund *went through many editions in Europe and the was contraband and subject to confiscation there into the early eighteenth century. The hymns are rendered here in free verse, retaining the sense and meaning, along with some of the rhythm where possible, but with no attempt to retain the rhyme scheme. All were taken from the most recent edition of the book,* Ausbund, das ist: Etliche schöne Christliche Lieder *(Lancaster: Verlag von den Amischen Gemeinden, 1984).*

Song #6: Poetic rendering of a letter written by Felix Mantz

1.
With joy I will sing,
My heart delights in God,
Who brings me the ability
To escape from that death
Which is eternal and has no end.
I praise you, Christ in heaven,
Who frees me from anxiety

2.
You were sent to me by God
As a model and a light,
Before my life is over you have

41

Called me to your kingdom,
That I may have eternal joy with God,
And love him from my heart
And all his righteousness,

3.

Which here and now is intended,
For those who want life.
His righteousness is praised and misused,
Without it nothing could endure.
This is what the scripture says:
Whoever resists it,
Poisons other people.

4.

One finds many people now
In this wide world,
Who preach God's word,
Yet are full of hatred and envy:
They are not full of God's love;
Their guile and deception
Is known to everyone.

5.

As we have been aware
In these final days,
Those who come in sheep's clothing
Are sometimes ravaging wolves,
They hate all of the pious on earth,
And hinder their way to life,
And to the true sheepfold.

6.

That is done by the false prophets
And hypocrites of this world,
Who both curse and pray,
Their conduct is totally wrong.
They call on the authorities,
That they should put us to death,
For they have forsaken Christ.

7.

I will praise Christ,
Who shows everyone patience,
He acts as our friend
And inclines his grace toward us,
He shows love to everyone
According to his Father's nature,
Which no false one could do.

8.

We should note this difference,
Listen carefully to what I say,
The lambs among the heathen
Seek only to honor God.
They are not detained by property or goods,
They are cleansed of this through Christ,
Who holds then in his care.

9.

Christ compels nobody
To his honor's glory,
It is only given to those
Who have freely desired it,
Through true faith and baptism,
Who work repentance with pure heart,
Heaven is for these only,

10.

Through pouring out of Christ's blood,
Which he did willingly,
It was not displeasing to him,
For he already knew that we
Would be gifted with divine power.
For whoever gives up his body,
Grows strong in God.

11.

Love alone is worthy
To God, through Christ.
Neither bowing nor inveighing helps,

It can be no other way.
Love alone pleases God;
Whoever does not show love,
Has no place in God.

12.

Pure love in Christ
Spares the enemy.
Whoever would be an heir with him
To him is also commanded
To show mercy
According to his Lord's teaching
And he will have eternal joy.

13.

Christ accuses no one,
As the false ones do,
They do not show Christ's love,
They do not understand his word,
Yet they want to be shepherds and teachers:
They will despair in the end,
Their reward is eternal pain.

14.

Christ hated no one,
Nor should his servants,
To remain on the true path
And to follow their Lord,
To have with them the light of life,
And be joyful in their hearts
Is the desire of all pious ones.

15.

Those who show hatred and envy,
Cannot be true Christians,
Nor those who bow to evil,
Nor hit with their fists.
To run after Christ as murderers and thieves,
To shed innocent blood,
Is a false kind of love.

16.
That is how one knows,
They do not stand with Christ,
They violate Christian practices,
Like all children of Belial,
As Cain did to his brother,
When God accepted Abel's offering,
Cain brought him into great need.

17.
Now I will close;
Note well, all pious ones,
It will do us well
To consider Adam's fall,
He listened to the serpent
And was disobedient to God,
And therefore death followed.

18.
The same will happen to those
Who resist Christ,
Those who look with carnal desire
And not with divine love.
And so ends this song;
I remain with Christ,
Who knows my every need.

Song #5: Written by George Blaurock

George Blaurock was born in 1492 and was educated as a priest. Blaurock was the first person to receive adult baptism among the Swiss Anabaptists. By that time (January 1525) he had already married. A fiery speaker, Blaurock was often very provocative, even to the point of publicly interrupting official church services to dispute with the preachers. Blaurock became a leading figure in the Swiss Anabaptist movement, for which he was repeatedly arrested, imprisoned and banished from various territories. By 1529, Blaurock had left the Swiss territories to work in Tyrol and South Germany. He was captured in Innsbruck in August of that year. He was questioned under torture and on September 6, 1529, he was burned as a heretic.

SWISS ANABAPTISM

1.

God's judgment is true
And none can break it
Who does not do God's will
Will be condemned

2.

You, O Lord, are merciful and good
Gracious you are found
Whoever does your will on earth
You recognize as your child

3.

Through Christ we give you praise and thanks
For all his blessings
And that for our life long
He protects us from sin

4.

The sinner receives a harsh judgment
To bring him to repentance
If he does not refrain from sin
God warns him with threats

5.

He comes in his glory
To take the judgment seat
Then they will suffer
No excuse will protect them

6.

His word shows clearly
That people must repent
Believe his word and be baptized
And follow his teachings

7.

So note well you sons of men
Cease from your sinning
Do not be senseless, godless and blind
For the physician seeks you

8.

It will be terrible for the sinner
Who is not circumcised
In eternal pain God will put him
And there in suffering he will remain

9.

For you, O Lord, are a righteous God
None will deceive you
You preserve from the second death
Those whom you love in your heart

10.

You, O Lord, are a strong God
Who opens up hell
And throws therein the godless rabble
Who have hated your children

11.

God, your mercy is great
To those who repent
You erase all their sins
Through Jesus Christ our Lord

12.

God bids the whole human race
To love and fear him
To follow his righteous servant
And he works his teachings in us

13.

The sinner mocks and scorns
When offered the love of God
This will be his undoing
For God will not be deceived

14.

Antichrist with all treachery
Sets against those who fear God
O God, please watch over us
And strengthen your weak vessels

15.

So have patience, you loving child
For the sake of my name
Even though you are hated
I will still your worries

16.

God the Father through his faithfulness
Will never forsake us
Renew us daily, O Lord
In our everyday living

17.

Through Christ we call on you
As through your tender suffering
We know your faithfulness and love
Along this our pilgrim's way

18.

Forsake us not as your children
From now until the end
Give us your hand, O Father
That we may complete our journey

19.

When our journey is ended
Then we will receive a crown
As is already upon your son
Who hung upon a cross

20.

The suffering is great and hard
Which is happening to us
Help us to thank you for it
And see it as a joy

21.

The Father has chosen us out of grace
And has not rejected us
Let us then, when our time comes
Receive the reward with joy

22.

Prepare us for communion
Through Christ your beloved son
Clothe us with your Spirit
Protect us from suffering and death

23.

If we would eat this meal
Who serves us at the table?
As all hearts know, this is done
By the one who made atonement for sin

24.

Blessed are those invited
To this communion meal
Remain steadfast with Christ until the end
In all tribulations

25.

Just as he suffered
Hanging on the cross
So now the pious ones
Suffer great violence

26.

For all who do not soil
These wedding clothes
The Lord has a crown prepared
And will crown them with it

27.

But those who are not dressed
When the king comes
Must stand off to the side
And not receive their crown

28.

They will be bound hand and foot
For they were unready
And they will be thrown into outer darkness
Away from this joyous occasion

29.

O Lord, give us perfect love
To walk unhindered
So that we remain inside
Before the door closes

30.

As it will happen to the foolish
They will cry out, Lord Lord
But they will receive no oil for their lamps
They will be excluded

31.

Blessed are those who remain alert
As were the clever bridesmaids
They will receive eternal good
And show the clarity of God

32.

When the king appears
With the trumpet blast
Then all of the elect
Will be taken with him

33.

Therefore, Zion, you holy church
Show what you have received
Keep from all sin
And receive your crown

Song #30: Written by George Blaurock

1.

Lord God, I will praise you
Now and Forever
For you have given me the faith
Through which I might know you!
You sent me your holy word

SWISS ANABAPTISM

Which, by your great grace
I find remains with me

2.

I have accepted you
As you know well, O Lord
Nothing will return empty
I hope, strengthen my spirit
That I may know your will
This makes my heart
Cry out joyously

3.

It would frighten me terribly
If I found it in me
A burden wanting to choke me
If you did not come
With your word of grace
I would be defeated
And suffer eternal agony

4.

Therefore I will praise
And glorify you eternally
Your name is high above
You always show yourself
To be a loving Father
You will not forsake me
You have chosen me as your child

5.

I cry to you, O Lord
Help me, my God and Father
That I become your child and heir
Out of love and trust
O Lord, make me strong in faith
For the building would go to ruins
If your help were not there

6.

For me not, O Lord
Be with me always
Let your Spirit protect and teach me
That in my suffering
You will always comfort me
And valiantly conquer
In the struggles of this battle

7.

The enemy attacks me
And hunts me down
In the field where I lay
Lord, you gave me the victory!
The sharp weapons of false teaching and coercion
Which the enemy brought up against me
Made my whole body quake

8.

Lord, you allow your mercy
Through your grace, help and power
Your Son aids this poor one
And makes me triumphant
O Lord, as soon as you hear me
You come with your strong aid
And defeat the enemy yourself

9.

Therefore I will sing
Praising your name
And eternally proclaim
The grace I have seen
Now I pray for all your children
That you protect us eternally
In the face of the enemy

10.

I cannot build on the flesh
It is weak by nature
I will trust in your word

That is my comfort and refuge
And because I have given up myself
You will help me in all need
To your peace

11.
In the hour of the final days
Which we stand before
Help us, O Lord, to carry
The cross according to your plan
Turn to us in all your grace
That we might serve
The Spirit in your hands

12.
I pray to you from the heart
Before all our enemies
O Lord, with all seemliness
However many they may be
Do not count their misdeeds against them
That have been done according to your will
This I pray, O God

13.
So now I take leave
From all my loved ones
In grace, lead us all, O God
Into your kingdom
That we may believe without doubt
And fulfill your holy work
Give us power unto the end

Song #7: Written by Michael Sattler

Michael Sattler was born in 1490 in Southern Germany. He was trained as a priest and became the prior of a Benedictine monastery. According to his own testimony, he was shocked by the unspiritual life of the monks and priests with whom he had contact. He finally left the monastery and married. He went to Zurich in 1525, where he joined the Anabaptist cause. He presided at Schleitheim in February

SWISS ANABAPTISM

1527 over the Anabaptist "conference," which produced the first unified Anabaptist confession of faith. By the end of that month, Sattler was arrested with a group of other Anabaptists. His trial was held in Rottenburg in May. The charges against Sattler, along with his innovative and able defense, have been the focus of various scholarly studies.

Sattler was condemned to a terrible death. The court stipulated that on his way to the stake, his tongue was to be progressively cut out, piece by piece. He was to have two pieces torn from his body by glowing tongs and burned five times with the tongs. Finally, he was bound with ropes to a ladder and pushed into the fire.

1.

As Jesus with his true teaching
Gathered to himself a small flock
He told them that each with patience
Should daily carry his cross

2.

And he said, You my beloved disciples
You should always be glad
On earth love nothing else
Than me and following my teaching

3.

The world will persecute you
And mock and scorn you
Hunt you and publicly say
You have Satan in you

4.

When others blaspheme and mock you
For my sake persecute and strike you
Be glad, for your reward
Is already prepared for you in heaven

5.

Look to me, I am God's son
And have always done well
I am the best of all
But was killed anyway

6.

Because the world called me
An evil spirit and seducer of the people
And denied my truth
It will not be easy for you either

7.

But do not fear the man
Who can only kill the body
But fear only the true God
Who has power to judge

8.

God tests you as gold
And holds you as his children
If you keep my teachings
I will never leave you

9.

For I am yours and you are mine
Where I am, there you should be
And who touches you touches my eye
And will be punished on judgment day

10.

Your misery, fear, anxiety, need and pain
Will then turn into joy
And you will receive praise and honor
Before the hosts of heaven

11.

The apostles took such on
You should teach it to everyone
Whoever will follow the Lord
Should expect the same

12.

O Christ, help your people
Who follow you truly
So that through your bitter death
They will be saved from all need

13.

Praise be to God on his throne
And to his beloved son
And the to Holy Spirit also
Who draws many to his kingdom

Song #36: Written by Annelein of Freiberg

Annelein of Freiberg was drowned and then burned in 1529. Nothing more specific is known about this woman, although some sources indicate that she may have been only 17 years old at the time of her imprisonment.

1.

Eternal Father in Heaven
I call to you from deep within
Do not let me turn from you
Hold me in your eternal truth
Until I reach my end

2.

O God, keep my heart and mouth
Watch over me, Lord, always
Do not let me part from you
Whether in anguish, fear or need
Keep me pure in joy

3.

My eternal Lord and father
I am your poor, unworthy child
Teach me and make me know
So that I can observe your ways
That is my truest desire

4.

To walk in your strength in death
Through tribulation, martyrdom, fear and need
Keep me in your strength
That I may never again be separated
From your love, O God

5.

There are many who travel this path
On which stands the cup of suffering
And also much false doctrine
With which they try to turn us away
From Christ our Lord

6.

I lift up my soul to you, Lord
I hope in you in times of danger
Let me not become a disgrace
So that my enemies have the victory
Over me on this earth

7.

They have me here locked up
I wait, O God, from my heart
With great desire
If you would only stir
And save your ones in prison

8.

O God Father, for your kingdom
Makes us like the five wise virgins
Who were alert
In waiting for the bridegroom to come
With his chosen band

9.

Eternal king of heaven
Give us eternal food and drink
Feed us with your truth
Which never spoils
For it is of spiritual nature

10.

If you hold back your food from us
Then all is lost and for nothing
We can accomplish nothing without you

We hope in you through your grace
That we have not been mistaken

11.

I do not doubt the power of God
Truthful is his judgment
He will forsake no one
Who is firm in faith
And remains in truth

12.

Be comforted, you Christians
And always be joyous through Jesus Christ
He gives us love and faith
God comforts through his holy word
And we must trust in it

13.

I bid God and his church
That he be today my guardian
For his name's sake
My Father, let it be so
Through Jesus Christ, Amen

Song #61: Written by seven people imprisoned in Gmund, each wrote one verse

1.

I cry to you from deepest need
O God, hear my call
Send your Holy Spirit to us
To comfort our deepest despair
As you have done to now, Christ
We rely on your command
But the heathen now want to kill us

2.

The flesh is weak, as you know
It fears the smallest pain
So fill us with your Spirit

SWISS ANABAPTISM

We pray from our hearts
So that we may remain until the end
And go bravely into suffering
And not fear the pain

3.

The spirit is surely willing
To undergo suffering
Hear us, O Lord
Through Jesus Christ your beloved Son!
We pray also for our enemies
Who know not what they do
And think not of your wrath

4.

We ask you, Father and Lord
As your loving children
Kindle the light through Jesus Christ
Even more in your little flock
That would be our hearts' desire
That for which we hunger and thirst
And would bring us greatest joy

5.

You have received us in grace
And made us your servants
This we have all done willingly
And fulfilled with your help
Keep us pure in your word
We want to be obedient to you
Give us aid and comfort

6.

You, Lord God, are my protection
We lift ourselves up to you
So it is but a small pain
If our lives be taken from us
You have prepared for us in eternity
So if here we suffer insult and blows
It will not be for nothing

59

7.

Body, life, soul and limbs
We have received from you
These we offer up to you
To praise and glorify your name
It is nothing but dust and ashes
We commend to you our spirit, O God
Take it into your hands. Amen

Part II:
South German
and Austrian
Anabaptism

Hans Hut

Hans Hut was undoubtedly the most significant early Anabaptist leader in South Germany and Austria. Hut had notable contact with Thomas Müntzer during 1524 and may have taken part in the Frankenhausen battle during the German Peasants' War. He was baptized by Hans Denck in the early summer of 1526. Sources indicate that he developed a very apocalyptic and chiliastic interpretation of Anabaptist ideology which barely altered the revolutionary hopes he had previously held. He seems to have expected that a Turkish invasion would finish what the peasants had failed to accomplish. Hut did teach pacifism, but it was an "interim" ethic which would end when the final trumpet blast sounded. Then the "saints," aided by the Turks and God's own angels, would rise up and overthrow the unrighteous ruling authorities and the rich. Hut was arrested in September of 1527 and died in prison soon thereafter.

Hut's major extant writing, "On the Mystery of Baptism," was preserved by the Hutterians. Hut was known to have taught that there were "seven judgments" of God. This writing deals with the first judgment. Hut's doctrine of "three baptisms" (of the Spirit, of Water and of Blood) was a major characteristic of his teaching; it echoes through the writings of many of Hut's followers. Another clear echo of Hutian influence is mention of the "gospel of all creatures." Hut's major formulation of this gospel is also found in this writing. According to Hut, all of nature points toward the need for suffering. Nothing comes to true fruition without suffering. The grape must be crushed, the animal must be butchered and roasted, the grain must be ground and baked. Likewise, the human being must suffer in order to become a worthy instrument of the will of God. Accepting the Christian faith, therefore, is a blessed but bitter internal experience. True faith is a very real struggle. Scholars have rightly pointed to the influence of Thomas Müntzer's "mysticism of the cross" on Hut at this point. Hut's *disdain for professional scholars and preachers, who earn comfortable livings for their religious work, is very apparent in this writing.[1] He sees them as following the dictates of their "bellies" rather than those of justice and right. In his "gospel of all creatures" we see the anguished wrestling of a semi-educated man trying to understand that age-old question, "Why do the wicked prosper while the good people do not?" Hut's "natural theology" of suffering is a landmark of Anabaptist spiritual writing. This translation is taken from document 2 in the source collection Glaubenszeugnisse oberdeutscher Taufgesinnter, Band I, ed. L. Müller (Leipzig: M. Heinsius Nachfolger, 1938).*

"On the Mystery of Baptism.
Baptism as Symbol and as Essence, the Beginning of a True Christian Life. John 5" (1526)
Hans Hut

To all brothers and sisters in the Lord, I wish you the fear of God which is the beginning of divine wisdom. The congregation of God is the true foundation of Christianity, the bride and the spouse of Christ, unified in the bonds of love through the Holy Spirit. These are the ones who with contrite hearts and spirit earnestly desire the righteousness of the crucified son of God. And all those who seek it will be satisfied. To these people I wish grace and peace through the Holy Spirit. Amen.

The final and most terrible times of this world are upon us.[2] With alert eyes we see and acknowledge that all which was prophesied and preached from the beginning through the prophets, patriarchs and apostles will take place, be restored and this is happening even now. This is as Peter told us in Acts. But the world (God have mercy) has absolutely no understanding of this, especially those who teach others but actually understand less than the apes, although they present themselves as scriptural authorities. In fact, the truth is closed to them sevenfold, for they will not suffer it to be opened up to them by a work of God. Actually they are God's enemies, as Paul said. Therefore, all that they teach and read is backward in order and a falsehood. Truth is for them most concealed and covered over. The poor man is being led astray, betrayed to all that is destructive and foul. No one believes this, even though it is spoken and proclaimed.

There is no worldly and debauched scholar alive who knows the judgments of the Lord. Because they are perverted they see everything as backward and thus they seduce both rich and poor with their jeweled tongues. Well then, those who will be misled will always be misled.

Therefore I admonish all godly people who seek after and love righteousness to earnestly safeguard themselves from all usurious, haughty and hypocritical scholars who preach for money. They do not look out for your good but only for their own bellies. We see that their lives are no better than any other worldly person and anyone who trusts them will be betrayed. They preach nothing but "faith." But they never say how this faith is to come about. So the world grovels before them. For where the order of divine mystery is betrayed, there is only frivolous error and nothing lasting. This can be seen in all things.

Therefore, my beloved brothers and sisters in the Lord, you must learn the judgments of God concerning His commandments and His word for yourselves and be given understanding from God alone. Otherwise, you will be led astray right along with the rest of the world. For they do not know the judgments of God, nor even what is meant by a judgment. So they say simply that it is impossible to know or grasp the judgments of God. They arm themselves in this with the words of Saint Paul, but forget what he said in the first epistle to the Corinthians, following Solomon. They also forget that David pled with the Lord to learn his judgments. And God earnestly commanded them to learn, keep and accomplish His judgments. If we are to do that, then we surely must be able to know what His judgments are. Oh, how wretchedly they seduce the whole world under the guise of the holy scripture with their false and worthless faith, a faith which brings no betterment of life. Anyone can judge and recognize this for himself from the fact that whenever two or three of them preach concerning the same scriptural passage, none of them agree in their exegesis.

Therefore, my beloved brothers and sisters in the Lord, if you truly desire to know the judgments of God and witness the Holy Spirit in truth, do not listen to the cries of those who preach for money. Rather seek the poor, those forsaken by the world and called fanatics and devils, following the example of Christ and the apostles. Listen to these. For no one may obtain the truth except he follow in the footsteps of Christ and his elect in the school of affliction, nor have the least part in following the will of God in the vindication of the cross of Christ. For the mysteries of divine wisdom cannot be learned in the rogues' galleries of Wittenburg or Paris. Neither can they be learned in the lords' courts while living on a comfortable stipend. For the wisdom of God does not dwell among those living in ease.

So our new Evangelicals, these soft scholars, have pushed the pope, monks and priests from their stools. But now that they have succeeded, they begin once again whoring with the villainous Babylonians in all greed, haughtiness, covetousness, envy and hatred and are building (God have mercy) an even more wicked Popery than before. They will not listen to a poor man or engage in scriptural arguments with such a one, for they do not want to be found lacking knowledge or unlearned.

Therefore, they conclude that all those who do not believe the way they do must be evil knaves, devils, false prophets and fanatics — just as happened to Christ. Well then, leave them in their pits with their idols and rulers, tickling their ears, so long as God allows. But their time is short and everyone will witness their shameful end.

I am moved by Christian love and brotherly concern to record the judgments which are necessary to the beginning of the Christian life, to the degree that God gives me grace, as a witness to all brothers and sisters in the Lord, those who hunger and thirst for righteousness, and not for the worldly, debauched people. For such judgments are incomprehensible to them, backward and upside down, heretical, despised and damned. Therefore, all brothers and sisters who love and desire the truth, when you begin to read such a written judgment, I admonish you not to despise it because there are parts you do not understand. For understanding has been made impossible for some because of the folly by which our new scholars have seduced and led them astray.

Therefore, if we are to come to a true understanding of such judgments, we must from the beginning become as children and fools. It is impossible for a carnal person to comprehend or to grasp the judgments of God in truth, when they are not in all parts placed into a proper order. Therefore, we want to begin first of all with the judgment of baptism, the beginning of the Christian life. We want earnestly to note and see how it was instituted and mandated by Christ and practiced by the apostles, with proofs from the divine witness of the holy scriptures, and not according to the good thought of human wisdom, as it has been up until now, even among those who celebrate the gospel. May God have mercy on all people, but especially the poor.[3] And help us, the cross of Christ. Amen.

If we want to arrive at a correct understanding and judgment concerning baptism, we must not rely on our human thoughts and toss aside the form and practice of Christ and his apostles. For God has forbidden us to do whatever seems right to us. Rather we should do only what God has commanded us to do and not waver left or right. So if baptism is to be practiced in right order as it was commanded by Christ and practiced by the apostles, we must with all diligence and earnestness take as truth the command of Christ. For he has instituted an order and a rule or measure which lays the proper foundation for Christian faith. Who has ears, let him hear! And if someone is offended, so be it.

First of all, Christ said, go into all the world and preach the gospel of all creatures.[4] Next he said, who believes, thirdly, and is baptized, will be saved. This order must be kept if we want to achieve a true Christian life and break the whole world to pieces. Where this order is not kept there is no Christian community of God but only of the devil, and the result is a world full of false Christians who champion what is not right and their perverted order.

First of all, Christ said, go into all the world and preach the gospel of all creatures. Here the Lord tells us how a person comes to knowledge of God and Christ—that is, through the gospel of all creatures. So our first task is to learn and understand just what is meant by this "gospel of all creatures."

But (God have mercy) the entire world knows nothing of it and neither is it preached in our time. It has been revealed to those poor in spirit, despised by the world, as it should be, and they preach it and speak about it. But to the soft and lascivious people, especially those who preach for money and boast about their preaching of the gospel, it is seen as the worst kind of foolishness and fanaticism. They call those who preach this gospel of all creatures the most evil sort of false prophets and rebuke them as lying spirits. Well, their day is coming. For now, as Paul said, the word of the cross is foolishness to those who will be lost. But for those of us who will be saved it is the power of God.

The gospel of all creatures is about nothing other than simply Christ the crucified one. But not only Christ the Head was crucified, but rather Christ in all his members.[5] This Christ is what is preached and taught by all creatures. The whole Christ suffers in all members. It is not as these scholarly Christians preach (those who would be seen as the best—as we constantly hear from them). They say that as the

Head, Christ carried out and fulfilled everything. But what then of the members and the whole body in which the suffering of Christ must be fulfilled?

Paul gives witness of this when he said, I rejoice in my suffering, for in this I restore what is lacking of Christ's suffering on my own body. Therefore soon, and it is already begun, these wise men will become as fools. For it pleases God to save those who believe through foolishness, nonsense and the preaching of fanatics—or so these clever types call us when they rant and roar about it. So, in a short time these wise and proud ones must yield to the poor in spirit, who they call fanatics.

Now understand and note well, my beloved brethren, what Christ called the gospel of all creatures. Above all, do not mistake it to mean that the gospel should be preached to the creatures, like cats and dogs, cows and calves or leaves and grass; but rather, as Paul said, the gospel which is preached to you in all creatures. He also shows this again by saying that the eternal power of God will be seen when it is recognized in the creatures or in the works of the creatures in the world.

So I say and confess here that the gospel according to the instituting of Christ, as Christ and his apostles preached it, that is, the gospel of all creatures, is yet unknown in our time, including by those who would claim to be the best. It is hidden and concealed from them because they do not seek the pure and clear honor of God. Rather, they look after their own honor and their own bellies. Even if this gospel were preached to them, they would only laugh at it and say we are crafty-headed fanatics.[6] Therefore my beloved brethren, mark well what is meant by the gospel of all creatures, as Paul called it when he said the gospel which is preached to you in all creatures.

The gospel of all creatures is nothing other than the power of God to bless all those who believe. If a person wants to understand and confess God's power and divinity, God's invisible essence, through the works or creatures of the creation of the world, then he must note and consider that Christ always communicated the kingdom of heaven and the power of God to the common man through the use of parables, pointing to a creature or to different handicrafts or different sorts of human occupations. He never sent a poor man to books like our scholars do, lacking all understanding. Rather he taught and witnessed the gospel to them through their work—to peasants by their fields, seeds, thistles, thorns and rocks. In the prophets God said that seeds should not be sewn among thorns. Rather, clear them out first, then plow and then plant. The power of God which is shown in this is the work of God in us. The power of God works in us as the farmer works his field. Christ used a field for his demonstration—and Paul said, you are God's field. Like the farmer working the field before he sows the seed, so God does also with us, preparing us for His word, so that it grows and bears fruit.

Jesus taught the gospel to the gardener by using the trees, to the fisherman by using the catch of fish, to the carpenter by using the house, to the goldsmith by using the smelting of gold—Matthew 13; Luke 13; 1 Corinthians 5; Galatians 5. He taught the gospel to the housewife by using the dough—Isaiah 5; Jeremiah 2; Matthew 20; Luke 20; John 15. He taught the gospel to the vinekeeper by using the vineyards, vines and grapes, Matthew 9; to the tailor by using the patch on old cloth, Matthew 13; to the merchant by using pearls, Matthew 9; Mark 2; Luke 10; Joel 3. He taught the gospel to the reaper by using the harvest, Isaiah 10; to the woodcutter by using the axe and tree, Ezekiel 34; Zechariah 11; John 10; Ezekiel 37; Hebrews 13; to the shepherd by using the sheep, Psalm 2; Isaiah 30; Jeremiah 18; Romans 9; Revelation 2; Ezekiel 34. He taught the gospel to the potter by using the clay, Luke 16; to the steward and overseer by using their accounts, Isaiah 26; John 16; Revelation 12; to the pregnant woman by using the act of birth, Matthew 3; Isaiah 41; Luke 3; to the thresher by using the winnowing fan, Psalm 44; Isaiah 53; Romans 8; to the butcher by using the slaughter, Romans 12; 1 Corinthians 12; Ephesians 4 and 5; Colossians 1.

Paul illustrated the body of Christ by using the human body. Christ always preached the gospel, the kingdom of God, by using the creatures and parables. In fact, he never preached without the use of parables. David also said, I will open my mouth and speak in parables.

The thing in all of these parables to note well is that the creatures are made to suffer in human work. It is through this pain that they reach their goals, that is, what they were created for. In the same way no human comes to salvation except through the suffering and tribulation which is the work of God in him.

So the whole of scripture and all the creatures illustrate the suffering of Christ in all his members. Therefore, the scripture is figured simply in the creatures. That is why God gave the children of Israel understanding of His will by use of the creatures and rituals and announced, preached and described it through Moses. God commanded that offerings be made to Him of oxen, sheep, goats, rams and bulls.

At the same time, God said through Isaiah that He does not desire sacrifices of that kind, for God said, the sacrifice of cattle, the blood of sheep, calves and goats, I never wanted. And through David God said, I do not want the bulls of your house or the goats of your stables.

Therefore, the precept of God is not in the commandment of sacrifice. It is in the power of the Spirit. The power of this commandment for human beings is that the human stands in relation to God as that which is sacrificed stands in relation to humans. It is for that reason that David offered to God burnt offerings such as rams, oxen and goats, and a calf for himself. Such ritual sacrifices are signs and witnesses that humans should offer themselves as living sacrifices. That is why God commanded that clean animals should be eaten. The power behind this is that humans are to give themselves to God to suffer according to God's will, just as animals suffer according to our will.

So when God forbids the eating of unclean animals, the power behind this is that one should not have dealings with unclean people, who are compared to unclean animals. For it is written that there is nothing unclean and all things are good. These rituals demonstrate clearly what the will of God is and are as much meant for us as for the children of Israel.[7]

That is why Christ spoke in parables. The importance is not in what is spoken but in the power and meaning. All animals are subjected to humans. If one wants to use an animal, it must first be dealt with according to human will—it must be prepared, cooked and roasted. That is, the animal must suffer. And God does the same with human beings. If God has use of us or will have benefit of us, we must first be justified and made pure by Him, both inwardly and outwardly; inwardly from greed and lust, outwardly from injustice in our way of living and our misuse of the creatures.

The farmer does not sow corn among thistles, thorns, branches and stones. Rather, he clears them out and then does the sowing. In the same way God does not sow His word in a person who is full of thistles and thorns—who desires only the creaturely. The concern about physical prosperity, which God forbids, must first be rooted out. The carpenter does not build houses out of uncut trees. He rather first cuts them down and shapes them according to his will. Only then does he use them to build a house. And this is how we are to learn God's work and will in relation to us. It is compared to how humans act in relation to a house before they move into it. We are the house (Hebrews 3).

Humans are often called a tree in the scriptures. If one is to become a house, one must be cut off from the desires of the world. With a tree, one knot points this way and another that way. That is how it is with human desires. One points toward property, another to wife and child, a third toward wealth and a fourth toward fields or knowledge, arrogance and worldly honor.

Therefore, we should note well our actions in relation to the creatures, for this is scripture to us. For the whole world with all creatures is a book which in our actions is like what is read in a written book. The elect from the beginning of the world until Moses studied this book of all creatures and gained understanding from it. Through the Spirit of God this understanding of nature was written on their hearts, for the whole of the Law is described in the actions of creatures. All people, including the heathen who do not have the written Law, are occupied with the creatures (as the Law shows us) and do the same as those who have the written Law. The scriptural Law shows how an animal should be slaughtered before it is offered to God. Only after that was it to be eaten. The heathen do that also, because they have the law of nature and do not eat living animals. Likewise, we must die to the world in order to live in God. The Law is like a lamp of light and the heathen also have their lights and almost the same rituals and commandments. That is why the Book of Moses describes these rituals of creatures—to remind and admonish people that in these things they may search out and learn the will of God.

Therefore, since the Law is inscribed in and demonstrated by all creatures, we may read it daily in our work. It is a book which concerns us daily. The whole world is full of descriptions of the will of God. Our own hearts give us witness of this when we avoid coarseness, worldly chaos and lusts. One may perceive through the work of the creatures God's invisible essence and eternal power. One may there recognize how God works with people and prepares them for perfection. One can there see how this can only happen by way of the cross of suffering according to His will.

That is why all creatures are subject to humans, and humans rule over them. For just as the whole Bible is written in terms of the creatures, so also Christ spoke and preached and demonstrated the gospel of all creatures through parables. This he did himself when he preached to the poor. He did not send them to book chapters, like our scholars do.[8] For all that can be shown in the scriptures is already shown in the creatures. Christ had no need of scriptures unless he wanted to prove something from it to the soft scholars.

When, according to the Lord's command, the gospel of all creatures is preached, a person is then brought to understanding in a reasonable and natural way. He sees it in his own work, that which he does in relation to the creatures. He can then recognize God's will toward him and may give himself exuberantly in obedience to Christ. For then he will realize that no person may come to salvation except by suffering the will of God in his own body and affliction, as God pleases to do.

Then he may believe that it must also be so with him and all people who desire salvation. This learning and understanding is the second part of the divine order, that part which Christ meant when he said, "and whoever believes." If the person understands the gospel of all things or all creatures and believes it, even that is not enough. For that is something any person may witness and prove. The third part of the divine order must follow. For as Christ said, "and is baptized" will be saved.

Baptism must follow after the other two parts. It comes when the person is ready to accept and suffer all that the Father through Christ has in store for him. He must have set his heart upon the Lord and forsake the world. He accepts the sign of baptism as a covenant of acceptance before the Christian community, to be received into the covenant of God, in the name of God, whose power and might have separated him from those things which the heart desires. For as Christ said, what is bound on earth will be bound in heaven. But no person can be accepted and taken in by the Christian community except he first has heard and learned the gospel, and believes and agrees with what he has heard. For this covenant is an agreement, a demonstration of divine love in relation to all brothers and sisters, in obedience to Christ with love, life, goods and honor, regardless of what evil the world says about him for it.

And where are these Christians? It is a small group. For if even two or three are gathered, Christ is there as witness among them. The mouths of even two or three are a genuine witness. A person is assured in baptism that he is accepted as a child of God, a brother or sister of Christ, a member of the Christian community and the body of Christ, because he has with faithful heart desired to come into such unity, according to the will of God.

For God commands his saints to gather together, and holds this covenant more dear than all sacrifices. God does not desire the sacrifice of goats, but rather offerings of thanks. He desires that each person offer his body for justification, as Paul said, and believe that God will not forsake him in times of need, but will rescue him from all need if he be led into tribulation. Such a faith, although it is not yet perfected and is yet unproved, will be counted to him as righteousness until it is justified and tried, as gold in the fire.

Baptism, which follows preaching and believing, is not that which makes a person godly. It is a sign only, a covenant, a parable and a memorial of this desire, which the person can remember daily in expectation of the true baptism. This baptism is, as Christ said, the water of tribulation by which the Lord makes us clean, washes and saves is from all carnal lusts, sins and unclean works and behavior. Just as we recognize that no creature can justify itself and come to its true purpose without becoming subject to humans, so also no person can justify himself and come to his true purpose, that is, to blessedness, but by accepting the baptism of affliction which God has shown and worked in the person and to which the person is subjected as justification. If a person is to be justified by God he must be still before the Lord his God and allow God to work in him as God wills. For as David said, trust in the Lord and have your hope in him, for He does all things well.

Therefore, the water of tribulation is the real essence and power of baptism, by which the person is swallowed up in the death of Christ. This baptism was not first instituted in the time of Christ. It has been from the beginning and is a baptism with which all friends of God, from Adam to the present, are baptized, as Paul said. Jesus accepted this covenant with God in the Jordan river. Here he demonstrated love to all people, in obedience to the Father, even unto death and became an example of one upon whom the baptism of tribulation is richly poured out by the Father. That is why the sign and the essence of baptism must be clearly distinguished from each other. The Christian community administers the sign or covenant of baptism through one of her true servants, just as Christ received it from John.

The true baptism then follows. God administers it through the water of tribulation and in return He offers the comfort of the Holy Spirit. God lets no one founder in this baptism, for it is written, He leads into hell and out again, He makes dead and then brings to life again. This is the baptism with which the Lord was baptized. Whoever would be a disciple of the Lord must be baptized and made pure in the Holy Spirit and be united by the bonds of peace into one body.

Therefore God makes His own blessed and worthy through the bonds of the new birth and renewal of the Holy Spirit in faith. God works according to His great mercifulness, and it is only through this same grace that we are justified and inherit the hope of eternal life. In this way one is washed, healed and made pure and reborn into the unblemished community before God. Not like one of our contemporary citizen Christians, formed by the usurious and greedy scholars. Just as the people are, so is the priest. . . .

That is why beloved David prayed to God to wash him and cleanse him of sin. And God graciously heeded him and, as we read, placed him in the waters of tribulation. He cried to the Lord for help. And from this deep abyss the sin was slain and he was made alive again in Christ.

Paul also admonished the brothers to suffer, just as they had seen him suffer. For the kingdom of God consists not in what is spoken or other external things, but rather in the power of God which God alone can give, which makes a person wholly new in senses, speech and heart in all actions and conduct. Therefore it is a false gospel which worldly and haughty preachers in our time are spreading around. That it brings no betterment of living but only vexation, I place before you to judge, brothers and sisters.

But blessed are those who hear the word and heed it. For a lamb of Christ hears the voice of the Lord and fears it. But whoever hears and does nothing is a fool and will never be righteous. Whoever, as the whole world now does, wants to come to God without the justification which is worthy before God (which is the suffering or cross of Christ) is throwing away the very means of justification (yes, Christ the crucified one himself). But they will not escape suffering, for no one comes to the Father without the Son, who is given in strict discipline.

Whoever would rule with God must be ruled by God. Whoever would do the will of God must give up his own will. Whoever would find something in God must lose much in Him as well. The world talks much now about freedom, yet remains in total slavery to the flesh. They will not give anything up, but only want to have more given to them. Oh, how masterfully they can fool themselves!

So now everyone is saying that each should "remain in his occupation." If that is so, why did not Peter remain a fisherman or Matthew a tax collector? Why did Christ tell the rich young ruler to sell all that he had and give to the poor? If it is right that our preachers want to have so much wealth, then it must be right for their followers! O Zacchaeus! Why did you so foolishly give away your wealth? You could have followed the example of our preachers and still be a good Christian! O beloved company, how easy it is to see who the scoundrels are! But this one thing is true, there is a Lord who will judge you.

A true and faithful friend of God, who daily places his hope and trust in the Lord, will have his heart strengthened so that he will be able to carry the cross of Christ. All that such a person suffers is Christ's suffering and not our own. For we are one body in Christ in many members, united and bound together by the bond of love. Christ accepts such a person as part of his own body. He witnessed to this when he said that "whoever touches you touches the apple of my eye." And elsewhere, "whatever you do to the least of these my own, you do to me." The affliction of Christ must be fulfilled in every member until the suffering Christ is brought to completion. Just as Christ is the lamb who was slain since the beginning of the world, so he will also be crucified until the end of the world. In this way the body is perfected in length, width, depth and height in the love of Christ. This passes all understanding, for in this Christ will be filled with all the fullness of God.

A person will prove his faith under the suffering and cross of the true baptism, justified and tried as gold in the fire. Through this a truly grounded faith of the kindness and mercifulness of God will be revealed. When a person is comforted by the Holy Spirit through all suffering and tribulation, he is then ready for the Lord and for doing good works. There is no other path than this for people, for truth will be revealed without betrayal.

The faith that comes by hearing will be counted to the person as justification until the time comes when that person is justified and made pure through the cross.[9] Then the person's faith will be conformed to the faith of God and united with Christ. And it is from this faith that a righteous man lives. Therefore, a great distinction must be made between this faith and the beginning faith. God's own faith is absolutely true, righteous and enduring, as He promised. Our faith in the beginning is like silver that is still embedded in the ore, full of spots and impurities. But still it is counted as genuine silver until the smelting, in which the impurities are taken out. That is why the apostles said, we believe, help our unbelief! But it is also possible to compare our beginning faith to unbelief. As the person finds himself in the fires of trial, he find much in himself that is neither faith nor trust. He feels himself cast totally into unbelief and thinks that he has been cast out from before the eyes of the Lord. Nothing can comfort him, no creature at all. It is as David said, my soul will not be comforted. And elsewhere also he said, I am cast out from before the purview of Your eyes. In this way, in what Christ called the "Sign of Jonah," the person is cast into the abyss of hell. Then, when absolutely nothing can bring him joy, he must simply wait until the comfort of the Holy Spirit comes upon him. Then he will be filled with joyousness as he forgets all worldly desire, joys and honor and counts them all as dung. Then the person returns from the pit of hell and wins joy and courage in the Holy Spirit.

The justification which really counts before God does not come from an untried faith. An untried faith only goes up until the time of justification, where it must be prepared and justified. Of course the whole world fears this justification like the devil and would rather pay with an artificial faith and indeed not go on to justification. Such righteousness is not preached by the world's preachers, for they themselves are enemies of the cross of Christ and of righteousness. They seek only their own honors and only whatever of God will serve their bellies!

God works his righteousness in us through the suffering of the holy cross which is laid upon each person. According to His promise, this reveals God's faith to our faith, so that we are able to believe that God is sure and His faith is demonstrated to our faith. Then all creaturely desires are rooted out and smashed. This is how the world's yoke of sin will be lifted, for then Christ governs and not the world. Then will the Law of the Father be perfected in us through Christ in all his members. Then there is the desire and love to do the will of God in true obedience.

To such a person His burden is light and His yoke sweet, and all that was impossible is made possible! Then may a person truly say, "Christ has blotted out my sin." But whoever does not submit himself to this discipline of the Lord, but rather remains attached to worldly desires, will be overcome and surrounded by a much greater shame and suffering. For then, even if in the midst of this suffering he cries out to God, God will not hear him but will scorn him in the same measure as he scorned. Therefore all who fear God should seek their comfort in the Lord and he will rescue them from all tribulation, so help us God through the bath of the new birth.

Now Follows the Essence of True Baptism

Now we want to say more about the baptism of the new birth. Christ showed this is not an external symbol but rather a bath of the soul which washes and cleanses the heart of all lust and carnal appetites. It is the slaying and stilling of all desires and disobedience in us which set us against God. Just as in the time of Noah, God slew the whole world through the flood, drowning all evil and washing it away; just as happened with Pharaoh and the Egyptians in the baptismal bath of the Red Sea, where they sank to the bottom like lead. Noah and his family went into the bath right along with the rest of the world, just as Pharaoh and his men went into the bath along with the people of Israel. But the results were very different. The evil go in but do not come back out. Because they are sunk in carnal lusts, neither the creaturely part nor themselves could be freed. Rather they gladly lived continually in the lust and love of the carnal. That is why they persecuted the elect, who unlike them are not mired down but rather strive to swim out. Like Peter, they work without ceasing to come to the shore or land and out of the turbulent sea of this world and out of the waters of tribulation and adversity to come to solid ground. They see that God reaches out His hand to help them out of it. So for those who seek renewal of their life, baptism is not a dunking and drowning, but rather a joyous rescue from the whirlpool or undulations or stirrings of our own desires.

Our living was so stormy. This turbulence is the battle between the spirit and the flesh which is in all people.[10] If in this battle against the flesh we are to still, free and defeat our greed, lusts, stirrings, demandings and rebelliousness, then the sweet water of carnal lust and greed must in the same measure be countered by the stirrings of divine righteousness, which in the contest will be acrid and bitter. For what was before in the creature was sweet, not from God but from himself, which is why he turned toward it.

Then a great turbulence arises in the conscience between spirit and flesh. The way to life is narrow if one is to come to new life in God and the new birth in baptism by the perishing of the old man. For then fear, trembling and trepidation falls upon the person, just like the fear of a woman in the labors of birth. When God passes such waters through the soul, there must be patience until one gains understanding and teaching. And finally peace in our world will be born from this assault on the flesh. Then, in the length of time, in the patient hands of God, humanity will be made a finished and ready seat and dwelling of God.

As now the cloudy water clears, the bitter becomes sweet, the turbulence becomes still and quiet. The Son of God appears upon the water, God stretches his hand and rescues the person from the whirl-pool and lets that person see that it was through his truth that he elucidated our darkness and the living water which is hidden within us, and from the kingdom of the physical, earthly man we are made pure in eternal life. The water which pierces the soul is temptation, consternation, fear, trembling and affliction. It is the baptism of suffering. That is why Christ went trembling into this baptism, before it was brought to perfection in his death. True baptism is nothing other than the struggle against sin throughout one's entire life.

The water of adversity washes the soul of all vestiges and traces of indolence and carnality. The baptism of John in water is incomplete and cannot free one from sin. For it is a prefiguring, a preparation and model of the true baptism in Christ. Therefore they must be baptized again in Christ. For Christ was also baptized with this figurative baptism, which in true essence began in him. That is why Christ was baptized, as an example to us that in him all was as it should be.

In the death of Christ we also have perished as members of his body. Consent is given under this symbol. As Paul said to the Romans, you are baptized into the baptism of Christ, that is, into the death of Christ. And since we are now buried with Christ, we receive the baptism of truth from the Father.

Christ accepted the baptism of John so as to humble himself before all men. He took our prideful nature, which is departed from God, upon himself and through baptism brought it again under God. In this he showed how a person must be baptized as a new creature in the slaying of our evil, disobedient, insolent nature, for the washing away of all sin and human characteristics. As Paul said, since you have been baptized in Christ, you have put on Christ. So all that was dead in Adam will be made alive in Christ.

But whoever will not be so baptized remains dead in Adam. Therefore, baptism is a struggle to conquer sin throughout one's whole life. Whoever now finds behind him the Pharaoh (that is, persecution, tribulation, fear and need) and in front of him the sea (that is, the helplessness of all creatures) and concludes that he has been abandoned by God and sees nothing other than death, stands in the true baptism to which he consented before God and his community or people by the symbol of baptism.

The world most certainly does not desire this baptism. That is why the baptism of the contemporary world is terrible villainy by which the world is deceived and Christ is denied. They will not let Christ work in them, to have the place cleaned where Christ should be living. That is why everything is backward and there is no true judgment on earth concerning the mystery of divine commands. Of course we would be happy if everyone found Christ and bragged to us about it. But nobody is willing to suffer with him. Of course if the Spirit of God were given in the uproar and debauchery of this world, the world would be full of Christians. But Christ is hidden and concealed to the flesh. He does not let himself be seen, as we notice, except in suffering the highest resignation, by which he shows himself to all his brothers. Here one finds the graciousness of God, the highest stage of divine righteousness and the beginning of divine mercy. Here a person becomes one with the person of Christ, the crucified son of God, purified and wholly united into one body. The person lives no more but rather Christ lives. Therefore Christ said, who will be my disciple and learn the will and way of God must accept the Father's discipline for disobedience and carry the cross on his back like Christ, and accomplish the will of the Father in the sense of suffering (so long as he remains under suffering) and accomplish God's will in the sense of actions. There is no other way that Christ will accept someone as his brother or the Father as a son. Christ, the crucified one, has many members in his body. And yet there is no member which does not bear the work, the suffering or the acceptance of suffering after the example of the head. Only by this means can one know Christ and no other. This is the power of God, who makes us pleasing to him. This suffering is the baptism in which he would let no brother or sister sink and be lost. Rather they should be made pure from it and cleansed from all stain and able to receive the graciousness of God. And he will be healed after this through the recognition of God's will.

The weakness of Christ angers and vexes the world, and yet no one may accept the sweet Son of God except he first taste the bitterness of justification. For Christ's life is so bitter, his teaching so high, his person so grim and foolish that indeed it may be said, "Blessed is the man who takes no offence in Christ."

Now, if there is little carnal desire, one will not remain long in the waters of tribulation. Rather the waters become clean, pure, joyous and pleasing, clear, so that one may can accept the Spirit of God in all fullness, to fulfill the will of God. We stand, like him, under obedience to the Father. It is proper, therefore, that we put our sin onto him. For the sin does not touch him for his own person's sake but rather he is afflicted above all for the sake of our sin and his soul was most horribly troubled.

Matthew and Luke spoke of baptism in terms of fire and spirit; John in terms of water and spirit; Mark speaks neither of fire nor water. Matthew and Luke call the Spirit of God "fire," while John speaks of the Holy Spirit as "water." Yet they are all in agreement. Water and fire in the scriptures are temptation, the sea of the world. Fire and water cleanse all things. In that time these were cleaning agents. Any cleaning to be done had to be done with water or fire. Whatever was delicate and could not stand the fire was cleansed from impurities by water. What was hard, like gold, silver, copper, iron or tin, was smelted in fire and cleansed of impurities.

The Spirit of God is portrayed for us as a contrast of water and fire in which the reason of creaturely work agrees with the obedience of Christ; water, which takes away uncleanliness, and fire, which consumes all dirt, cleansing and purifying from all impurities. The power of God does this as well in its working toward truth through the suffering of tribulation. And whoever does not hear the voice of God in the water must hear it in the fire.

God thrusts us into various temptations to root out carnal desires in us, and God works in us the renunciation of the whole world in order that He may help us and use us for His work. It is like an impure piece of gold, which cannot be used by a goldsmith until it is smelted in fire and the grime is burned away and consumed. And what passes through the test of fire is pure and good.

Therefore God puts all disobedience into the fire and changes the spirit in the flames. He likes fire and gives His commands from the fire. He calls Himself a consuming fire which consumes all things and burns in Himself. That is why He will have no foreign fire in His house for His offerings and incense.

All living creatures display the judgment of water and spirit. For all are conceived and born in water. But if they remain in the water, they will drown and rot. Therefore, baptism has its time and end and epoch, just as the first birth has its time and end and also its epoch.

All creatures are born in essence through water, until their perfection. And without baptism none can achieve a fulfilled life and be blessed.

But this infant baptism of the contemporary world is a pure invention of men, without God's word or command. It is a silly betrayal and insidious shame of all Christianity, an arch-rogue's cloak of the godless. For in the whole of scripture not a single sentence can be brought forward to defend it. It is so groundless that, however much they try to hide it, they all are brought to silence.

According to the word of Christ and all of scripture, one should baptize nobody except one who gives an ardent and trustworthy account of his faith. Where this sign of baptism is accepted, it symbolizes the coming baptism of suffering. It is in this sense that one may say, "without baptism there is no salvation." But infant baptism is not only unnecessary, it is the greatest hindrance of truth.

Leonhard Schiemer

Leonhard Schiemer was born in Upper Austria and became a Franciscan monk. But he became disillusioned with monastic life and left the order after six years. Having learned the tailor's trade, he arrived in Nikolsburg in Moravia during the time when Balthasar Hubmaier was preaching there. From Moravia, he went to Vienna, where he made contact with the circle of Anabaptist associated with Hans Hut. On his second day there, he accepted adult baptism from Hut's aide Oswald Glaidt. This was in the spring of 1527. He soon became a preacher among the Anabaptists in Upper Austria, and in their name he traveled to Salzburg, Bavaria and Tyrol to spread the teaching. He was captured in Rattenberg, Tyrol, in November of 1527. By that time, he was already being called a "bishop" of the Austrian Anabaptists. He suffered some seven weeks of imprisonment, during which time he was repeatedly questioned under torture. His major writings were written during this time. He was beheaded in January of 1528.

Presented here are two of Schiemer's extant writings, "Three Kinds of Grace," and "Three Kinds of Baptism," documents 5b and 5d respectively in the source collection Glaubenszeugnisse oberdeutscher Taufgesinnter, *Band I, ed. L. Müller (Leipzig: M. Heinsius Nachfolger, 1938). The impact of Hans Hut on Schiemer's thinking is very apparent as well as that of medieval monastic piety and mysticism. Of special note is Schiemer's distinction between externals and internals in terms of the Christian faith and practice. Thus, we believe "in" God and not simply "on" God. That is, through our faith and disciplined practice, the community participates directly in the living being of God. Both of these writings were done from a prison cell.*

"Three Kinds of Grace Found in the Scriptures, the Old and New Testaments" (1527)
Leonhard Schiemer

The whole world is talking about the word *grace*, particularly the scholars. They have taken notice of the fact that the scriptures speak of something called grace. Yet they are unable to say what it means. These great scholars compare it to the word *Chimera*, or *Ens cognitum*, which they learned from Aristotle. They say that it exists in essence only when it is spoken or thought about. But if one ceases to speak or think of it, its essence also ceases. It is called *entia secunda intentionis*, or *secundum intentionem*, or *ens reale*. Words are used like *genus species proprium differentia, accidens propositio categoria*, etc. And then they say this cannot be translated into the vernacular because the vernacular is unable to express such a high and mighty concept. It is so high that it can never be "realia," for *res* or *realia* means something, a thing. But grace is no thing, not something, but exists only so long as one thinks of it. So it is in fact no-thing. And those who can clamor on the most about this nothing we call masters and doctors!

And so it is with these scholars, for their sophistication does not come from God.[11] Rather, what knowledge and sophistication they have is stolen from Christian books. Jeremiah spoke of this kind, saying, "I am against the prophets who steal from one another words supposedly from me" (Jeremiah 23:30). They are not sent by the God of heaven but rather from the god of the belly! That is why they have nothing to say. They are not of Christ's elect and therefore they cannot witness to the world. For their works are evil. They are of the world and the world does not hate them (John 7). They are of the world and are loved by the world (John 15). They are like any wood cutter earning his living. For they sell their preaching to make a living from it, like any other handworker. And you can know them by their fruits. For the Lord says that a good tree cannot bear evil fruit. And as God spoke through the prophet, "As the rain and the snow come down from heaven and do not return to it without watering the earth and making it bud and flourish, so that it yields seed for the sower and bread for the eater, so is my word that goes out from my mouth; it will not return to me empty, but will accomplish what I desire and achieve the purpose for which I sent it" (Isaiah 55:10–11).

But these belly-preachers cannot point to anyone whose life has improved because of their preaching. And they know not their sheep.

83

As the Lord said, a good shepherd knows his sheep by name (John 10). Such are the true master and doctors of the holy scripture.

So they have landed upon a word, *faith*, which appears often in scripture. Also such words as love, communion of the saints, ceasing from sin, brother, neighbor, Holy Spirit, grace of God, justice, law, Christ, spiritual, preaching, baptism, communion, hope, peace, repentance, falling into sin, prayer, righteous Word of God. And so they simply stole these phrases. But if you ask them what these all mean, they can only say that you must have faith (John 24). But if you ask them what faith is, they are left speechless. They are unable to give account for their faith (1 Peter 3). They speak of love and faith. But if you ask them how one comes to love and faith, they don't know. If you ask them if they know Christ, they know him only according to the flesh. As the Lord said (John 6), their ignorance knows no end.

Whatever you ask them, they have something to say. But they don't know the difference between the inner and outer word (2 Corinthians 5). When pressed hard, they acknowledge that a Christian must be taught by God. Then they unashamedly insist that they are taught by God. But their fraudulence is clear. Ask them where God's schooling takes place or what one learns there first, and they have no answer at all. The same goes for the concept of grace, about which I will be writing.

I write alone to my brothers and sisters, the blessed of the Lord. For we each are to share with each other those gifts which God has given and to hold these in common, as it was done by the apostles (Romans 4; 1 Corinthians 12; Acts 2 and 4). For if a brother or sister has something, it should not be held by that person alone but shared with others.

Three Kinds of Grace Found in the Scriptures, the Old and New Testaments

First of all, it must be understood that the kinds of grace are clearly distinct from one another. For as John said, "We have received grace upon grace" (John 1:16). And Christ said, "For everyone who has will be given more, and he will have an abundance. Whoever does not have, even what he has will be taken from him" (Matthew 25:29). And the unworthy servant will be thrown into outer darkness. The three kinds of grace must remain distinct and not mistaken for one another. And where the scripture speaks of the first type, it should not be confused with the second or third type.

Furthermore, it is not my intention with this writing to unlock the scriptures for the godless. For it is sealed to them with seven seals which on the lamb who is slain may break (Revelation 5). Who does not have the key of David (that is, the cross of Christ), to him it remains sealed for eternity.[12]

Concerning the First Grace

"In the beginning was the Word and the Word was with God and the Word was God. He was with God in the beginning. Through him all things were made; without him nothing was made that has been made. In him was life, and that life was the light of men. The light shines in the darkness," etc. (John 1:1–5). That means that all believe through the word, not through John the Baptist, as Luther translated it, but through the light. It was a true light which is a light to all people who come into this world.

Here again Luther mistranslated—"through his future in the world." Check this against any Latin or Hebrew Bible. For Luther comes to Christ, to God, to faith, to the light. He does not want the light to be in him but only next to him, among him, on him. So therefore he translates, "the word became flesh and dwells among us." Luther hopes in God and believes in Christ. But we have the word in us, not only among us.

Now the text speaks of the light of grace. It was in the world and through it was the world made, but the world knew it not. But to those who know him, he gives the power to be children of God, etc.

And further, in his glory he received grace upon grace. For through Moses the Law was given, and grace and truth through Christ. The Law is the first act of grace; Christ is the second act of grace. But because John says that through Moses we are given the external Law, while the light or word dwells in us internally, he is expressing his view that the outer is a witness to the inner. Moses was an external conduit of the internal first grace, and Christ is a witness to the internal second grace. For he also said that John the Baptist was not the light but a witness to the light. To help us understand this he also said (Matthew 6) that the eye is the light to the body. If the eye is sound, the entire body is given light. But if the eye is unsound, the entire body will be in darkness. Furthermore, the Lord says that if your body is in the light, with no trace of darkness, it will be as a bright flash.

From this I conclude that God enlightens all people of this world.

So if anyone chooses to forsake this light and snuff it out, he cannot blame God for his own damnation. This being the case, the entire direction of Lutheran teaching, from which one might say, "I lack God's grace. I want to do what is right but God is guilty of withholding His grace from me, etc." is nothing short of blasphemy. It sets the entire scripture on its head to say that God gives His grace to one person and withholds it from another. Look what Peter said, "I now realize how true it is that God does not show favoritism but accepts men from every nation who fear him and do what is right" (Acts 10:34–35). And also it says (Acts 17) that God is not far from us, for in God we live and move and have being. Also Paul said (Romans 1) that God's invisible essence, God's power and divine nature, can be seen in the creation itself if one is open to that truth. For while they recognized that there is a God, they neither worshipped God nor were thankful. Instead the became lazy in their thinking and while holding themselves to be wise, their foolish hearts remained in darkness.

Later on Paul says (Romans 2) that God is no respecter of persons. Those who sin without the Law will be lost without the Law. So the Gentiles, who do not have the Law but do by nature what the Law requires, are a Law to themselves and show clearly that they have the Law written in their hearts. Their consciences and thought will declare them guilty or innocent on the day when God will judge what is held in secret through Jesus.

Christ said (Matthew 22) the whole Law and all the prophets can be summed up in these two commandments: You shall love the Lord your God with all your heart and all your soul and your mind and strength, and your neighbor as yourself. These two highest commandments are described in the Old Law, for there the Lord said, "Now what I am commanding you today is not too difficult for you or beyond your reach. It is not up in heaven, so that you have to ask, 'Who will ascend into heaven and get it and proclaim it to us so we may obey it?' Nor is it beyond the sea, so that you have to ask, 'Who will cross the sea to get it and proclaim it to us so we may obey it?' No, the word is very near you; it is in your mouth and in your heart so you may obey it. . . . This day I call heaven and earth as witnesses against you that I have set before you life and death, blessings and curses. You must decide as you come into the land God has promised between evil and death or good and life" (Deuteronomy 30:11–14 and 19). Therefore, love God and your neighbor—that is the true kingdom of God. As John said, "Let us love one another, for love comes from

God. Everyone who loves has been born of God and knows God. Whoever does not love does not know God, because God is love" (1 John 4:7–8). That is why the Lord said that the kingdom of God dwells within you. So it is certain that there is a light in every person that shows to that person what is good and what is evil. But until that light shines in children—that is, until they know the difference between good and evil—they remain innocent and will enter into the promised land. In this case we are not referring to the earthly land of Canaan but rather the heavenly Jerusalem (Hebrews 11). For David and Samuel "had not yet received the promise," even though they were in the land of Canaan. This is further shown in Ezekiel, where it says, "You were blameless in your ways from the day you were created till wickedness was found in you. Through your widespread trade you were filled with violence, and you sinned. You have lost your holiness with your great misdeeds" (Ezekiel 28:15–16). Christ said, "Let the little children come to me, and do not hinder them, for the kingdom of heaven belongs to such as these" (Matthew 19:14).

Now this light does nothing other in people than to show them what is good and what is evil. Because God in His eternal goodness does not forsake anyone, He did not allow the godless hypocrites to remain silent. He rather allowed them, like Baalim's ass, to speak the truth—such as the ten commandments, the twelve articles of the Christian faith, the Lord's Prayer—which contain these two commandments of love. Whoever keeps them will be saved. Whoever is true in little things will be given great things (Luke 16).

Therefore, God does not hide from the scholars, these Lutherans and Zwinglians, so that they in turn conceal the commandments of God. I cannot say how it is in the lands of the Turks and the heathen, for I have never been there. But I am sure of this in my heart. God plays no favorites—every person who repents is acceptable to God.[13]

But although this light is in every person, people hold themselves differently in relation to the light. These differences can be distinguished in three forms.

First, as the light shines in their darkness, their flesh, they try as much as possible to snuff out the light. This light is not the sun shining in the western sky. It is the eternal, living word. The darkness is our flesh and blood. The light strives toward the good, but the flesh strives toward all that is evil. The soul stands in the middle. All of us—except Christ—have at one time or another turned our soul toward the flesh.

So we are all dead of soul. But Christ is the doctor who brings us back to life through his word. Through the power of his word we have health, but not final perfection (Romans 7). This first sort of person resists this light, so that the conscience is wholly destroyed (Acts 7). God will be concealed and God's power removed from whomever wantonly strives against the Holy Spirit.[14] Because they pay no heed to the conscience God gave them, God gives them over to do all that is shameful, all that is unjust; to whoring, anger, greediness, evil; to that which is full of hatred, murder, quarreling, cunning; to become poisonous gossips, slanderous, wicked, haughty, financiers, disobedient to parents, enemies of God; to foolishness, untrustworthiness, unfriendliness, obstinance and unmercifulness.

Those who know the righteousness of God are not on their own. It is as with the rooster who cried when Peter denied Christ. For then Peter realized that he had sinned and ran out of the courtyard and wept bitterly (Matthew 26). But this first kind of person, when he hears the rooster of the heart crowing, binds the rooster's beak so as to muffle its cries. He treats the rooster as an enemy. After doing this over and over, the cries are finally heard no more and the person loses all fear of sinfulness. Sinfulness is embraced and nobody can put the fear of sin back into him. These sorts of people make the best, most independent soldiers of war. For without any fear they murder, kill and rob. They are the ones who are the first to attack and make good swordsmen, dancers, knights, singers, gamblers, abusers, great hangmen, bar maids, bishops and archbishops, abbots, traitors and liars. The Lord's will is concealed from such as these.

Of such type the Lord said if even the light in you is darkness, how great is the darkness in you! To the impenitent people it is forbidden even to speak the word of God. For they are like the dogs and swine of whom it is written, "You should not give what is holy to dogs nor throw pearls before swine," etc. (Matthew 7:6). For they simply trample it all under foot and then tear their teacher to pieces. They will kill the one who has taught them the most, killed like any common criminal and left forgotten in the dust.

The second kind of person reacts sleepily to the light. They do not tie up the beak of Peter's rooster and refuse to let it speak. When their conscience speaks they are frightened. But they salve it. That is, although they are not totally genuine, they are amiable people. Of these the scripture says they have a lukewarm spirit. Then it says,

"Would that you be hot or cold! But because you are lukewarm, I will spit you out of my mouth!" They are like the five virgins (Matthew 25) who act in all ways like a Christian. But they lack the oil of the Holy Spirit; they fear God, but only halfheartedly. They have many of the qualities which people respect—wisdom, understanding, counsel, strength, sophistication. They are inquisitive, asking many questions and wanting to experience everything.[15] But such people are a danger to us. For they appear often as an angel of light, as good Christians— that is, until it comes time to bear the cross! Then they are like the sour grapes of winter (Isaiah 5), which look like good grapes in every way but are too late in ripening. They are slow in coming, and when they arrive the door is already shut. Only then do they pray fervently for entrance!

So in times of persecution, they fall away, for they do not recognize their fundamentally wretched state. We don't want people like this in our community. For they come among us with seductive talk. But let them grow until time for pruning and none of them will remain faithful. Of this kind the Lord said (Luke 12) that the servant who knows the master's will and does not do it will be severely punished. That is his reward.

Therefore, a good leader among us should learn to differentiate the spirits well. When such a person seeks counsel and reflection, then let him reflect. But when he demurs from it, it will be within him like an expended coal.

The third type of people set their hearts on the word of God when they experience this light. With all diligence they set themselves against sin; they pray and listen to much preaching. They read much and ask many question, all with a true heart. And although they have made themselves an enemy of sin, they find that on their own power they are often defeated by sin. But when this happens they spend hours in pain and truly humble themselves. God sends grace upon grace to these ones (John 1). Toward these God is gracious and merciful. Of these the Lord said, "This is the one I esteem: he who is humble and contrite in spirit, and trembles at my word" (Isaiah 66:2). Also David wrote, "A broken and contrite heart, O God, you will not despise" (Psalm 51:17). Of these Christ said, "Come to me, all you who are weary and burdened, and I will give you rest" (Matthew 11:28). And it is also written, "The Spirit of the Lord is on me, because he has anointed me to preach good news to the poor. He has sent me to proclaim freedom for the prisoners and recovery of sight for the blind, to release the oppressed, to proclaim the year of the Lord's favor" (Isaiah 61:1–2; Luke 4:18–19).

Truly these mourning ones, having no rest in their hearts, find no comfort in any other writings or teachings than the word of God. They are burned by a burning fire and have no peace until they are enlightened by God as to how and in what way they can flee from sin. These people know that the peace they need is an internal peace and that they cannot simply go their merry way with an external appearance of peace. They know what they need and do not forsake the first grace, the grace that has revealed to them their sinful state. And it is to these alone that the second type of grace is promised.

Concerning the Second Type of Grace

Blessed are those who hunger and thirst for righteousness, who want nothing other than to become righteous. For they will be satisfied! Blessed are those who cry and mourn, for they will be comforted! This is what the second grace is—righteousness. To create a person out of nothing is a great work of God. And to justify a sinful person is no less a great work of God. But that cannot take place outside of Christ, who through his conception, birth, death and resurrection in us, when that happens, is our righteousness. Christ said, "Whoever would be my disciple, follow me!" (Luke 9 and 14). And again, "Without me you can do nothing" (John 15). Peter said that whoever suffers in the flesh ceases from sin. The first light is our guide to the second light, which is Christ, the light of the world. When his Spirit comes into me, I am no longer under the guide's tutelage, but under grace. There the works of the Law, of sin and of death cease and the Law of the Spirit, of faith and of life begins.

This Spirit, is given only to those who have taken up the cross and seek the Lord (Hebrews 12). One cannot simply graft just any kind of branch onto a tree. Likewise it is impossible for Almighty God to save me without the cross. For the cross is the blessedness of God-self. And I love God and seek joy and trust and assurance of life in nothing other than God alone. My heart yearns not one bit for that which is of the creatures of this world. For if God has given me the gift to trust, have joy in and to love only Him, but I love, trust and have joy also in the things of this world, it is as though I have taken a marriage vow but held something back. That God cannot allow, and it would not be good if God did allow this. For then God would not be God. God would be denying Himself. And this is not possible. For this reason God is a jealous God and gives His honor to no other. It is like the bridegroom who, once he has taken his bride to wife, is no less attentive to the marriage vows than he was before.

If we have left behind that which is creaturely and love it no more, then it follows that the Lord must prune us of the creaturely fruits. That is, God must take from us that which is creaturely and take us naked and pure into the second birth, where we are given his Spirit and taught to know and love him.

But this cannot happen without pain, suffering and anxiety.[16] Not that God wants us to suffer. Rather, God forgives us and is patient with us, in much the same way that a physician, in order to bring healing, must endure the stench of the sick person.

Such suffering and pain is a result alone of our unfaithfulness. It is this unfaithfulness which causes agony, for it keeps God from us. It is like when a man separates himself from an adulterous wife. It causes him pain, but it is nothing other causing him this pain than the great love he still carries for her. So in the same way, when God sends the loss of a wife, of children, father, mother, brother, sister, of property or wealth, of health or even of life itself, the pain this causes us is a result of our unbelief. That is to say, it is because we are not yet firm in the belief that it is for our own good and that something even better awaits us. As Christ said, "And everyone who has left houses or brothers or sisters or father or mother or children or fields for my sake will receive a hundred times as much and will inherit eternal life" (Matthew 19:29).

And there are even greater modes of unbelief which torture us— such as when we experience such godless thoughts as "Will God forget me? Will God remain true and faithful to me? God has favorites and will not support me as He has the other." Or other such foolish and unbelieving thoughts such as, "If I give all to God, what assurance do I have that I will not perish? If I remain with the world, at least I have some security and will not perish foolishly." Or again some thoughts like, "If I become a Christian, or remain a Christian, God may not even see to my basic needs. At least if I become or remain among the worldly, I am free to see to my own basic needs." Or again, "If I become a Christian, my family will starve to death; if I refuse, at least they will remain taken care of."

Here is my answer. Of course if you are so concerned about such things you are surely no Christian but remain among the heathen. And these thoughts will continue to cause you agony until your belief is separated from your unbelief. You need a powerful refinery, much effort and a strong smelting solution! For an uncrucified Christian is like untested metal or a house before the timbers are even split.

The only thing separating us from the love of God is our own recognition of it! If one knew it, that God is the highest of all which is good, it would be impossible not to love God alone above all else. In fact, to know God truly is to love God so dearly that it would be impossible to hold something else dear beside God, even if threatened with eternal punishment! Yes, if I knew God truly, I would experience in my soul and spirit such a pure joy that this joy would surge through my body and make even my body wholly without pain or suffering, immortal and glorified. So if a person is cleansed of the love of all that is creaturely, it extends even to the flesh, which God holds in the sleep of the saints until the resurrection of the dead (1 Peter 1). But to know God truly, the covering or mesh which obscures the divine light in us, that is, the creaturely nature, must be removed (Hebrews 11). The more, for the sake of Christ, this creaturely nature is taken from us, the brighter shines the light and God's word. So anyone who gives himself to God under the cross is a child of God (2 Corinthians 1).

But this alone is not the end! He must also separate himself from all that is not of Christ and love and be in fellowship with those who have likewise given themselves to God. For these are then his true neighbors. They must hold in common to all the gifts which God has given them, whether gifts of teaching and understanding or of goods and wealth or anything else. Anything God has entrusted to him must be made available for the use of the community, just as it says in our articles of faith and in all the scriptures and as we see in particular in the actual practice of the twelve apostles (Acts 2, 4 and 5).

Third, he becomes obedient to the brotherly discipline (Matthew 18). As we have it in our articles of faith, it says "Refrain from sin!" (Romans 12). For what is not bound and taken in by the community of Christians is also not bound or assumed in heaven (1 Corinthians 5, 12 and 16; Matthew 18). As John said it, "For anyone who does not love his brother, whom he has seen, cannot love God, whom he has not seen" (1 John 4:20). Also, the Lord said, "By this all men will know that you are my disciples, if you love for one another" (John 13:34).

So the second grace is the cross. Whoever asks for this grace is asking for the cross. Those who pray for this grace pray in the name of Christ. But the heathen (and by this we mean all those who call themselves Christian but are not) write the name of Christ on a little piece of paper and then pray to the paper! They have certainly never come to Christ. Christians can say in all truth, "Jesus Christ is our Lord." But these heathen, on the other hand, have another lord. So when you place the truth right in front of them, they answer, "It is forbidden by the lords!" Ask them who these lords are and they answer, "The ones of Austria" or "The ones of Bavaria." So I say to them, why do you then lie to God and say, "I believe in Jesus Christ our Lord!" For Paul said, "No one may say that Christ is Lord except through the Holy Spirit" (1 Corinthians 12:3). Also Paul said, "Whoever does not have the Spirit of Christ does not belong to Christ— he is no Christian" (Romans 8). The one who prays truly prays as the Lord himself showed us, saying, "God is Spirit and all who would pray to God must pray in spirit and in truth."[17]

Therefore, all those who have not surrendered themselves with life and all else they have under the cross of Christ and in the community of the saints, and have not been released from their sins by the Christian community, are of the devil and the Antichrist (1 John 4). They blaspheme, rebuke, curse and mock God our creator every time they open their mouths. And this they call praying! But God will be prayed to only in spirit and in truth. These heathen, these "Christians," pray neither in spirit nor in truth. For their father is the devil, a liar from the beginning, who never could endure the truth.

Now I will speak of the third type of grace, which no one may receive before he has received the other two graces. Many people make the error of seeking this third grace without wanting the other two.

Concerning the Third Type of Grace

The Lord has made it very clear in the form of a parable. A man goes out from Jericho and falls among thieves, who leave him almost dead. Along comes a priest, who takes no pity on the poor man. The same happens with an evangelist. But it is the scorned Samaritan who comes to his aid, cleans his wounds with wine and oil, etc.

I have been speaking mainly of the wine (of suffering). Now I want to speak of the oil of joy. It was of this oil that Saint John said, "But you have an anointing from the Holy One, and all of you know the truth. I do not write to you because you do not know the truth, but you know it and because no lie comes from the truth," etc. (1 John 1:20–21). And then a little later he says, the anointing you have received from God remains with you, and you have no need of someone to teach you. What the anointing teaches you is truth and not falsehood. So hold fast to what you have been taught.

Concerning this oil, the Lord also spoke, calling it "the comforter, the Holy Spirit, which my Father will send in my name. This one will instruct you and remind you of all I have told you." This oil is the Holy Spirit. The Holy Spirit, however, teaches nobody who has not already despaired of all human comfort and wisdom and offered his heart up to God alone. No one can be comforted or strengthened by the Holy Spirit until he has forsaken and relinquished all human comfort and strength. That is why the Lord said you should not allow anyone to call you "master." But our Master, Christ, takes no one to be his pupil or disciple who has not forsaken and hates all that he once had and can take up the cross daily and follow after him. In hope one must wait upon the comfort of the Lord, as it is written in many scriptures, especially in the Psalms, prophets and Isaiah. Even the Lamentations of Jeremiah show that Christian strength comes only from that stillness which does not soon fall away or despair of the word of the Lord. We are to be long-suffering and expect the comforting Holy Spirit even in the midst of the worst agony and misery.

This is the illness of which Paul spoke when he said, I am strongest when I am ill. He also said that just as the sufferings of Christ come upon us, so through Christ much consolation will be given us as well. This is what Christ meant when he said, "You will see me only a short while and then you will not see me." When the apostles asked him for clarification on this, he answered, "Truly, truly, I say to you, you will weep and cry and the world will rejoice in this. And when they kill you they will think they have done God a favor. But I will not leave you as orphans. I will come to you," etc.

Worldly living starts out joyously and ends in eternal sorrow. But our kind of living begins in sorrow. Then soon the Holy Spirit comes, anointing us with the oil of inexpressible joy. But we need not only wait for God to comfort us. Rather, each Christian can comfort another and speak words of comfort to those in tribulation. That is why God said through Isaiah, "Comfort my people and be comforted says your God. Speak words of affection to Jerusalem," etc.

Of this oil James said, "If someone is sick, call the elders together and let them pray and anoint him with oil in the name of the Lord.

94

And the prayers of believers will help the sick one. The Lord will comfort him and forgive him of any sins he has committed," etc.

James is not referring here to some kind of cooking oil. The elect saints who even now in Salzburg are praising God daily with their martyrdom could bathe in tubs of such oil and would not thereby be strengthened to remain stable in their faith. It is only the comfort of the Holy Spirit which tempers their suffering in martyrdom. The apostles were anointed with this oil, and we are as well in our time.

"Three Kinds of Baptism in the New Testament Clearly Outlined" (1527)
Leonhard Schiemer

In the entire holy scripture of the New Testament I find no other seal of faith than baptism. But when one speaks of baptism, it is understood to mean water baptism alone. And this is the basis of errors. For John said that there are three which bear witness—the Spirit, Water and Blood, and these three are a unity.[18] One should not be confused with the others, and there is a particular order for them, just as God has created order in all things according to their measure, number, weight, etc.

The first baptism is when one becomes obedient to the Father, just as Christ was obedient to the Father even to death on the cross. For as John said, "He will baptize you with the Holy Spirit." Christ also was so baptized, for John saw the Holy Spirit come upon him like a dove. Here one yields body and life to God. Such yielding cannot happen without the Holy Spirit. Therefore it is a sure and strong witness that one has received the Holy Spirit when he yields himself totally to God.

The second baptism is the baptism of water, for as the eunuch said to Philip, "There is water; why should I not now be baptized?" Furthermore Peter said, "Can anyone object that these now be baptized with water, since they have received the Holy Spirit?" And thus was Christ also baptized in the Jordan river, just as others were.

But the scriptural experts will have nothing of such externals. They see clearly how we are burned, beheaded and drowned, and they privately support us. But publicly they disavow us. But the Lord said, "Whoever denies me before men, I will deny him before God my heavenly Father." And Paul said, "If one believes in his heart he will be saved, and as he confesses with his mouth, he will be blessed."

Now you great scholars, doctors, academics, monks and priests, who care nothing for "external things," just how would you demonstrate to others that you are true disciples and followers of Christ except by feeding the hungry, giving drink to the thirsty, clothing the naked, sheltering the poor, comforting the sick and imprisoned, washing feet and showing love to one another? This baptism is not for Jews, Turks or the heathen. It is only for those who are elect of Christ, called into the office of the gospel. That is, it is for Christians.

The third baptism is the baptism of blood. Of this baptism the Lord said, I must yet be baptized with another baptism. And how distressed I will be until it has taken place! This is also the baptism he foretold to the two sons of Zebedee when he asked, "Can you drink the cup I must drink and be baptized with the baptism with which I must be baptized?" For this is the true test of a Christian. An untested Christian is like untested or unhardened metal. If there were someone who could spare me this baptism, that would indeed be a beloved person to me! Indeed, if the cross of Christ were not there at the door, the Lutherans would put no more importance on baptism than on eating meat. Christ received this baptism from Judas, Caiphus, Herod and Pilatus, the high priests and the religious scholars. And in our time there are plenty of children of Judas and Pilatus and hypocrites to spill this baptismal water.

To sum up, the baptism of water is a seal of faith and of the indwelling covenant with God. It is as when one writes a letter. When it is finished, it is sealed. But no one will give his seal to a letter without knowing what it says. When you baptize a child, you are sealing an empty envelope. Who does not believe will be damned and needs no baptismal water to get into hell. Who would baptize first and teach later is like one who scrubs the barrel first and only then asks what the purpose of it is.

In short, there are no grounds for the baptism of children in the holy scriptures. Christ called no one to baptism who had not accepted the teaching of the gospel. That is why the Lord said that any plant which is not planted by the heavenly Father must be pulled out. Since God did not plant child baptism, there cannot be much disputing the fact that it must be rooted out. You should also not say that you have been baptized twice, for thereby you are acknowledging that this papal child's bath is a baptism.[19]

I would never want someone to teach me goldsmithing who was

not himself a goldsmith. And I would not want a non-Christian teaching me the way of Christ.

We must turn to Christ with humble heart and earnest prayer. There one will experience all truth. For otherwise it helps nothing even if one studies all the books and runs all over the place, like a sow in a sugar beet field, studying everywhere. As one who has tried it himself, I can give personal testimony of this.

I, brother Leonhard, give witness to what is true, to what I have experienced personally. God is no respecter of persons. Rather, to anyone who turns to Him, He gives grace, ability and comfort.

Hans Schlaffer

Hans Schlaffer was a highly regarded Minister of the Word among the Austrian Anabaptists. He had become a priest by 1511, serving in that capacity in Upper Austria. He came under Luther's influence rather early and resigned from the priesthood by 1526. Soon after this he came into contact with Hans Hut. During the next year he spent time in Nikolsburg in Moravia as well as Upper Austria and Bavaria. During a short stay in Nuremberg, he also had contact with Hans Denck. Although he was never associated with any one particular congregation, his influence among the Austrian Anabaptists stemmed from his epistles and short doctrinal writings, which were circulated and highly respected among them. Schlaffer was apprehended in Tyrol in December of 1527. He was beheaded in February of 1528.

Presented here is Schlaffer's instruction as well as two prayers which have survived. These are document 6a in the source collection Glaubenszeugnisse oberdeutscher Taufgesinnter, Band I, ed. L. Müller (Leipzig: M. Heinsius Nachfolger, 1938). The impact of Hans Hut on Schlaffer is obvious in his formulation of the three witnesses to faith and his explicit mention of the gospel of all creatures. In fact, at points his writings are paraphrases, or even verbatim renderings, of Hut's own writings. But like Leonhard Schiemer, Schlaffer flavors the Hutian teachings with a more spiritual and less apocalyptic attitude. Even so, his clear understanding was that in accepting the Christian faith, one accepts the cross of suffering and agony, even unto death. The call to become a disciple of Christ was indeed a blessing. But it was not clearly understood by anyone who did not at the same time experience dread and anxiety because of what it would entail.

"Instruction on Beginning a True Christian Life" (1527)
Hans Schlaffer

O Almighty and Merciful God! Because all of humanity lives in evil, blindness and error, and hatred fills the world, I pray to you to save all tenderhearted people from such blindness and error. Draw us to your wonderful light. Bring us to that light which alone is Jesus Christ, your eternal and only son. O Lord, with this light enlighten the darkness of our hearts. Help us to sincerely desire truth and to live and walk in this truth. For Christ alone is the way, the truth and the life. Outside of this light there is neither truth nor life, only empty error, lies and death. Let it shine forth before the world and the eyes of humanity.

O heavenly Father! Give us understanding so that we may flee from injustice and grasp the way of righteousness, against which the largest part of humanity has fought since the beginning of the world. Only a small remnant has chosen the truth and remained steadfast in it. For it is the narrow way which few travel. O Lord, who does not shutter in awe before your marvelous works and the judgment you have shown in these final days, by which you bring comfort to the world! But the world will not receive it. Therefore, eternal God, send us your Holy Spirit to teach us in our hearts the truth, that we may pray to you in Spirit and truth as our savior Christ taught us to pray— Our Father In Heaven.

That which Christ taught us is now mouthed externally, verbally, by all so-called Christians. But it is denied constantly in their hearts and truth by their feigned deeds. This any tenderhearted Christian can easily see for himself in view of this prayer. For although the world prays "Our Father," it is easy to see what kind of children they are; how much love they have for him and what kind of life they lead; how much they keep his name holy; how much the kingdom of God comes to them and how much his will is done; how much hunger they have for daily bread (that is, the word of God); how much they forgive sins among themselves and how much they desire to be protected and delivered from evil.

From all this we see clearly whether or not one is a true Christian. For not everyone who cries "Lord Lord" will enter into the kingdom of heaven, but only those who do the will of the heavenly Father. Of this I am quite sure. If I had all the so-called Christians of the world in one pile (if this were possible) and asked them if they are Christians, and they were to answer truly, they would say, "I don't know," or "I hope so," or "I hope to become one," or some such answer. And even if one answered "yes," that could only be because of confusion in his heart. For his heart and life do not show the slightest trace of Christian deeds. In short, these so-called Christians are actually worse than Turks or heathen, to which they give witness among themselves. For no people under the sun blaspheme the name of God, God's suffering, martyrs and death more than these so-called Christians. I will not speak of how blasphemous they are with their public displays of adultery and whoremongering, drunkenness, pride, greed, brawling and gossip. They are not Christians and have no desire to order their lives according to the teachings and commands of Christ, which are nothing other than the commandments of God the Father. They have no desire to remain in Christ and follow his footsteps. They are more wicked than any "unbelieving" people on earth, God help you. Amen.

Whoever will be a true Christian must first be convinced by the truth and recognize fully that all of his previous deeds and thought are evil, sinful and damnable in light of God's commandments and the teaching, life and example of Christ and his disciples. He has been hateful and sinned in his heart and life and works and continues to do so. Indeed, he must know that in his own power it is impossible to live and do as a true believer or Christian should.

Moses said in the Law, and Christ in the gospel, that truth exists in the mouths of two or three witnesses. Therefore, we have here three witnesses as an instruction and testimony to a true and blessed Christian life. These are the creatures, the scriptures and Christ.

The First Witness: The Creatures

In the first place all that is created, the creatures, which God created for the use, requirements and needs of humanity, witness to and teach a Christian life blessed by God. No creature is created for its own sake. That is, no creature lives and dies for itself alone. It lives and dies according to the will and pleasure of humans. That is why Christ commanded his apostles to preach the gospel of all creatures. This he did himself in such parables as the trees, the vineyard, the fields, the seeds, branches, bread, fish, hidden treasure, oil, lamps, clothing and many other things. He never preached without using parables.

His disciples undoubtedly did this also. As Paul said, he has become a servant of this gospel. The others did as well. Here is an example. A hen or fish or other animal, if you want to eat it, cannot by its own pleasure and will be prepared, that is, slaughtered, skinned, feathered, made presentable, threaded or cooked. You must do this. It must suffer according to your will. You must clean it according to your will. The animal does nothing but stay still and endure your will and work. And so what for the animal is to the highest degree contemptible (that is, when you chew and swallow it) is for you the best thing. This is what you must consider and learn from other creatures as well. Think how wine or bread must suffer before you can eat it or use it. When we use the creatures and such for no higher purpose than to fill the belly and to nourish our stinking bodies, we are no better than Turks or heathen. Indeed, we are like the dumb animals themselves, as David said it. Here is another parable about a field. So long as it is overgrown with grass, thistles and thorns, no seeds are sown in it, as the prophet said.

Now look how much work the field must suffer before it is ready for seeding. Likewise, a wild tree brings forth wild fruit. For it to bring forth good fruit, it must be husbanded and cut down to a stump. After that a good branch can be planted. Likewise, nobody farms in a field which is not his. Nobody plants a tree in a garden he does not own, as the prophet said. Now we are according to our nature (that is, as soon as we come to know the difference between good and evil) a bad tree and are unable to make ourselves good, just as a field cannot farm itself or a tree cannot husband itself. A farmer or gardener must do that. So God alone must make us spiritual, righteous and worthy for his praise. We must endure this and be still before him (as the field for the farmer or the tree for the gardener) and suffer his work and discipline. As God himself said, turn to my discipline and I will give you my Spirit! Learn my word, for it is the good seed in the field and the good branch of the tree. But because we are a stranger's field and stand in another's garden, God will not plant his seed in us nor graft his branch in us. Only when one renounces all that he has can he become a disciple of Christ, etc. That is what is meant, taught and preached by the gospel of all creatures—it is the power and will of God and his divine work to make us holy from his grace and mercy through faith in Christ, as the Lord commands. For the creatures are the book and living letters or scriptures which can be read and understood by all of humanity. Because of this, nobody will have an excuse before the Lord on the final day of judgment.

That is why Job could say to speak with the earth and it will answer, ask the fish and it will answer. The birds of the air and fish in the sea are witnesses to you. Paul said that God's invisible essence, his eternal power and divine nature can be seen in the works of creation in the world, if people seek the truth. Therefore, all are without excuse. For though they knew that the One God exists, they failed to honor, praise and thank him as God. Rather, their thoughts were foolish and there hearts were darkened. Although they thought of themselves as wise, they were fools. Paul also said that the unseen will be known by what is seen.

Here one sees clearly what should be known and understood concerning the creation and all of God's creatures. Namely, by what is visible, we see the invisible (the power and wisdom of God) and the work that God (and not we ourselves) works in us for our justification, salvation and making us worthy for the honor and glory of his kingdom through his son, Jesus Christ.

So for a Christian person all things are pure, such as eating, drinking, sleeping, waking, putting on or taking off, all undertakings whether in relation to self or others. For in all things he does not seek to do his own will but only the will of God. In all things he stands ready and willing to be subject to God and to endure God's work in him. It is just as all the things with which he deals and uses for his needs must suffer and endure according to his will and work, although of course the creatures do this unwillingly because they are subject to his vanity (which is why they themselves also wait with groaning, yearning and longing for the liberation of the children of God in hope, as Paul said). That is also why the flesh of human beings rebels against the spirit. Even so, there is no more condemnation in those who belong to Christ. They no longer walk according to the flesh but according to the Spirit. That is, the flesh no longer rules over them but rather the Spirit. In the use of creatures and in all other of the works of God which he perceives, the Christian is always ready to be subjected to the will of the Lord. The preaching of the gospel of all creatures is proclaimed to these ones and is able to be understood well by them without the need for honed skill and higher wisdom. All that is needed for understanding is a pure, obedient, good-willed and humble heart set upon God, as the scriptures attest in many places.

Much more could be written about the creatures. I hope, however, that a tenderhearted person, who desires Christian truth and a life blessed by God, will himself be able to observe it more loftily and diligently than I can present it here.

The Second Witness: The Scriptures

Let us now hear about the second witness, the scriptures.[20] From Abel to the apostles, the entire scriptures speak of the suffering of the elect. That is why "the lamb has been slain since the beginning of the world."

Let us keep in mind how our ancestors, such as Abraham, Isaac, Jacob and others, were blessed. They came to their faith through much tribulation. There was hardly a greater persecution suffered by men than was suffered by the prophets, such as Isaiah, Jeremiah and others. They were persecuted by their own fellow believers (that is, the Jews of old) and were even killed, just as happened to Christ himself in the gospels. Here one should take special note of the eleventh chapter of Hebrews. There the apostle goes through the scriptures, pointing out what the faithful had to endure, and how, through their faith, they were finally victorious.

Paul said that all that is written is written for our learning or demonstration, that we might have hope through patience and trust in the scriptures. Patience is part of suffering, and all of the scriptures speak of suffering. Patience without suffering is not patience, any more than fire is fire without heat and light. Trust is embodied in the promise of God to bring aid and assistance in time of suffering. Of that the scriptures are full. "I will be with you," says the Lord, to bring release in tribulation and to glorify you. Likewise, God is near to those who have a repentant heart and will sustain those of humble spirit.

Christ said that those who mourn will be blessed, for they will be comforted. We might also add that those who now laugh will later weep and mourn. Likewise, he said that you will have anxiety in the world, but in me is peace. Likewise, he said that you will weep and mourn while the world rejoices. You will grieve, but your grief will turn to joy and no one will be able to take your joy from you. So then, it is through much anxiety and tribulation that we come into the kingdom of heaven. Likewise, every child whom a father loves, he disciplines. Only illegitimate children, who will inherit nothing, are not disciplined by the father. Look through the letters of Paul, Peter and James. You will find nothing there but the suffering of Christians. Likewise, in the Revelation of John, which points toward the end times, you will find it also. There it speaks of the patience of the believers and saints, those who hold to the commandments of God and faith in Jesus.

I admonish you through the mercy of God to be tenderhearted Christians. A true Christian knows above all to search the scriptures, for this is how the Lord himself differentiated between true and false Christians.

The Third Witness: Christ

Christ's life was a model witness that we ought also to live and walk as he did, each according to his abilities. As Peter said, Christ suffered for us, leaving us a model or example that we should follow in his footsteps. He also said that because Christ suffered in the flesh for us, so we should arm ourselves with this same attitude. The one who suffers bodily is done with sin and will not live for human desires but will live for the will of God. It is enough that we have spent the past part of our lives doing as the heathen, living in debauchery, lust, drunkenness, orgies and detestable idolatry, etc. Now heathens think it strange that you no longer follow them in this flood of dissipation, and they heap insults upon you. But they will have to give account to him who is ready to judge the living and the dead.

Now seek God's will. It is easy to see from these words of Peter who is and is not a Christian. Debauchery, orgies, drinking, blasphemy and idolatry (and Paul calls greediness a service of idols, etc.)— whoever is burdened with these things for a long period of time in this world (and there is even a saying about such—that the devil has spit them out on the floor) are surely not Christians, as Peter said. Paul also said that among you there should be no immorality, impurity or greed. Such things are not proper for the saints. Nor should there be foolish talk, coarse joking or anything which is not helpful, causing only irritation. These things also have no place among the saints. Rather, let there be thanksgiving. This you should know already— that no immoral, impure or greedy person has any inheritance in the kingdom of God.

Paul also says that those who are Christians, who are of like mind with Christ and have armed themselves for suffering, do not mix themselves into worldly entanglements. They have nothing in common with works of darkness, only works of light. They are not ashamed of Christ their master or his word. They are disciples of his word, each according to the measure of grace received. Therefore Christ will not be ashamed of them before God, his heavenly Father and all of the angels. As Christ himself said, "Whoever loves his life will lose it; but whoever scorns and denies his life on this earth for my sake will gain eternal life. Whoever will serve me must follow me. Where I am my servants will be also. And whoever serves me honors my Father as well." And again the Lord says, "Whoever will be my disciple must deny himself, take up the cross daily and follow me." In short, a Christian is a follower of Christ. That much is sure, even if the whole world comes to end and doom (as will surely happen and, I believe, very soon!). For with God, as Peter said, a thousand years is like a day. Therefore Christians, hold your heads high and peacefully await your redemption, for it is coming. Christ will return to judge the living and the dead.

The Father teaches, seeks and wills that all people will be saved, for he teaches and seeks all people. When a good-hearted person is instructed in the truth through all creatures, through the scriptures and through the teachings, life and example of Christ, he finds in his heart that this way and no other leads to salvation. Nor can there be another way. This is confirmed in his heart. The gospel of all creatures is preached to him and he is instructed and made a disciple. To him repentance and forgiveness of sins in the name of Christ are proclaimed. And he yields his whole heart to this faith. As the Lord said, whoever believes also believes that faith is a work of God in human beings. Through this faith God has made a covenant with humanity and humans with God. For as God himself said, I will be your God and you will be my son or daughter, my servant, along with all the other chosen sons and daughters. Therefore, keep my commandments, live and walk according to my will. There is much written concerning this in Moses and the prophets.

This is not the ancient covenant which God made with his people, the Hebrews. The ancient covenant was sealed in rams' blood and is a prefiguring of the new covenant. This is a true covenant, as Jeremiah said. And Christ himself called this a New Testament, sealed with his blood which was shed for the forgiveness of sin. It is not enough simply to declare this covenant with words. Rather, it is a work of the Spirit in the hearts of people. It is the baptism in which Christ was baptized, that is, in Spirit and fire.

What a holy and blessed covenant this is, which no human has the power to either sanction or hinder, for it is eternal! God created it through Christ, his only son, and built it with his servants. For this they were chosen and sent by God, not by humans. As David said, "Gather to me my consecrated ones who have kept my covenant by sacrifice." And Christ himself witnessed to this covenant in many sayings to his disciples, without regard to permission from any emperor, king, prince or any other worldly authority. This covenant is not against them, but is actually for them. For their power extends only to the physical body and possessions and not to the soul. Christ alone is ruler of his kingdom and will be so eternally. In this kingdom there is neither distinction nor difference made between people.[21]

Neither Christ nor the apostles sought permission to preach from the Roman emperor or his representatives in Syria or the rulers of any other country. Even if they had, the permission would have been refused. If any of them ever became Christians, the biblical writings do not say—except that it is more difficult for a rich man to enter the kingdom of heaven than for a camel to go through the eye of a needle. But what is impossible for humans is possible for God.

Oh, would that God would only have it be known to all in authority how true Christians think of them! They would then surely desire and wish in their hearts that their whole country would be full of Christians, if that were possible.[22] But I fear they would not believe it. Well, the day of the Lord is coming, when all things will be revealed. Nothing is so secret or hidden that it will not be made known.

There would be more to say here concerning the covenant between God and the believers, but it would take too long. In summary, then, I understand this covenant to be the baptism of Christ in the Spirit and fire, as I said before.

Spirit is assurance of mind in the grace and mercy of God for the forgiveness of all previous sin, no matter how many or how serious. For Christ has taken them all away. The Spirit of God gives witness to our spirit that we are children of God. It is by this Spirit that we are able to address God as *Abba*, loving Father. Only one having the Spirit of Christ can do this and is a Christian.

Fire is the ardent love in the heart for God and for the neighbor. It is the willingness to suffer anything for the will of God, which is encountered because of this truth. Even death cannot turn the person from witness to this truth. This burning love for God is next directed toward the neighbor, the brother and sister, not just in words but in deeds and truth. It also results in good deeds toward enemies and persecutors. As Christ himself taught, it is by this that the world will know that you are my disciples, that you have love for one another. Paul said that the love for one's neighbor works no evil. It does not break marriage vows, does not lead to unchastity, does not covet, does not bear false witness or any other acts of evil. That is how one may know who are Christians in this world. This is enough said for now concerning faith, covenant and the inner baptism of Christ.

Now, when the Lord said to baptize, I understand this to mean baptism of those who have already believed. In Matthew he also said to baptize in the name of the Father, Son and Holy Spirit. Here also I understand this to mean those who have already been taught. In such cases he is speaking of water baptism, the external sign, which is only proper. But this is most vexing to the world.

Note then what is proper concerning water baptism. Christ instituted and commanded this order—that there first be preaching and teaching, followed by belief, and then followed by baptism.

First of all it must be understood just how strenuously God has forbidden us to turn his word around. So the word or commandment of Christ is just as important, for he is himself the eternal word of God. His word is the word of the Father. Heaven and earth will pass away, but not his word. Therefore, we do not want to change or turn around any part of his word. We want to remain steadfast in his command and order. Through his grace he has given us this understanding, and it does not matter that the popes, church fathers or councils have ordered and decided something different. It is a much surer and more true foundation to build upon Christ and his teaching than to rely upon the church fathers or councils. For on that final day, Christ will sit in judgment, not the popes, fathers or councils. It does not matter how old a tradition may be. Christ and his word are older still, for he was the son of God from eternity and will remain so into eternity.

Secondly, we practice baptism only after belief and knowledge of Christ because Christ himself was baptized by John the Baptist in his thirtieth year. Only then was he led by the Spirit into the wilderness to be tempted by the devil. He was victorious over the devil, which is no small mystery. After all, a Christian life is not child's play! It requires seriousness, truth, courage and holiness. It is not the kind of easy sport which the world encourages.

Thirdly, water baptism is a sign by which Christians give recognition and outward confession. It shows first of all that one has a Christian, brotherly love for others; and secondly (in obedience to Christ's command) it shows that one is ready to take part in the church's teaching, admonishment, help, discipline, exclusion, binding and loosing, etc. This is not a small thing among Christians but the most necessary, if the church, community or assembly of Christ is to be the groom's bride, without spot or wrinkle, a holy mother, as it is often called in scripture and elsewhere.[23] Why did Christ cleanse and heal them with his blood if not that they then be able to live according to his teachings and commands, inwardly blameless before God, among themselves and before the world?

We do not confuse salvation with external baptism. For Christ said that if one does not have faith, he is condemned. He said nothing there about baptism. Likewise, one finds in the Acts of the Apostles that when Peter preached to the heathen, he proclaimed Christ and gave proof from the scriptures. Then those who received and believed in this message received the Holy Spirit. And only then were they baptized. For the one whose heart is ready, there is plenty of good teaching concerning external water baptism in the apostolic history. But I fear that those who do this and are yet guilty have already been judged, just as the Lord said and as Isaiah said, etc.

But there is one more baptism, which comes as a result of water baptism. That is the baptism of blood. Of this the Lord said, "I have yet another baptism to undergo, and I am greatly distressed until it is completed." Here he meant the baptism of suffering, the shedding of his blood. That is why he asked the disciples if they were willing to be baptized with that baptism with which he would be baptized. Here he was speaking to them of suffering.

There are three that testify on earth: the Spirit, the water and the blood. And these three are in agreement, for there is but one faith, one baptism, one God and Father of us all and of our Lord Jesus Christ.

To sum up, God has again in these last and most dangerous times, through his son Christ, erected a public Christian and holy community, and it is his will that it be made known to the world by the external sign of baptism.

Because of this, the world rants and rages against it and knows not how or why God has brought judgment against his own house. In this all writings of the prophets, of Christ and the apostles are being fulfilled and brought to conclusion. The judgment is against God's own house first of all, and then against the whole world, which does not recognize this fatherly and rightful affliction. Their leaders will not acknowledge this, and therefore they must suffer eternally another judgment and punishment.

But God will protect, through his son Jesus Christ, all who in this time humble themselves before his powerful hand and suffer with patience this fatherly discipline. Amen.

Repent and be baptized in the name of Jesus for the forgiveness of sin and you will receive the Holy Spirit.

From prison in Schwatz, the nineteenth day of December in the year 1527.

"Two Prayers" (1527)
Hans Schlaffer

O Almighty, eternal, merciful God! We give you praise and thanksgiving that you have chosen us to be your children and have opened up to us the mysteries of the divine will. For you have hidden these things from the wise of this world, O Father, according to your pleasure. We ask you to make us able to drink fully the cup you have placed before us. We pray for all those in authority in this world, that you enable them to use the sword you have given them for the protection of the good and punishment of evil. Watch over them, so that they do not mingle their hand in the blood of your saints. And give us the strength to accomplish your divine will. We pray for all the brothers and sisters who are in prison or suffering affliction and disgrace. Strengthen them according to your divine will. Amen.

O Almighty, eternal God, we acknowledge our weakness and ask you to strengthen us with your Holy Spirit to deliver us from human fear. O eternal God, forgive us from all our sin. O Almighty Father, we pray also for our enemies. Forgive them, for they do not know what they are doing. We pray also for all people of good heart, for they hunger and thirst for your divine righteousness. Satisfy them with that food of eternal life which never spoils. O eternal, heavenly Father, we give you praise, honor and thanks that you have graciously called us out of the terrible darkness of this world into your wonderful light, which you have kept hidden from the wise of this world but have revealed to the common person.

O eternal Father, we pray for all the brothers and sisters. Keep them steadfast in your divine name, that they may be able to keep your commandments, unwavering until the end, able to drink fully that cup which you have given us. We pray also for all lords, princes and people in authority. Enlighten them in your divine truth, that they use the power you have given them to protect the good and punish the wicked. And stay their hand from the shedding of innocent blood.

O eternal Father, we pray that you send us workers for your vineyard. For the harvest is great and the workers are few. We pray also for all missionaries sent into the world. Strengthen them with the power of your Holy Spirit. Extinguish from us all human fear so that we may proclaim your word without hesitation. Keep us in your holy name and do not allow us to turn from the spring of living water, neither in the present nor the future, high or deep, in death or in life, nor toward any other creature. Make us firm in true faith until the end. We pray these things through your loving son Jesus Christ, who taught us to pray this in his name: Our Father in heaven, let your name be kept sacred. Let your kingdom come and your will be accomplished on earth as in heaven. Give us each day our daily bread. Forgive us our sins as we forgive those who sin against us. Keep us from temptation and deliver us from evil. For yours is the kingdom, power and glory in eternity. Amen.

Hans Denck

Hans Denck was born about 1500 in Bavaria and was an outstand-
ing leader among the South German Anabaptists. He was well educated, with a scholar's knowledge of Greek, Latin and Hebrew. He
studied at Ingolstadt and Basel and was more a literary scholar than a
theologian. At age 23, he was appointed to the rectorship of a school
in Nuremberg but was soon banished from the city for questionable
religious views. By that time, Denck was already becoming disillusioned with the Reformation doctrine of justification, since it seemed
to him to result in license for ungodly living. Denck was moving in
the direction of an ethical spiritualism, tinged with influence of the
mysticism of Thomas Müntzer. His motto was, No one may truly know
Christ except one who follows him in life. Denck lived in Augsburg for
about one year, until October of 1526, employed as a language teacher
for children. It was there that he met Balthasar Hubmaier, and Denck
was probably baptized by Hubmaier. When Hubmaier moved to Moravia, Denck became the leader of the Augsburg Anabaptist congregation, which numbered about eleven hundred people. There is evidence
that it was Hans Denck who won Hans Hut to the Anabaptist cause.
Denck was soon openly opposed by the Lutheran clergy and, desiring
to avoid a public dispute, he left in November. He stayed in various
locations, arriving in Basel in September of 1527. By that time, Denck
was very sick and he died of the plague in November of 1527.

Presented here are two of Denck's major writings, "Concerning
True Love," and "The Divine Order." These stem from 1527 and
were both published in the source collection Quellen zur Geschichte
der Täufer VI: Hans Denck Schriften, ed. Baring/Fellmann (Gütersloh: C. Bertelsmann Verlag, 1959). Both writings demonstrate the
influence of medieval mysticism as well as classical learning, on Denck's
religious thought. In these writings, Denck defends the freedom of
the will and pleads for true holiness of living. Institutional religion can

be, in Denck's view, a hindrance to true faith, which is based on the immediate love of God. In both of these writings, we come face to face with the conflict within a young and learned man to express as clearly as he can that very personal spiritual experience which has taken hold of his life and soul.

"Concerning True Love" (1527)
Hans Denck

Love is a spiritual power. The lover desires to be united with the beloved. Where love is fulfilled, the lover does not objectify the beloved. The lover forgets himself, as if he were no more, and without shame he yearns for his beloved. The lover cannot be content until he has proven his love for the beloved in the most dangerous situations. The lover would gladly and willingly face death for the benefit of the beloved. Indeed, the lover might be so foolish as to die to please his beloved, even knowing that no other benefit could come from the act. And the less his beloved acknowledges his love, the more passion the lover feels. He will not cease in his love but strive the more to prove his love, even if it will never be acknowledged.[24]

When love is true and plays no favorites, it reaches out in desire to unite with all people (that is, without causing division and instability.) Love itself can never be satisfied by lovers. Even if all lovers were to desert their loving, even if the joy of loving were no more with them, love is such a richness in itself that it was, is, and will be satisfied into eternity. Love willingly denies all things, no matter how cherished. Yet love cannot deny itself.

If it were possible, love would even deny itself for the sake of love. Love would allow itself to cease and become as nothing so that love's object could become what love is. We might even say that love hates itself, for love selflessly desires only the good of others. If love were unwilling to deny itself for the sake of the beloved, it would not be true loving but a form of selfishness in love's own eyes. Love knows and recognizes that total giving for the sake of the beloved is good. That is why love cannot deny itself. Love must finally love itself, not selfishly, but as loving what is good.

The spark of love is found in many people to a certain degree, although it seems to have been extinguished in many more of our contemporaries. Yet we may be sure that because love is spiritual and human beings are but flesh, no matter how small this spark of love may be, it comes not from a human source but from the source of perfect love. God, himself uncreated but the Maker of all things, is this love. God cannot destroy himself, but all things will be broken by God. For God is eternally immutable. This means that God must love Godself because God is good. God is sufficient within Godself, yet were it possible, God would gladly become as nothing for the sake of those in need.

Humanity could not comprehend such love if God did not show it to them in particular people. Such people are called holy and children of God, for they favor God, their spiritual Father. This love is more readily understood by human beings when it is most perfectly shown. The more perfectly this love is comprehended, the more attractive it becomes. Salvation is nearest to those most attracted by this love. Therefore, the person in whom it pleased eternal love to show itself most clearly is called the savior of his people. Not that it would be possible for one of humanity to save others. But God is so perfectly united in love with this one that all that God would do is done in him. The suffering of this one is the very suffering of Godself.

This person is Jesus of Nazareth, promised in scripture by the true God and fulfilled in his time. All the qualities proper to love were publicly demonstrated in Israel in the events of his life through the power of the Holy Spirit.

Even now, though our time seems without love, we may also know that this has been accomplished. We acknowledge this highest love and may be sure through the Spirit of God that the love of God toward humanity and humanity toward God cannot be shown more perfectly than has happened in Jesus. For in him God had such compassion for the world that God willingly renounced his righteous judgment against us for our sinfulness, asking only that we not despise that which is shown to us in the human aspect of Jesus—that is, as he was led by God and not his human nature. In doing so, a person who loves God most truly and as much as possible can help his neighbor to also know and love God.

Whoever wants to know true love can receive it no better than through Jesus Christ. Indeed, it cannot be known except through him. Salvation is not limited by flesh and blood or time and place. But it is not possible without these. For just as a person must be saved by God, so God also cannot save a person except through his humanity. All who are saved are one in spirit with God. But that one who is most perfect in love is a forerunner of those who are being saved. Jesus is not with us himself. But in all times God has been pleased by those who, in his name, follow and are obedient to those who teach his will. The more clearly it is taught, the more rightly it can be followed. But it has never been more perfectly taught than by that one in whom it was perfectly accomplished. That one is Jesus Christ, whom God sent to lead both Jews and Gentiles together out of spiritual bondage. But now in our time, he is denied not just by Jews and pagans, but by Christians themselves. All people who sought and found the way of God are one with God. But this one who never strayed from the way of God was always united with God. He was one with God's Spirit from eternity. Yet he was born as a human being and, other than in sin, was subject to all human failings.

That is why it is written that all who are saved must be saved through this Jesus to behold the perfection of the Spirit. This is the one aim toward which all who are being saved should seek. Only to the extent that one beholds the perfection of the Spirit is one saved. The closer one comes to it, the farther one is from condemnation.

What is taught and done by love is truly good and right. Without love, nothing is truly good and right. Whoever knows what is good and right, yet teaches something different, even if it seems good it is evil and useless. That is how it is with the teachings and works of Moses, David and the patriarchs. They were good. But where they displace love (that is, Jesus) they must be considered dross for the sake of that which is better. For indeed they are dross when you consider what they lack and how they could be improved. When Moses killed the Egyptian who was beating the Israelite, this was in a sense good, for his passion was for justice and against injustice. But if Moses had known and possessed perfect love, he would have given himself to be killed in place of his brother. But he would not have strangled the Egyptian, the enemy of his brother. Therefore the teachings and Law of Moses, which said an eye for an eye, to protect the innocent by force, to defeat evil with force, and concerning usury, divorce, oath swearing and so on, were good teachings and law for the people of Israel at that time (out of whom God would create and bring forth a new Israel.) But if it had been possible that (before Jesus) one would have presented a more perfect teaching and love, and the people had been disposed to accept it, then the previous love would have had to fade. Then, anyone who would have resisted or spoken against the new way would by this show the uselessness and evil of the old teaching.

We can see then why it is written that works of the Law cannot

114

justify anyone before God. The justification by faith which is worthy before God far surpasses the works of the Law. For perfection forsakes the concessions contained in the Law.

The righteousness of faith is prepared and yearns to restore to the Lord God all that belongs to him—that is, all our possessions and capacities. Legal justification, on the other hand, consents to no more than what is expressly written in the law and takes advantage of every possible concession it can squeeze out of it. So those under law are slaves who do no more than is explicit in the law. But those under faith are called children of God, for they do all that they are able to do for God's sake, which is more than could be made literally explicit. They therefore have the benefit of God in that God has not given them an explicit or written law, but asks only that they love God. A slave under obligation to his master must get up at four or five in the morning and work until late at night. But the master's son gets up and retires as he chooses, without obligation. But while the slave gives no thought to the fate of the master, the son remains by his side through all dangers, even unto death. Therefore, the slave cannot remain indefinitely in the master's house, be blessed or enjoy peace with his master, unless he first becomes a child or household member. Then he no longer thinks of obligations or rewards, but only of how and in what ways he can please his lord and best carry out the lord's will. Not that the obligations that the Lord made with his people Israel in the Law of Moses were wrong. But it is wrong to oppose the Lord's purpose to lead his people to an even better way through Jesus, the firstborn in the Spirit. The way of Jesus was not against the Law, though it sometimes seemed to be. For all slaves are obligated to be true and devoted to their lord. After all, it is also explicitly written in the Law that one should love God with all one's heart, soul and abilities (that is, with all one has and is capable of). Jesus taught and did exactly that. All of his teachings and deeds stand in this aim and purpose. Therefore, all who follow him in his teachings and deeds are promised eternal life. But there is very little written in the Law about eternal life, for as said above, the slave does not remain forever in his master's house. His time of service is limited.

Now one might object that nothing can be added to or taken away from the Law. In other words, it is improper to elevate that Law in love, thereby reducing and not observing its practices.[25] Yet to this one must reply that love is the very essence of the Law, which nobody can practice too perfectly or understand too profoundly.

Whoever daily grows in love does not add to the Law but rather fulfills it more perfectly. Love means to know and love God, surrendering for his sake those things which are so valued by people after the flesh, and to accept and bear those things which run counter to the flesh. Therefore, one can understand that in the old and new Law (as they are called) there is only one love. But in the new Law it is more perfectly explained and shown to God's people through Jesus the helper. The old Law had become a source of bondage because the people lacked understanding. At the same time, however, they were partially gathered in by God (like bondsmen) in that they were obligated to service. In the same way that the covenantal sign, circumcision, was given without regard to human desire for it; all descendants of Abraham were duty-bound to the Law, whether they wanted to be or not. But the new Law is a matter of becoming God's children. Therefore, all who are under the new Law are not forced to be there by other people. Rather, they are drawn to it in the deepest part of their soul by the merciful God, the true Father. He makes known to them his most perfect will, which is love itself. This was exhibited in Christ Jesus and was and is proclaimed through the good news of his magnificent resurrection.

Baptism, the sign of the covenant, will only be given to those who by God's power through knowledge of true love are invited to it, who desire it and are willing to follow. They will be uncoerced by other members and relatives to remain in this love—only love itself may constrain them. As it is written in the Psalter, "Your people will be there of their own will!"

That ceremonies prescribed in the Law are no longer practiced is not a result of a command, but is a freedom permitted by love. The holy patriarchs of old sometimes must have broken these ceremonies also. Yet they were without blame because they were excused through love. Out of true love, Jesus was silent about these things, neither commanding nor forbidding. It was as if he wanted them to understand that one can come to this love without such ceremonies. For one without love, these ceremonies are of themselves of no benefit. But whoever has this love and understanding should practice and observe them even as Jesus did. But when preaching the gospel of love to the Gentiles, it is unnecessary to teach them such things. For if they take on love, they will know how to act in terms of such rites when they need to. It is also unnecessary to throw this in the face of Jews when preaching love to them. For otherwise love may become the source of tearing down love. Love gives its friends freedom from such rites because they love the Father in truth, even if they once stood under the kind of obligation which a slave owes his master.

Now it might be asked why love forsakes the old ceremonies only to replace them with new ones such as baptism and the Lord's Supper. It is because these are only a confession and remembrance. In these rites the children should confess and remember from where and to what they have been called. They have been called out of the world to God to serve God in holiness and righteousness, as Zacharias, father of John the Baptist said.

Holiness is once and for all to separate oneself from this evil world and the impurities of the flesh to serve only the Lord God. This is the meaning and witness of water baptism. In baptism one confesses the old way of living as useless and desires from then on to walk in a new way of living. Righteousness is, as was said, to give each person his due. Because we owe everything to the one Lord God, everything we have and do in body and soul, honor and worldly goods, we should give for his name's sake. We should risk everything in highest submission. It should be with all children as it was for the firstborn. He was transformed into our nature that we might become one bread, broken for one another. Since he became bread for us and was crushed and baked for our benefit, we should remember this in the breaking of bread.

That is why we break bread often but baptize only once. For initiation into the new covenant happens only once, even if it is sometimes transgressed and recommitment is needed. It is like a child born to his father. He may run off and then return, yet he remains his father's child. He need not go through the birthing process again. But the fruition of the covenant of righteousness must be strived for constantly and acted upon.

The ceremonies of baptism and breaking bread were not instituted that salvation would depend on keeping them. But where they are held, one should do so earnestly. Although they may appear to be rather foolish and simple to the world, the Lord does not want them to be scorned. The Lord practiced these things himself. He fulfilled all works of righteousness, from the smallest to the greatest, as an example for us. By doing these things he wanted to show us that nothing is too simple to be used as a remembrance of something of great value.

This then is a summation of the teaching of Jesus Christ. By this all contention which arises concerning the truth may be settled by those who have a heartfelt desire to understand. Whatever teaching is not built on the foundation of love should not be maintained in favor of love. Whoever knows this principle and yet teaches otherwise cannot be defended by love. Even if he tries to defend his teaching by love, saying in effect that it is done for love's sake, it can come to nothing. The children of love should not act contrary to love for the sake of love. In such things the wise need wisdom and all friends of God need love, so as not to replace God's love with human love. To love someone other than through God's truth and love is actually a form of hatred. It is more loving to hate someone for the sake of God's love! Of course you cannot hate someone for the sake of love. But this means earnestly to censure him and, if he will not take heed, with deep sorrow to avoid him. This is the basis for separation between the children of God and the children of the world. Indeed, this is the basis for the banning or exclusion of false brothers, which also clearly must occur for the sake of true love. Otherwise we would have to deny the foundation of the covenant of the children of God, which is holiness and separation from worldly company. This is what happens in baptism, as was said before.

From what has been said, then, it is easy to see what to make of things like infant baptism, vows and oaths and governing evildoers. God tolerated these things in the world to bring about improvement (though this does not apply to infant baptism, which God never willed). But among those who know the truth (or at least assume they know the truth) God does not cause these things to happen any more than God causes any sort of evil.

Truth strongly witnesses to the spuriousness of infant baptism. The most important task of disciples of Jesus Christ is to teach and make disciples of the Lord, seeking above all else the kingdom of God. When you baptize before a person has become a disciple you are by that act saying, in effect, that baptism is more important than teaching and knowledge. In the eyes of God this is a terrible error. So if teaching is more important than baptism, let baptism wait until teaching has taken place. To baptize before teaching is saying that baptism is more important, but this is contrary to Christian doctrine. Now some say they give priority to teaching for those willing to listen. But in his commission, Christ did not say to go to the Jews and preach but go to the Gentiles and baptize! One does not baptize Isaac because his father Abraham is a disciple! The commission says clearly, "Go forth and teach, making disciples of all nations, baptizing them (those who have become disciples!) in the name of the Father (who draws them to him) and the Son (who now leads them) and the Holy Spirit (through whose power they are made firm in fulfillment of the Father's will)." In short, just as Christ is Christ before anyone believes in him, so teaching is done before baptism. Where there is no Christ there is no faith. So baptism without teaching is not a true baptism.

Oaths and swearing should not be done because no human has power to keep them. What a friend of God knows to be right should simply be done, so far as he is able, without oaths and promises. He might ask the Lord to help him accomplish something. But he should not make presumptuous promises, as if the Lord were obligated to do what he wants the Lord to do. Humans do not have power over a single hair! Therefore, if someone swears that he is able to do something, he either acts brazenly without understanding, or if he does understand, then he acts as a hypocrite—that is, he says something which in his heart he knows is not true. As scripture says, "You cannot make even one hair white or black," and "Do not fall into hypocrisy!"

Now some say that God himself swears oaths and that is not wrong. So we should swear as well, for it is written, "Be perfect, even as your Father in heaven!" Here is the answer to that. If we could be as sure as God that we have the power to keep our word, then we could swear as God did. We might say the same for killing and governing, if we could do them like God, totally without revenge or self-seeking. But we cannot. The only person who could have done this purposely did not do it, as an example to us. For his time had not yet come. So we should abstain gladly from such things and follow the one through whom we come to the Father, the Father we could not know without such a mediator.

You should not be too quick to say yes or no. For if you say yes as a guarantee or assurance, this is really a kind of oath, in that by doing this one expects what was promised to be fulfilled as God's will. Then you must break your word if you cannot keep it. If you do right this will not happen—as Paul did when he apologized before God to the Corinthians that despite his promise he was not able to visit them.

This is all that needs to be said concerning swearing about future events. As for testimony concerning things past, according to the Lord's teaching we should do it simply, using as few words as possible—yes or no. For we must answer to God for anything we say. One might call on God as a witness that what he says is true, as Paul did. But do not forget never to use God's name frivolously. This is forbidden in the Law and also in the New Testament, where we are forbidden to swear at all. It is not wrong to use God's name in itself. In fact, love requires all her children to do so that God might be known and alone be eternally loved and praised.

No Christian who wants to bring honor to his Lord can use force or be a ruler. For the governance of our King consists only in teaching and in the power of the Spirit. Whoever truly acknowledges Christ as Lord should not act contrary to his commandments. And Christ has commanded his disciples to deal with evildoers in no way other than to teach and admonish them for their own improvement. If they will not listen, one should leave them alone and avoid them. Those who are outsiders (that is, unbelievers) do not concern the community of Christ, except that Christians hope to serve by teaching. Not that power is wrong in itself, in view of how wicked the world is. It can serve as God's wrath. But love teaches its children something better — that they should serve the grace of God.

It is the nature of love never to desire the worst for anyone. Rather, love seeks to serve for improvement wherever that is possible. The head of a household should treat the household members as he himself would want God to treat him, that is, not contrary to love. And if it would be possible for a governor to do the same, he might also be a Christian in that position. But because the world would not tolerate this, a friend of God should not be a ruler. He should leave that position if he wants Christ as Lord and Master. One may love the Lord in any station in life. But he must not forget what is proper for one who loves the Lord — to forsake all violence for the Lord's sake and to be subject to others as unto the Lord.

Now one might say that John the Baptist, when asked by the soldiers what they should do, did not tell them to give up their profession. Here is the answer to that. The Law and the prophets lasted up to John. John did not come to overthrow the Law. Only the Light himself and he alone could do this — that is, as far as it was to happen. John was not the Light, but a witness to the Light. The one who takes away sin may also take away the Law — that is, Jesus Christ, the Lamb of God, to whom John pointed. John preached the wrath of God for repentance to those who would not keep that Law. But Christ preached to them grace and free forgiveness that they might live without rebuke in God's good favor.

All that is written here flows from the perfect love of Christ, and from it one may perceive who has the Spirit of the Lord. Whoever understands and yet teaches otherwise is a true Antichrist. And whoever cannot understand it does not know the Lord. Although the whole world does not tolerate this teaching, it is a comfort to all of God's children. God is stronger and mightier than the whole world or the prince of this world, the devil himself. God is faithful and will not allow harm to come to those who trust him.

Woe to anyone who shrinks from the truth to avoid scandal and yet claims to be doing right. For this is love of the devil. He blinds his children and seeks to blind the children of God also, so that they fear men more than God. Whoever wishes to avoid offending the Lord should first see what the Lord commands and then not fail to do it for any reason. Stand on the solid rock, don't trip on it!

The person who teaches a command and then does not hold it himself and allows others to break it is the real offender! He will have the least place in the kingdom of heaven. What can be said of one who violates all or most of the very commandments he himself teaches? Never forget that one who teaches in the Lord's name must himself be a disciple of Christ. A disciple of Christ never acts without sanction or neglects the Master's commandments.

Oh, all of you who long for love, seek love and you will find it! For the Lord God offers it freely to all whose hearts desire it. Whoever longs for love prepares for the wedding. If he lacks the proper dress, the bridegroom will see to it that no shame is brought upon him. But woe to those who come to the wedding in worn-out garments, when atonement has already been accomplished.

"Divine Order and the Work of His Creatures: To Destroy the Artificial and Hypocritical Excuses of Those Falsely and Corruptly Chosen, Giving Room for Truth to Fulfill the Eternal and Unchanging Will of God. Colossians 1; Ephesians 1" (1527)
Hans Denck

To all readers and listeners, I say with Christ (John 7): Whoever desires to do the will of God, those who are dead to sin will know clearly those teachings which come from God. For it is impossible for such a person to be deceived by a false spirit (John 7; Matthew 7; Mark 3; Ephesians 6; 1 Peter 2 and 4; 1 John 2 and 5; Hebrews 10; Romans 2 and 5).

To the company of the Lamb, John says, "The anointing you received from the Holy Spirit remains in you and you do not need anyone to teach you. But as his anointing teaches you about all things, it is real and not counterfeit."

To the scholars, Christ says in John 5, "You diligently study the scriptures because you think they have life. These are the very scriptures that testify to me, yet you refuse to come to me to have life."

To those who do not know God and yet lament the futility of all things (Romans 8) I say with Moses and Paul, "Evil and vanity you see well. But the good for which you yearn is not far from you, nor too high or hard for you to obtain. It is in your heart and mouth. Although it is contrary to your manner, you think and speak of it and cannot be purged of it. But it cannot benefit you so long as you oppose it. But if you follow it, you will be marvelously led by it from all your doubts."

To all of the elect who seek after God in their innermost being, I, Hans Denck, a servant of Jesus Christ, wish you endurance. In the fear of God, may you know his almighty power, judgment and wondrous deeds. Amen.

Beloved, you find beginning among you the work of the eternal and invincible God. Your hearts have been to some degree secured and will lead you from all selfish pursuits of this carnal life. You know yourselves how vain and erratic this life is. Be careful then that you do not throw it as chaff to the wind, that it blow over your heads (Psalm 7; Ecclesiasticus 27) and you be blown away with it (Psalm 1). You consider this treasure of life to be of little value. But if you do not use it well, there can be no excuse (Matthew 25). Know that he who has given you this treasure acts mightily and takes the profits for himself. If you fear him, can you not then trust him? (Psalm 115). Say what you will, you know the truth. The more you flee from him, the more he pursues you (Psalm 139). Why then do you not use this treasure?

If you say that you cannot do anything profitable with it, you do not speak the truth. For there is no treasure so insignificant that nothing profitable can be done with it (Matthew 13). You simply don't want to try (Matthew 23). Why not? Lazy as you are, you will not make the effort. You fear putting your backs into it (John 16). Eating and drinking and indulging yourselves you know only too well. Who taught you that? You say it is your nature, you must do it. Oh, brothers! You do the Almighty injustice! For you know that he is called Good, just the opposite of these things! And yet you blame him for your evil deeds (John 8), saying that he made you that way? (Romans 9). You say it is written (Romans 8), "For those God foreknew he predestined for salvation" and no others. Beloved, examine these words carefully and do not misuse them to your own condemnation (1 Peter 3). The word of God is itself easy and clear (Psalm 19). But in our darkness we do not always grasp it (John 1). For we are a self-seeking people (Matthew 10). That is why Peter so truly admonishes us not to be too quick with Paul's letters. But it serves us right. For we want to learn the word of God from ever more books. But then we deny it in our hearts, even though scripture itself, which we receive as liars and thieves (John 10; Jeremiah 23; Isaiah 22; Revelations 1 and 3) gives abundant witness that this is wrong (Deuteronomy 30; Romans 10).

So now we want to summarize briefly the Divine Order and contrast it with the works of creatures since the foundation of the world. We hope to show by this comparison how wrong those people are who, without the command of God (Psalm 50) speak of the covenant and mysteries of God, of which they have no understanding (1 Corinthians 13). They would teach the right path to salvation, yet they have never walked this path or even wanted to do so (Philippians 3). They say they believe—and as they believe, so do they speak. They have never cast off their old way of living or accepted a new way of living. Brothers, whoever has ears, let him hear! And if any of you lacks wisdom, ask the Lord in truth and humility and he will give it to you (James 1). Amen.

Concerning Foreknowledge and Predestination.
God's Mercy Is Without Partiality

We know that God is truly good. If God were not good (God forbid!) God would not be God. But because God is good, God has made all things good (Genesis 1). Therefore, to the extent that humans are evil, they are without God (Psalm 10; Ephesians 2) and do not belong to God (John 8). There was once no death. Human beings brought death upon themselves through their own guilt. It was not created by God (Wisdom of Solomon 1). Yet God remains who God is, namely Good (Exodus 3). God causes the sun to shine on both the good and evil people (Matthew 5) and gives everyone reason, grace and power to be transformed (Matthew 19; 2 Peter 3; Ezekiel 33; Wisdom 11 and 12).

No person has a need to sin (Ecclesiasticus 15). The Light, the word of God, shines in every human heart in this world. It is there from the beginning, giving power to those who accept it to become children of God, inheritors of the kingdom of the Father (John 1). But for those who do not accept it, this Light is a light of judgment and condemnation (John 3 and 9). Just as God does not cause anyone to sin (Ecclesiasticus 15), it would not be fitting to compel anyone to serve God against that person's will. God wants to be served in freedom (2 Corinthians 9; Ecclesiasticus 35). God would that every person be saved (1 Timothy 2 and 4; 2 Peter 3). But God also knows that many will choose condemnation (Romans 9). If God's will were executed without any kind of ordering restraint, God would simply speak the word and it would be done instantly (Matthew 8; Luke 7). But that would be without regard to God's justice. For God to coerce would be to set Godself against God's own will and mercy. God cannot do that.[26]

What does it mean, then, that God hated Esau before he was even born and had done no evil? (Romans 9). The answer is in Isaiah 48. "I knew well how treacherous you would be. Therefore, I called you a rebel from birth." Why did God love Jacob? The answer is in Jeremiah 1. "I knew you even before I formed you in the womb. Before you were born I set you apart." God knew beforehand that Jacob would not be a sinner (although he did indeed sin, Ecclesiasticus 31). That is why Jacob was loved by God. The sinfulness of Esau and all corrupt people has been known by God from the beginning. God also knew of their death and punishment. But God does not punish the innocent (Genesis 8). God knew from the beginning of Jacob and those who choose righteousness. God also knew of their reward, the kingdom, which was prepared for them since the foundation of the world (Matthew 25; John 14). But even so, nobody receives the crown without effort (2 Timothy 2).

The Two Ways of Humans — The Way of Life and the Way of Death (Matthew 7)

It is a constant struggle for a person to deny himself in the obedience of faith, overcoming the evil in which he is entangled (Romans 7; 1 Corinthians 9). The reward is true knowledge of God and God's Anointed (John 15 and 17). The friend of God knows that the victory is not his own. It belongs to God. It is not accomplished with sword and bow but by the power of the Spirit of God (Psalm 44). Such a person is content with God (Psalm 4) and stands upon the solid rock (Matthew 7). No foe can harm him. No spirit can lead him from the peace of God's Spirit, to which he has been intended (John 10). In this contentment he knows no disharmony. Living or dying are of equal value (Philippians 1; Galatians 6). For he no longer lives for himself but for his King, for how he might bring others to this place of the King (Romans 1; John 17).

Sin is disobedience and unbelief (John 16). Sin is human self-seeking without regard to justice, which is gladly discarded if it means suffering any inconvenience (Matthew 23). The consequence, however, is a hardening of unbelief (Romans 9) by which a person frees himself into wickedness (Psalm 1). The person hates all that is good and takes pleasure and desire in what is wrong. And then he wants to say, "Why has God created me so wicked? I can do nothing about it! Of course I would want to be saved. Anyone would. But if God wants me saved, let him do it!" (Isaiah 45; Romans 9).

His pact is then with the Abyss (Isaiah 28). And when he encounters a righteous person, the nearer that person is to God, the more he hates him. And finally he says to himself, "Hey, all this about eternal life and damnation is just a lie and pure fiction. We live and we die. That's all there is to it" (Wisdom 2).

Concerning Hell, Conquered by God, Which Is Correction by the Just Hand of God (Psalm 77)

Once the godless person has come to the point of saying this, he enters that place of Hell to which he was destined (Proverbs 9; Psalm 115). This is not to say that he has to remain there (Psalm 77). For the Lord can even free from Hell. Damnation has no impenetrable roof on it! (Job 26). For nothing is more powerful than the strong arm of God.

In the highest justice, which we call God's anger, God may inflict upon us the pain of Hell (Psalm 18). This way we may recognize our own misery and cry to God for help in our time of need (Hosea 9). As Paul said in Romans 11, "For God has bound all people over to disobedience so that he may have mercy on them all." The word of God works this way when it is clearly preached to the person under condemnation, "You have done this yourself! Do not blame others for what you have brought on yourself! Your suffering is fair and just!"

And when that person sees the truth of these words, he is partially free already (John 8). He can then either continue in his wickedness or offer himself up to his suffering. The more he resists his suffering, the more damnation he brings on himself, until he finally sinks into death. But the more he humbles himself and cooperates with the mighty hand of God (1 Peter 5) the easier it is for the Lord to accomplish his work. A person may feel he will be totally torn apart when this work is done in him. He thinks his emptiness and hunger will never be satisfied (Amos 8). He sees himself very distant from the bosom of Abraham (Luke 16). He may well know that he is getting what he deserves, but he may not yet know how close beside him God (Jeremiah 23) and his mercy on all people are (Ecclesiasticus 18). Now both Abraham and his own conscience (that is, the Spirit of God who instructs his conscience) speak to him only of justice. The justice of God and God's almighty mercy are still separate things in his mind.[27]

The Eight Beatitudes (Matthew 5)

The Lord places us in the deepest abyss of Hell, making us poor in spirit (Matthew 5) and thinking that we shall surely perish. But then blessings begin to well up before we even know it. For during this unspeakable weeping and moaning, when we can see nothing else than that God has totally forgotten us and turned his back to us (Jeremiah 18) and will neither accept nor hear our cry and plea (Psalm 22), suddenly the rays of dawn break through! (Genesis 32). The comfort of God's mercy is like rain on the parched land! (Ecclesiasticus 35).

Then with great joy, in tenderness and patience, the chosen person can say, "Lord, now I can see how you have only sought what is best for me in all of this trial and affliction! Your rod and staff have comforted me (Psalm 23). Had I known this before, even a thousand times my affliction would not have been too much!" In other words, he now is able to take heartfelt joy in the justice of God. His desire and thirst for unity is so strong that he totally forgets those who have opposed him and done him wrong and wants only to forgive them. His heart and soul are made pure and he forgives the whole creation—especially those who have, according to human standards, deprived him in some way.

Then this new "Israel" (. . . for he has struggled with God . . .) may see God freely, face to face (Genesis 32) in the brightly shining morning sun. He sees (I witness to this!) the one true God as God really is. This is the fulfillment of Psalm 85, where it is written, "Love and faithfulness meet together; justice and peace kiss each other." After all affliction we first begin to believe and understand that God is good since the beginning of time. When this understanding and trust springs forth on the earth—that is, from earthly human beings through the word of God—we see divine justice. That is, we see that it is no longer ourselves but the Spirit of God who dwells and works within us. That spirit which we stole as thieves from God has been returned to the Father. From that moment on there is contentment. For the friend of God no longer considers only himself. His concern is for others. If they are receptive, he helps them find contentment. For their sakes he is again discontented (although actually for him there is no more discontentment). But what this means is that he has a heartfelt desire to show his highest love for the brethren (John 15; Genesis 3).

This chosen one is then no longer a useless servant (Luke 17) who only barely fulfills his obligations to the master. He becomes a faithful servant and friend to his master (Matthew 25), going far beyond what the letter of the Law requires of him. He wants to serve the Lord even at great cost to himself—something the Law could never expect from him. He does not do this by himself. Rather, he has experienced and learned it from his Prince, Jesus of Nazareth. For just as the word which was born of the Father in eternity in this same Jesus accomplished mercy in the most unmerciful circumstance, it accomplishes this in him also according to the measure of his faith (Romans 12).

The Separation of God's Will from Human Will

There are these two, God and humanity. And because they are not the same, each acts for good or evil, according to its nature (Isaiah 55). Now of course God is not the cause of sin. That insinuation comes from a devilish spirit. But God does punish, and since this is in opposition to what we like, it is perceived by us as "evil" (Isaiah 45; Amos 3). Nor do human beings truly do good (Galatians 6; Isaiah 46). God alone is good. But human beings do seek truth, and there is good in that truth.

The more a person sins, the further he is separated from God (Isaiah 59; Luke 16). To become one with God, a person must suffer that which from the beginning God wills to work in him. For up to then it was God who suffered because of that person's human nature

127

(Isaiah 1; Romans 9). Now God actually neither works nor suffers (James 1). God's work and suffering are done through the word which from the beginning, through his Spirit, was born of God or flowed out from God. So long as time and space continue, this word continues its work (Luke 1; Daniel 7).

God suffered in the people of Noah's time the sins of an evil world, right up until the Great Flood (Genesis 6). Then God began to work righteousness in those in whom God had previously endured sin, right up until the death of Jesus Christ. Through his suffering, Jesus became one with God and God's word (Luke 24; Acts 17; Psalm 18). In the Spirit he descended into the place of the dead to preach this same message to the unbelieving spirits there (1 Peter 3) to perfect the work begun by those who believed (1 Peter 4). Indeed, the Lamb that suffered in Christ has suffered since the beginning of the world (Revelations 13) and will suffer until the end of the world (Matthew 25). Even the Lion of Judah (Genesis 49) who is victorious in Christ (Revelations 5) was victorious in the elect from the beginning (Numbers 23 and 24) and will be so until the final enemy is conquered (Isaiah 30; 1 Corinthians 15). The Lamb and the Lion are at once the word of God, filling the whole world (Jeremiah 23; Wisdom 1). This word is in our hearts (Deuteronomy 30; Romans 10). It is not there to be dormant, but to do the will of the Father (John 4). When we seek only for ourselves and take no heed for this word, it suffers within us to our condemnation (John 3). So the word is working in us even when we don't know it (John 9).

The Reuniting of God's Will and Human Will

In deepest damnation we let ourselves and everything we touch be torn apart with unutterable pain (Job 7). It is like a pregnant woman who must resign herself to the pain of giving birth. She resigns herself willingly, knowing that she will not rejoice in the child until she sees it alive (John 16). This is the eye of the needle through which no camel can pass (Matthew 19). We could never do this ourselves. We must let God, to whom all things are possible (Luke 1), do it for us (Philippians 4).

So long as the elect deem themselves to be something without knowledge and love of God (Galatians 6: 1 Corinthians 13), God prods and disciplines them until they admit that they are nothing and this false "something" is shattered (1 Corinthians 3). Only then is the needle's eye, the narrow gate leading to life, wide enough. The yoke of Christ (which in the world's eyes is bitter and unbearable) becomes for them easy and light (Matthew 11). The more one resists this burning fire, the more in conflict he becomes (Job 9) and Christ cannot help him (John 3), even though Christ has already suffered for him (1 John 2). But the more he renounces his possession, the faster God is able to accomplish his work (Wisdom 6). Then, even though he has been affected by Adam's fall into sin, it can do him no harm (Jeremiah 31; Ezekiel 18).

Whether Human Will Is Bound or Free

The closer, the more like one is to his original created self, the freer he is. The deeper one is in damnation, the more he is bound (Matthew 5 and 18). But no matter how free one is, one cannot do good except by suffering (Philippians 2). And no matter how bound one is, one may yet freely allow the word to work in him (Matthew 23).

Whoever says that God has not given him the grace to become more faithful is a liar—like all people are (Psalm 116). But this is a lie against God, who has generously poured out his grace on all people (Psalm 119 and 145; Isaiah 18 and 33; Wisdom 11; Ecclesiasticus 1 and 18; 1 Timothy 2; 2 Peter 3; Matthew 18) as well as, even more so, his wrath (Romans 5; Exodus 20). Otherwise, the godless would be innocent. They claim to be innocent, but this is not true (John 9; Romans 3; Psalm 57).

The corrupt person looks out for himself. He does not want to give up anything. And indeed he may find nothing in all eternity (Psalm 1; Matthew 10). He wants to perform and be victorious but does not want to suffer. He wants faith but does not want to know what faith is. He wants to be saved but wants to know nothing about damnation. He wants life but wants to know nothing of death.

It is from this that we find two contradictory views. On the one hand, some say that they have freedom of the will. Yet they are unwilling to do even the smallest thing to please God. On the other hand, there are those who say that do not have free will because they see that they cannot do what is right. Yet they choose not to allow the word to work in them (Matthew 23).

In themselves, both of these views are true, but they are both false also. For both speak of the human being as if there were no other foundation than in himself. One is boastful and arrogant about human freedom, while the other seeks only excuses—"God is finally responsible."

The first view, that the will is free, is an obviously brazen and foolish claim which gives no place for the fear of God. It arrogantly assumes I can do whatever I want to do (James 4; Proverbs 12 and 28). The second view is a kind of sham humility and craftiness that would have us believe that honor is being given to God and not to oneself. Yet it certainly is no denial of self—in fact, it increases selfishness. This is in the eyes of God the highest form of arrogance and pride. God knows the innermost workings of the heart, both its subtle and obvious sinfulness (Psalm 7). Whoever cannot see the similarities in these two views is not yet ready to fundamentally comprehend what the Spirit has to teach. For if someone does not know himself yet—his abilities and inabilities—how can he learn knowledge of God? (John 3; Wisdom 9).

In short, in the same measure that a person seeks only after his own benefit, the Spirit of God testifies in his heart and conscience that he is doing wrong (Wisdom 12). Whoever denies himself does right. Not that we are able to do what is right ourselves (1 Corinthians 6). But the word which is present in all creatures frees us to become children of God if we believe in him (John 1).

That Human Will Is Free When in Agreement with God's Will

To believe is to obey the word of God, whether living or dying, in full confidence that it is the best (Hebrews 11). Whoever does this cannot go wrong, even if mistakes are made. Such a person fulfills the Law of God to the highest magnitude, even if at times the Law is broken. Such a person seeks what is holy in heaven and on earth without regard to how it affects him personally.

For such a person there is no Law (1 Timothy 1), for he has become a Law unto himself (Romans 2). Such a person can do anything, but will only do what is beneficial (1 Corinthians 6). Such a person is one with Christ, even as Christ is one with the Father (John 17). Therefore, whoever slanders him is slandering the Law and the Word of God itself (James 4). For the word of God instructs him in all that he does (John 14; 1 John 2). He does nothing except it comes from the Father (John 5).

Therefore, he can count all of his deeds as good. Not that he is perfect and without error (Philippians 3), for his flesh will still struggle against the Spirit (Romans 7). Yet he knows that in truth his struggle is for the good (Romans 8). The grace of God is sufficient for him (2 Corinthians 12), and he prays daily concerning his sins (Psalm 32) and strives for that perfection which he has already partially achieved (Philippians 3). The Lord accepts him and counts him among the perfect, giving him the knowledge that he was chosen from the beginning. God seals this election with his Spirit, which is poured into the hearts of all the chosen ones (2 Corinthians 1). Then he may say in truth and without fear, "You are my Father, I am your child!" (Romans 8; Psalm 89).

The Guiltlessness of God Against His False Accusers (Psalm 52)

If the deeds of the Lord God were beyond good and evil, as some of these unfaithful servants claim, God could not judge and punish the world (Genesis 18) without judging and punishing Godself (God forbid!). Rather, the devil, God's enemy, in the end (as is already happening) will be defeated by his own lies. His kingdom will fall before the elect of God's kingdom (1 Corinthians 15). Therefore God, the Lord of Lords, said, "Surely the arm of the Lord is not too short to save, nor his ear too dull to hear. But your iniquities have separated you from your God!" (Isaiah 59:1–2; Jeremiah 5).

Who has ears, let him hear! Who has eyes, let him see! Beloved in the Lord, open your hearts! For the Lord has clearly said, "I am merciful and powerful enough to help you. But know also that I am a just God. If my strength and goodness is to benefit you, you must first know my justice, and that you don't want!" Examine yourselves well, brothers. See how you will be held responsible before the Lord, face to face on that great day of his glory (Isaiah 20).

You say that the Lamb of God has taken away the sins of the world (John 1). So why then go on sinning? Sure, you would rather just believe in him than make any effort yourselves. You want to say, "So he has taken away the sins of the world? Well and good! I'll be glad to believe that. Just so it doesn't disturb the peace!" Oh you miserable lot! What kind of Christians are you anyway? The Antichrist and his sort also confess that Jesus Christ is come in the flesh (1 John 4). But just like you, they give him no place in their lives! I tell you truly (and not I, but the Lord God, the Just and Almighty) that God's mercy, which you take for granted, will be made bitter enough. He

131

will punish your transgressions with the rod and your evil deeds with plagues (Psalm 89). The surer you are of yourselves, the harder it will be! (1 Thessalonians 5).

Can you have Christ as your king, the son of the living God (John 6) and not have him rule your lives? (Luke 19). Can you be a servant of God and not respect him? Can you be God's children and not honor him as your Father? Can you honor the Father and disrespect his son? (John 5). If you spurn and mock the very way of living which he led, you disrespect him, just as hypocrites and unbelievers have done since the beginning (1 Corinthians 1).

Beloved, don't be that way! Rather, give God glory, even as Achan did when, having sinned, he let himself be stoned to death (Joshua 7). Say, "Yes Lord! We have sinned! Remove the sin from us with your righteousness! Work your mercy in us! For this sin we would gladly die and be burned—just do not see us as your enemies!"

Sacrifice! Sacrifice to justice and hope in the Lord, for there is no excuse for you! I tell you in the Lord, you are able. You have been long able to endure the Lord's work, if only you were willing. From that moment when you desire what is right, the eternal Lord is ready to give it to you (Isaiah 18 and 33; Wisdom 6).

The Trinity, Unity and Triune God

Oh, how good is the God of Mercy! God stretches out his hand the day long, calling all to himself. And if even one answers, God is filled with unspeakable joy (Luke 15). But let us not deceive ourselves—God is also just. God cannot show his love for those who do not fear and love him (1 Samuel 2; Isaiah 66; Psalm 5: Proverbs 8). Even so, God has a wonderful love for everyone (Wisdom 11). If God showed his love to those who oppose him, he would be (God forbid!) giving to dogs what is sacred (Matthew 7), which we are not to do.[28]

"Wake up, O sleeper, arise!" (Ephesians 5). Do not let the corrupter attack you! (Jeremiah 6). For the Lord is stronger and mightier than all of his foes (Isaiah 42). Heaven and earth will pass away, but God's mercy and justice will be fulfilled (Matthew 24). The Lord himself has vowed that, regardless of opposition, this is true. The Lord said that every knee shall bow and every tongue confess (Isaiah 45; Romans 14; Philippians 2). The good will of God will be proven (Job 23; Psalm 115; Isaiah 46; Wisdom 12). But the lies of God's foes will come to shame and corruption (Psalm 1 and 112).

Concerning the Outrageousness and Idolatry of Church Ceremony,
Which Does Not Worship God in Spirit and in Truth

Above all else we need to examine whether we truly are seeking the kingdom of God and his justice (Matthew 6). We ought to celebrate in God (Isaiah 1 and 66) and ask the Lord to work in us and govern our lives. For he will wonderfully teach us his way (Psalm 26). But we boast of our faith without knowing what faith really is. Our works and way of living are not godly and in accord with the Spirit. They are rather carnal and in accord with the flesh (Romans 8; Philippians 3).

We carry on about external things like wife and child, clothes and possessions, eating and drinking, rocks and wood, wax and oil, water and wine, bread and meat. And to what purpose? It seems that even at our best, our lives are no more than gluttony and drinking and all kinds of heathen lusts and carousing. But the Lord your God says, "I do not want your festivals and offerings! Take your meat and bread and all the church's pomp from me! I have had a belly full of it and can't stand to see it anymore! (Isaiah 1; Daniel 9; Mark 3). I never told your ancestors that I wanted such things (Jeremiah 7). I never commanded you to make sacrifices of calves and sheep, after which you think you are free to then go and serve idols in all injustice and villainy! (1 Samuel 15). You yourselves are the calves (Malachi 4) and sheep of my pastures (Psalm 79). I want you as an offering; but that you do not understand (Psalm 4 and 51; Ecclesiasticus 35; Romans 12). I did not command you to break bread together like a pack of dogs. I gave you my beloved son as the true bread (John 6) that you might also become bread such as he is (1 Corinthians 10). As he was broken for you and gave his life for you in total love, do this also then for one another (John 15). Likewise, I never intended that you wash your body and leave your soul in the mud, or to return to the wallow like a sow in the mire!" (2 Peter 2).

Brothers, the Lord has called us to holiness, not to disunity and such superficiality, with no respect for God (1 Thessalonians 4).

As you tithe your mint, dill and cumin, do not forget that above all else God commands justice, mercy and faith (Matthew 23; Proverbs 11). Justice, to punish the sinner without favoritism (Exodus 23); mercy, that you can love your enemies and forgive their transgressions (Matthew 18); and faith, so that you do not take offence at God for his judgment, but trust in his mercifulness (Proverbs 3, 13 and 23). Do you not know that without these things, ceremonies are a yoke of worldly bondage? (Galatians 5).

That is why even though you talk long hours about external elements of the world, you can come to no conclusion. And what conclusions you do make are as fleeting as straw in the wind (1 Kings 14; Matthew 11; Luke 7).

The foundation of faith must be firm. Then the building will stand, in spite of wind and water (Matthew 7). This firm foundation has been laid by God. See only that you do not reject it, as did the dishonest builders (Psalm 118). And do not persecute this foundation, like the fierce dragon (Revelations 12). Seek it rather in the temple and seat of divine glory, that is, in your heart and soul (1 Corinthians 3 and 6; 2 Corinthians 6).

Concerning the False Peace Which the Scholar Proclaims and the Peace of God Which May Be Expected in Tribulation and Anxiety

The dishonest builders are the people who work foolishly to build their walls of stubble, hay and wood (1 Corinthians 3). Then the master builders—the scholars and false prophets—come along and cover the wall over with slackbaked mortar (Ezekiel 13). They are like unclean animals with cloven hooves and do not chew the cud (Leviticus 11) because they say, with neither thought nor understanding, "Peace, Peace! Just believe and you will be fine! All is well!" (Jeremiah 6, 8, 14 and 23).

Oh, you miserable folks! How can you trust your souls to such foxes? (Ezekiel 13). But the true shepherd and protector who can preserve you, you will not trust even for the smallest crust of bread! They lead you astray with smooth talk and flattery, my people. They take you on a path of corruption (Isaiah 3).

But because you drank from the seductive cup of the great harlot (Revelations 17), you must now drink the cup of divine wrath which is prepared for those who defiled themselves with the harlot (Psalm 75; Jeremiah 25 and 49; Revelations 18).

Drink of it in his name and wait for him through the night. He will wondrously comfort you in the morning!

Part III:
Hutterian
Anabaptism

Peter Walpot

Peter Walpot was born in 1521 in Tyrol. Although a "second generation" Anabaptist, he joined the movement at a very young age, for by the age of 21, he was already recognized as a Servant of the Word among the Moravian Hutterites. Although not formally educated, Walpot was widely read in the Bible and church history. By 1547, at the age of 26, he wrote the "Five Articles" which, along with the Rechenschaft of Peter Riedemann, was the earliest systematic formulation of Hutterian belief and practice. When Riedemann died in 1556, Walpot became the clear leader of the Moravian Hutterites. He was elected to the office of bishop in 1565. These were years of peace and prosperity for the beleaguered Hutterites and have become known in their histories as the "Golden Years." Aside from sending out missionaries, the Hutterians under Walpot's leadership consolidated and regularized their communal economic practices, established their educational system for children and began to gather together the historical material which would become their "Great History Book," which has been a key document not only for Hutterian history but for the history of the early Anabaptists in general. Walpot died a natural death in 1578.

The Hutterites have taken their name from their early leader Jacob Hutter, a Tyrolean hatmaker, who was publicly executed by burning in 1536. The communal impulse was present among all Anabaptists. But it was among the Hutterians alone that this impulse was developed into an economic communism in which private possessions were actually forbidden and condemned as evil. Therefore, while they exhibited similar depths of spiritual concern and commitment as other Anabaptist groups, Hutterian spirituality holds a unique place among Anabaptist religious thought. The Hutterian "Bruderhof" system of economic community came into its fullness only in the second generation, when a lull in the persecution against them allowed the freedom they needed to attend to its development. Hutterian communal groups continue to this day in North America and represent the oldest continually existing communal experiment in human history. The development of the Bruderhof economic system took place under Peter Walpot's leadership.

While short writings and letters remain from the first generation of Hutterians, it is in the second generation that the true essence of Hutterian communal spirituality appears in written form. Presented here is Walpot's "True Yieldedness and the Christian Community of Goods," which is part three of his larger work, "The Great Article Book" of 1577. This translation is taken from the source collection Glaubenszeugnisse oberdeutscher Taufgesinnter, Band II, ed. R. Friedmann (Gütersloh: Güterloher Verlaghaus Gerd Mohn, 1967). In this writing we see both Walpot's spiritual vision of yielding the individual will to that of the community and his defense of the Hutterian communal ethic against its detractors. Even in these "Golden Years," maintaining the communal life of the Bruderhof was not an easy task. There is certainly a judgmental flavor to Walpot's writing, which could be interpreted as bordering on self-righteous inflation. Nevertheless, considering the terrible persecution which the Hutterians had suffered and the witness of nearly five hundred years of communal existence they have given the world, the integrity of their spiritual vision, emphasizing internal surrender and the conquest of selfishness, which Walpot's writing capsulizes, speaks for itself.

"True Yieldedness and the Christian Community of Goods" (1577)
Peter Walpot

To have one, let the other one go.

"Love the Lord your God with all your heart and with all your soul and with all your mind. This is the first and greatest commandment. And the second is like it: Love your neighbor as yourself. All the Law and the Prophets hang on these two commandments" (Matthew 22: 37–39).

"And he has given us this command: Whoever loves God must also love his brother" (1 John 4:21).

HUTTERIAN ANABAPTISM

"Just as gold is tried in the fire, so are humans tried in the ovens of humiliation" (Ecclesiasticus 2).

God's word would not be so difficult if not for human selfishness.

1.

The Lord commanded Israel: Above all, there should be no poor among you (Deuteronomy 15). How much more should this be fulfilled in the full community of goods among the New Testament people.[1] For if the Old had been fulfilled and sufficient, no place would have been sought for another Testament (Hebrews 8).

2.

Israel had six years in which to gather its fruits, each for himself (Leviticus 25). But the seventh year was designated as a free year, a year in which the land is given a Sabbath celebration for the Lord (Deuteronomy 15). During this year the people were not to gather. Rather, what grew in the seventh year was held equally for all, the house father and his servant and maid and day-worker and family and foreigners, the beasts and animals of the fields. Whoever had been bought was in this seventh year given freedom with all kinds of gifts and offerings. Likewise, whoever had loaned something to his neighbor and brother may not in this year exact anything for it. It must be given up. For it is a glorious, nuptial feast proclaiming of the Jubilee Year of the Lord. This year of release was to be a model of the time of the New Covenant in Christ. For that was the true Jubilee Year, the acceptable year of the Lord. As the apostle of the Lord himself understood it, they would be freed who all their lives had been held in the slavery and power of the devil. Therefore, out of Christian love, we also should hold all goods which God has bestowed upon us in common enjoyment with our neighbors, brothers and families and not hold them as private. For now is an even more glorious, nuptial feast proclaiming the year of redemption than it was in the Old Testament. Yes! It is the year of Grace!

3.

Humanity will hold a great Sabbath (Isaiah 66). Yes, they will have a continual Sabbath and will lead a most holy life on earth, when they rid their nature of two words—"mine" and "yours." These words have been and are today the cause of many wars. From where comes

139

war and bloodshed, quarreling and fighting, envy and hatred, disunity and disruption, if not from private possessions and greed?[2] For whoever deals in mine and yours, that is, with possessions, becomes a friend of avarice. For there are two daughters born to the infamous leech (Proverbs 30) and they cry out "Give to me!" Just as the earth never has its fill of water; the fire never says "enough!"; the person with dropsy, the more he drinks, the more thirsty he becomes; the devil, death and hell are never satisfied, so long as there are people on earth; like these, the more possessions one has, the more one wants. Whoever wants much feels the lack of much, and whoever covets much feels is left wanting much. That is actually the most poverty-stricken and dissatisfied kind of life on earth. And Christ, at home with those who walk in the true Sabbath, Pentecost and Easter, will have none of it.

4.

The Lord said to Israel, the priests should have no inheritance. I shall be their inheritance. In Israel they shall be given no possession (land), for I am their possession (Deuteronomy 10; Numbers 18; Joshua 13). This is in harmony with the whole people of Jesus Christ, who are, in fact, a royal priesthood of God and Christ. This priesthood maintained itself with that sacrifice which, once offered up, no longer belonged to the one making the sacrifice (1 Peter 2; Revelation 1). This now pertains to the Christian Church.[3]

5.

As God the Lord brought the children of Israel out of Egypt and into the wilderness of sin (Exodus 16), He gave them bread from heaven, called Manna. They gathered it, some much, some less. They measured it with an *omer*. The ones who gathered more had nothing left over and the ones who had less lacked nothing. What was held in reserve had worms growing in it by morning and it stank.

So now, as God has led the Christian Church out of the Egypt of today and into the wilderness of this world, the rich should have no more than the poor and the poor no more than the rich. Their provisions should be held in common and for the use of all. Nothing should be held back. This is the meaning for us of this prefiguration, as Paul himself said and as Christ himself taught anew when he broke bread for the multitudes in the wilderness and gave them of it to eat in common (Matthew 14 and 15; John 6).

6.

David, the royal prophet who foreshadowed the kingdom of Christ, said, "Listen, O daughter, consider and give ear: Forget your people and your father's house. The king is enthralled by your beauty; honor him, for he is your lord" (Psalm 45:10–11). In this he teaches and indicates true abdication of temporal possessions and worldly household.

7.

"The Lord announced the word, and great was the company of those who proclaimed it: Kings and armies flee in haste; in the camps men divide the plunder" (Psalm 68:11–12). This is what took place in Acts 2 and 4.

8.

When the evil men of Belial said that the one hundred who remained behind during the raid on Ziklag should not share in the booty won there, David said, "Do not be like that, brothers, with what God has given us. Who will agree with you on this? The share of those who went shall be the share of those who remained behind. It should be divided equally." And since that time to this day that has been the custom and Law in Israel (1 Samuel 30; Deuteronomy 20; Numbers 31; Joshua 8 and 22). How much more should this be the custom and law among the children of the New Testament! What God has given them should be divided equally.

9.

Isaiah the prophet said clearly long ago (Isaiah 23:17–18), "The Lord will deal with Tyre. Yet her profit and her earnings will be set apart for the Lord; they will not be stored up or hoarded. Her profits will go to those who live before the Lord, for abundant food and fine clothes." So at the final judgment Christ will say to those who are his own that what they have done was done as unto him. But to those on his left, he will say that they did not do it and therefore have earned eternal punishment (Matthew 25).

10.

"There will be seven women (that is, the number of churches and nations) who want one man (Isaiah 4). And they will say, we will hold our food and clothing in common. Only we want to be your wives (or

141

betrothed or companions) and be spared this terrible rebuke"—
namely, the word of God in our consciences.

11.

"Aliens will join them and unite with the house of Jacob. Nations will
take them and bring them to their own place. And the house of Israel
will possess the nations as menservants and maidservants" (Isaiah 14:1–
2). That signifies coming into true community. In Isaiah 49:18 he says,
"All your sons gather and come to you. As surely as I live, declares
the Lord, you will wear them all as ornaments; you will put them on
like a bride."

12.

"Surely the islands (that is, the heathen) look to me; in the lead are
the ships of Tarshish, bringing your sons from afar, with their silver
and gold, to the honor of the Lord your God, the Holy One of Israel,
for he has endowed you with splendor" (Isaiah 60:9). The same is
shown when Peter cast his hook into the sea and drew out a fish which
had a coin in its mouth, which the Lord had him take to the temple
to pay for the two of them (Matthew 17).

13.

"Aliens will shepherd your flocks; foreigners will work your fields and
vineyards. And you will be called priests of the Lord, you will be named
ministers of our God. You will feed on the wealth of nations, and in
their riches you will boast. Instead of their shame my people will
receive a double portion, and instead of disgrace they will rejoice in
their inheritance; and so they will inherit a double portion in their
land, and everlasting joy will be theirs" (Isaiah 61:5–7). Just as Christ
spoke of finders of hidden treasure in the field (Matthew 13) they go
with joy (notice! with joy!) and sell all that they have and buy the field.

14.

Micah the prophet said, "Rise and thresh, O Daughter of Zion, for I
will give you horns of iron; I will give you hoofs of bronze and you
will break to pieces many nations. You will devote their ill-gotten gains
to the Lord, their wealth to the Lord of all the earth" (Micah 4:13).
Who are these threshers? (Hear what the scripture says!) "You shall
not bind the mouth of the oxen which tread out the grain." Paul asks,

"Does God care for the oxen? Or was this written for our sakes?" It is surely for our sakes that it is so written.

15.
"Behold the feet of those who bring good news and announce peace from the mountain! O Judah, celebrate your wedding festival! Make your freewill offerings!" (Isaiah 52:7f.).

16.
Zachariah the prophet foretold of a time (that is, with the New Covenant) when in the temple of the Lord there would be no tradesmen or businessmen (Zachariah 14; Matthew 21).

17.
Sirach, the wise teacher, said, "Invest your treasures according to the commandments of the Most High and your profits from it will be greater than gold. Put your alms in the hands of the caretaker and you will be protected from evil" (Ecclesiasticus 29). That is, put your wealth to the use of your brothers and neighbors and don't bury it under a stone.

18.
Many are the calamities which happen because of gold and money, and you have all seen such ruin. Punishment awaits those who sacrifice to and serve this foolishness. By this measure, then, who among the rich will be found free of punishment?

19.
John the Baptist, the forerunner of Christ, also taught community. For when he came and was asked by the people, "What shall we do, then?" he told them that whoever has two coats should give one coat to another person who has none, and whoever has food, do the same (Luke 3). See how clear it is!

20.
The devil falsely claims earthly and temporal power as his own possession (Matthew 4; Luke 4). For as he showed to Christ the kingdoms of the world, he said, "All is mine." The children of the devil do this as well, all those who have the maliciousness of Belial in their hearts. They try to gain and amass the wealth and possessions of the temporal

world for themselves. But among the children of God this should not be so. Rather, among them, what God has given should be held in common and for the use of all.[4]

21.

The Lord called as his disciple Simon Peter and his brother Andrew; also James, son of Zebedee and John his brother. And he said to them, "Follow me!" (Matthew 4; Mark 1; Luke 5). And they left their nets, their boats and their father and followed him. See then how Christ places demands on one's possessions and how these men left their parents and friends and followed him in the way he led, the path of yieldedness and community.

22.

Christ spoke saying, "Blessed are the poor in spirit" (Matthew 5; Luke 6). The poor in spirit are those who have relinquished their possessions and left them behind for the sake of Christ. They possess nothing anymore but stand and persevere in the community of the true Christian Church. It follows that the opposite of these are not in a state of blessing.

Here is not meant by "poor" those who have nothing as a result of their own laziness or those who have nothing because they have gambled, whored or been drunkards, or those who have nothing and yet are as wicked as any other person.[5] He means those whom the Spirit has made poor (2 Corinthians 6). In the same way that the Spirit led Christ into the wilderness to be tempted by the devil, so the Spirit leads these ones into poverty where, like Christ their master, they have nothing themselves. That is what is meant by "poor in spirit." Therefore, whoever dreads this poverty, you should dread them. And whoever shuns this community, you should shun them.

23.

Christ said to his disciples, "You are the light of the world. But not a light under a basket which is useful and a light only unto itself. You are rather a light in a lamp which is useful to the whole house." You do this with your good works. He also called them salt, that they should be useful to the community and show to all what good things they have received from God. The light or salt or yeast is of no use to itself. Its usefulness is rather in its relation to others. In the same way, our usefulness should be directed toward others and not ourselves.

Where the salt does not make salty, there is no salt, but something less. So when we do works of love and kindness we become an example of good works to others.

24.

No one may serve two masters (Matthew 6; Luke 16). For you will hate the one and love the other or obey the one and despise the other. You cannot serve God and Mammon—that is, earthly possessions and riches. For like a lock, the love of and concern for money occupies the heart. Therefore, you should not strive for surplus and then seek to justify it. For Christ said that it is impossible to serve and nurture both of these two masters. So don't say that it is possible! For one master commands you to deny yourself. The other master says to take for yourself what is not yours and keep it for yourself. One master says you should be in community; the other says you should be selfish and possessive. So how is it possible to bring these two stubborn things into agreement? Whoever is a servant of Mammon is certainly no servant of Christ. You must be finished with the one master in order to serve the other.

No one can go two directions at once; no one can put his foot in two places at once; a bird can only sit on one perch at a time; no one can cook two stews in the same pot; a sick person cannot become well by both water and fire. One of these must be gone. *To have one, let the other one go.* No one has more than one heart. And no one can love and serve God and at the same time love and serve earthly possessions and riches, money and wealth. For then they have their god, which is, as Paul said, their own bellies (Philippians 3). They trust and serve wealth as God himself. If day and night they care for house and field, land and water with the highest diligence and greatest care and most earnestness, they cannot give even the tenth part of that diligence, care and earnestness to God and His service. We are redeemed by Christ. Therefore we should not now serve money and wealth and cling to them but rather give them to God's poor. In this way we will not end up in the place where the rich man was thrown and punished (Luke 16).

25.

"Do not store up for yourselves treasure on earth, where moth and rust destroy, and where thieves break in and steal. But store up for yourselves treasures in heaven, where moth and rust do not destroy, and where thieves do not break in and steal. For where your treasure is, there your heart will be also" (Matthew 6:19–21). The temporal is fleeting, here today and gone tomorrow. Today there is a beautiful flower, tomorrow a dry piece of dust. Today there is a burning fire, tomorrow cold ashes, useless soot, smoke, which is soon forgotten and swept out of the fireplace. Nothing remains, all is consumed and makes no more difference. We may achieve nothing by the temporal. This is why Christ said, "Where your treasure is, there is your heart also." For it is surely true that where one places his treasure, there he also places his soul. The selfish person can hardly maintain that he can both possess his treasures and riches and at the same time have his heart and mind set on God. For that is impossible. They may say with their mouth that they are ardent, but their heart follows after its own good and greed. For that is their treasure. One sees this in many who serve and honor temporal, earthly things. They would give up their faith before they would leave their riches behind.[6] They are really worse than the heathen, for they have Christ in their mouth but their heart is on the money purse. They are idol worshippers of the worst sort.

26.

Someone might ask, so what happens then if I renounce all my possessions? Christ said, "Look at the birds of the air; they do not sow or reap or store away in barns, and yet your heavenly Father feeds them. Are you not much more valuable than they?" (Matthew 6:26). In the same way Elijah was fed by ravens and the five thousand were fed with five loaves of barley bread (Matthew 14:13ff.; John 16). So therefore, don't worry. For these are the things which the heathen do, each providing for himself regardless of the others. You should seek first the kingdom of God and His righteousness and these other things will be given you, even if you don't have provisions stored up for days and years like the rich. He will care for us as He did for Adam before the time Adam had to worry about food and clothing. Caring belongs to God; work belongs to us. It is through community that God cares for our daily needs and relieves us of greed. For we belong only to Him and our concern is only for the divine.

27.

Community is also taught in the Lord's Prayer. Christ taught us not to ask for our own bread. Not "give me my bread," but "give us our bread," that is, the communal bread. It is a false supplicator who prays, give us our bread, but then treats the bread received as his own! Whoever has his own shouldn't ask of God. Paul the apostle wrote (2 Thessalonians 3) that whoever lives in disorderly fashion and will not work, but goes around as a busybody, should eat his own bread, as a punishment to his shame.

28.

Whoever lives in wealth is false in his confession of faith. For the Christian faith sets up a holy Christian Church and a community of saints. Where there is no community of saints there is no true and worthy Christian Church. Therefore all lie who say that community is unnecessary and has no foundation in doctrine (Acts 2 and 4). For it is indeed an article of the faith and instituted by Christ and the Holy Spirit and his teaching. Therefore, just as it is necessary to hold to the Apostles' Creed, the Lord's Prayer and Holy Communion, it is also necessary to hold community of goods. Community is no simple oddity, which the apostles tried out for novelty. Rather, it is divinely earnest and just as right and proper now as it was in Jerusalem and elsewhere.

29.

"Enter through the narrow gate" (Matthew 7), Christ said. "For narrow is the gate and small is the way which leads to life, and few find it." A life of Christian community is the narrow gate. For the carnal man it is a small needle's eye. Indeed, it is an oven of yieldedness in which the person is tried like gold in the fire. That is why there are few who enter this narrow port or find this small way. They always think it is too difficult for a person to be so unencumbered, giving up everything. They simply cannot believe this and therefore will never enter into the narrow door or gate, before which one must give up all things. But the broad way with the wide gate is that of the society of the possessive life of the world, full of selfishness and greed. There are many who go that way, indeed, the whole world. As the saying goes—merchants are drawn to where the money is. In other words, people are drawn to greed and possessions and therefore mock the humble Christ who said you cannot serve both God and Mammon.

30.

"The birds have nests," Christ said to those he called to follow him and be his disciples (Matthew 8). "And the foxes have holes, but the Son of Man has nothing of his own on which to lay his head." He was saying here, in effect, that in order to be his disciple one must become yielded and forsake his possessions. For the servant is not greater than the master, nor the student greater than the teacher. So it is a false disciple, a weed sown by the enemy, who does just the opposite, and not only has something on which to lay his head, but also has money and wealth, and like the foxes and birds, possesses his own house and home.

31.

"Whoever loves father and mother more than me is not worthy of me. And whoever loves son or daughter more than me is not worthy of me. And whoever will not take up his cross and follow me is not worthy of me" (Matthew 10). So then, if a person is not worthy of him who loves parents and friends—these most necessary bonds of blood, nature and familial duty—more than Christ, and one who loves his own soul (and there is nothing closer than that) more than Christ, how much more unworthy is the one who loves his possessions more than Christ! For Christ said to sell all that you have and give to the poor (Matthew 19). Such a person is totally unworthy of this Christ and his glory and will have not part in his Holy Communion.

32.

Christ said that there are those who have been sown among thorns (Matthew 22; Luke 8; Mark 4). If someone hears the word and then goes out and is concerns himself with the anxieties of this world and the deceptions of wealth, he chokes out the word and makes it unfruitful. That is why the two do not belong together. If the thorns thrive and grow, the word will be choked out and erased from the heart. But if the word grows and thrives in the heart, so must selfish riches retreat. Therefore, it is a fraud to try to hold and possess both of these two. For just as thorns are unfruitful, so are riches. And just as thorns tear and stick whatever they touch, so also does the urge for riches. That is why the rich are on a thorny and wrong track. And finally, just as among thorns snakes and scorpions are hidden, so it is also with the deceptions of riches and possessions. Therefore, one should allow the word of God to whip like a switch and, with the true community, root out the thorns. Put them in the fire of the Holy Spirit and let them burn up. Hunt down those innumerable unclean animals so that, like good fieldhands, we keep the field clean and have an even footpath.

33.

Christ said, "The kingdom of heaven is like a treasure hidden in a field. When a person finds it, he goes out and with joy sells all that he has and buys the field" (Matthew 13). Therefore, whoever does not sell all he has cannot buy it. He didn't say "from the abundance." He said, "all." Therefore, whoever has found the word of God, the divine truth, through faith, should forsake everything and rid himself of all that is temporal and win the hidden treasure. And he also said this will be done with joy, not with sorrow, like the rich young ruler. For the kingdom of heaven, he said, is worth it fully.

34.

Christ also said that the kingdom of heaven is like a merchant looking for a good pearl (Matthew 13). And when he finds a precious pearl, he sells all that he has and buys it. This is the same idea as above. For in the same way, if you find a pearl and need an amount of money to buy it, the amount of money is no longer for your use. You can no longer do anything with that money. Your gain must be in the pearl. So if your pearl is the word of God, the divine truth, you will give all your goods for it and hold to this pearl alone. It is in this pearl that you will seek your riches, your treasure and your gain. But if you find your pearl and do not buy it, saying that the amount of money is more precious than the pearl, you buy yourself into damnation. Seek your security in the one for whose sake you give your money and not in your money itself. Take your money and buy the treasure, the pearl. Otherwise, for that money, you will be damned along with the unworthy servant who hid his money in the ground (Matthew 25).

35.

Christ also taught community by example. He fed first the five thousand and then the four thousand who came to him in the wilderness. He sat them down on the grass and broke bread with them in common and fed them the bread and fishes (Matthew 14 and 15; John 6). That the disciples, who had very little—just five loaves and two fishes and then seven loaves—were very willing to share with others is a lesson to us that when we forsake house, country and friends to follow the word of God into the wilderness, that even today we should hold all of our temporal goods in common and lay them out for common use out of love for our neighbors.

149

36.

"If anyone would come after me, he must deny himself and take up his cross and follow me" (Matthew 16:24; Luke 14). Christ's own blood is more than a remittance for money and goods and for renunciation of one's own will. For as a people we belong to God and not to ourselves (1 Peter 2; 2 Thessalonians 2). So how much less can someone say that something is his own, or that he owns or possesses something "with the rights of a Christian?" Therefore, whoever says that he would like to follow Christ or be a disciple of Christ without forsaking all that is creaturely and without denying himself does not really believe in Christ.

37.

The Lord said to Peter, "Go and throw your hook into the sea and take out the first fish you catch" (Matthew 17). "Then open its mouth and you will find a coin. Take this coin (note! take) and give it for you and me." This mystery means nothing other than that those who believe are fishers of men, drawing people out of the world with the preaching of the word, enabling them to use their fortunes for true community and for use of the common need, just as the church of Jerusalem. That is what is meant by the "for you and me." So even the seas bring forth gifts in the name of the Lord, as Isaiah said (Isaiah 60).

38.

The rich young ruler asked what he must do to be saved. To this Christ said, "You have fulfilled all the commands of the Law, but you lack one thing. To be perfect, go and sell all that you have, give it to the poor, and you will have treasures in heaven. Then come and follow me" (Matthew 19; Mark 10; Luke 18). So it is part of perfection to sell all and give to the poor. For love (which this young man lacked) is a bond of perfection (Colossians 3). Love brings about perfect yield-edness and community, not just in part or half but wholly and perfectly.

Therefore it is clear that those who hold onto their wealth— unable to renounce their possessions and place them before the spiritu-ally poor for the common use—are not able to become disciples and followers of Christ. To sell all is a general commandment and not a new counsel. So the person who keeps his property and possessions does not obey Christ. Christ also has no place among his elect for those who keep their wealth. For just as a water spring which is stopped up and cannot flow out is soon stagnated, so it is with the rich who keep their wealth for themselves. For when wealth is possessed and kept selfishly, the heart will be concerned only with silver and gold, which discolors and destroys. If you could imagine the heart of a greedy person, it would look like a piece of cloth which is eaten by a thousand moths. It is chopped up by worries, rent by sin and falling apart. For just as a physician cleanses the wounds before they will heal, so God also must first of all remove from his followers all idols to which people cling and cleave and in which people place their hopes, that which they love on the side or before God.

The idea of almsgiving, however, should not be taken to mean that poverty itself brings salvation. What brings salvation is the following of Christ's word and command. That is why one must first renounce his goods, for without that nobody is able to follow Christ. And whatever one gives up for the sake of Christ here on earth will be given back in the kingdom of God. But whoever loves riches will not have profit of them, says the wise Solomon (Proverbs 5).

39.

That he should give up his wealth was certainly a narrow gate for the rich young ruler, and he left very sad (Matthew 19). Therefore, Christ said: Oh, how hard it is for the rich to enter into the kingdom of God! I say to you, it is easier for a camel to go through the eye of a needle than for a rich man to enter the kingdom of God. For just as it is impossible for a camel to go through the eye of a needle, so is it impossible for a rich man to become small enough to enter into the kingdom of heaven. For if we must become as children, who have nothing, to enter the kingdom of heaven, then a rich man must give up much before he is like an animal small enough to go through the eye of a needle. That is a hard saying. But even harder still are the hearts of those who hear this and will not empty themselves but would rather hang onto their wealth and greed. Here is where we get the phrase—the Word of God would not be so difficult if not for human selfishness.

40.

The disciples of Christ, who were poor and had already given up everything, trembled for the whole world and asked, "Who then can be saved?" By this they meant that there would be very few who could accept this and follow. But Jesus summoned them and said, "With humans it is impossible, but for God all things are possible." By this he meant that no work or power of humans is able to free one from temporal possessions. But God is able to give grace to enable this and forgive His own and help them want to swim out of this water. Therefore, you rich and selfish people, how long will you be stained and troubled with your thick filth, how long will you be weary and heavy laden and have no rest for your souls? (Revelations 2; Matthew 11).

41.

Peter said, "See, we have forsaken everything to follow you" (Matthew 19; Mark 10; Luke 18). And even today a follower of the Lord should be able to say this. The Lord said, "Anyone who for my name's sake has forsaken house, brother, sister, father, mother, spouse, children or fields will have it returned a hundredfold and win eternal life." This was Adam's transgression, that he wanted something other than what God wanted. He loved the creaturely and in this he scorned his creator. And all people have fallen with Adam in the love of the creaturely. Christ leads us from this love of the creaturely back to his Father. He calls us to repentance, saying that one should forsake, for the sake of God's will, all that which is loved more than God. We should turn our hearts from the creaturely and once again fasten it on God.

Therefore we see that this does not mean that one is to remain by his house, home and possessions. For this strongly hinders discipleship to Christ and does not allow the word to remain alive and become fruitful. Think now. If someone says he will teach you the art and good way by which you could keep the fruits of the earth from spoiling for many years, beloved, what would you be willing to do because you want to keep the fruits of the earth from spoiling for these many years? Well, Christ here teaches a way such that all you have can be yours in eternity as a heavenly treasure, not just your external wealth but your very body and soul! Therefore the preacher also said, "Cast your bread upon the water and in time you will get the return" (Ecclesiastes 11). Share with seven and eight, for you do not know what sort of misfortunes may come to pass on earth. It is a great plague to hold one's wealth for selfish use, says the preacher (Ecclesiastes 5).

So, whoever forsakes all things will find all things. When we give up the physical in exchange for the spiritual and heavenly, we suffer no harm. This is a good exchange indeed! The farmer ventures a few seeds because he expects from this a great harvest. How much more should we do this with our things in relation to our expectations. Let

152

us not rob heavenly things for the sake of filth, or drive our ships to shore full of straw and chaff. For in this we fill the devil with laughter but prepare for ourselves eternal sorrow. Therefore the prophet Isaiah said, "He feeds on dust and his heart is deluded. He can neither free his soul nor say, 'Should deception be in your hand?' "

42.

Jesus went into the temple of God and drove out all the buyers and sellers. He overthrew the changers' tables and the chairs of the dove sellers and said to them, "It is written, my house shall be called a house of prayer. But you have made it a den of thieves" (Matthew 21). For Christ will not have business dealings, buying and selling in his house, as the prophet already said (Zechariah 14). This buying and selling is a sign by which each person may recognize the false church, in which he sees these very things which Christ drove out with the lash.

43.

"You shall love the Lord your God with all your heart, that is the first commandment. And the next is the same, you shall love your neighbor as yourself" (Matthew 22; Mark 12; Luke 10). This little word "yourself" contains within it the idea of true community and all works of love and mercy which one person can show another person. Indeed, to love your neighbor as yourself is the measure of true community and all good things. Where God has poured out this kind of love in the heart a person, true community is learned through the Holy Spirit and in the bonds of peace (Romans 5). There one seeks no advantage over the neighbor but rather mutuality and common concern for each other.[7] It is not loving your neighbor as yourself when one seeks to hold and possess one's wealth out of selfishness. For love is the bond of perfection (Colossians 3), a golden Debir in front of the temple of God (1 Kings 6). For to love one's neighbor as oneself is not to have part, or even half, but the whole in common and to give all things for the common use. Anything less is a heathen and false love, not a Christian love.

44.

Such love and community in the church, which is called his body, is the clear desire of Christ, according to the gospel with which he concluded his final sermon. For on that glorious and abruptly coming day he will say: Come unto me, you who are blessed of my Father, and take possession of the kingdom which was prepared for you before the foundation of the world. For you fed me, you gave me to drink, you sheltered me and clothed me, you visited me when I was sick. For truly, even as you have done this for the least of these my brothers, you did it unto me. But you cursed ones on the left side, go to that eternal fire which was prepared for the devil and his angels. You did not feed me, you did not give me to drink, nor shelter me, nor clothe me. You only took concern for yourselves, fed yourselves, gave drink and clothing to yourselves, only sought your own welfare and your own possessions, you did not desire to shelter and take me in, but only yourselves. For what you have not done for the least of these of mine, you did not do for me nor desire to do for me. For the same way that we act toward our neighbors and the members of Christ, that is how we will be deemed by the Lord. How many people nowadays wish that they would have lived in the time when Christ was on the earth, that they would be able to dwell and live with him and show him good works. But see how much more we can do. For he said what we do to the least of these is done as unto me, who welcomes you welcomes me (Matthew 10). Therefore, we should consider that day when we will stand before the judgment seat of Christ and ask him for mercy and for part in his kingdom. For then Christ will announce his own. And whoever will not be made an inheritor of his goods must remain silent before him.

45.

Christ demonstrates this as well by parable when he said, "Just like the man who was going to a distant country, he called his servants and entrusted his property to them. To one he gave five pounds, to the second he gave two pounds and to the third he gave one pound. He gave to each according to his ability. They were to trade and lend and put the money in an exchange bank. But the one who held his money in a cloth was thrown into outer darkness" (Matthew 25).

We may understand by the talents or pounds that each should give according to what he can or should do, whether it be in admonition and preaching, or in giving money or temporal possessions as he has received (for this is also lent by the Lord), or if you can in some other way be of service to your neighbor. Nothing is more pleasing to God than that you live your life in service of the common Christian good. Those who do this give joy to their Lord. But those who hide their pound in the cloth are those who serve their neighbors neither with words nor their temporal possessions. They do not desire community because they have a piece of Belial in their hearts. They want to keep everything for themselves, which benefits nobody. Such selfish and deceptive servants will be thrown to ruination.

46.

As Jesus travelled through the land preaching the gospel, the twelve went with him, as well as certain women who he had healed of evil spirits and sicknesses (Luke 8). These were Mary, called Magdalene, Joanna, the wife of Cuza, the manager of Herod's household, and Susanna, and many others who helped to support them out of their own means. See then, that these women enabled them by means of the community of goods!

47.

Watch out and guard against all kinds of greed. For no one's life consists in the abundance of his possessions (Luke 12). For it is greed that continually desires more than the neighbor and other members. Christ told a parable about inequality, about a rich man whose field did very well. Just as he thought things were well with him, the devil required his soul in the middle of the night. That is how it goes, said Christ, with those who gather treasures for themselves but are poor in God. For you are not rich if your soul is poor. Likewise, if your soul is full you are never poor.

48.

Sell what you have and give alms (Luke 12). Make yourselves purses which do not wear out, a treasure in heaven which will never decrease, where no thief comes and which you will have in eternity. Here once again he teaches that we should give away property and temporal things and strive for what is heavenly and eternal. But he does not mean the kind of alms which the world gives. For if one gives something to a wandering beggar who is just as full of vice and ungodliness as any rich man, one cannot say that this was done as unto Christ.[8] For such a beggar is neither a member of Christ's body nor surrendered to him. Of course there is nothing wrong with such charity and human sympathy. But Christ spoke of true alms, giving all that you have, within the community of the saints.

49.

Christ likened his calling of the Christian Church to a banquet. For we are wedding guests and banquet guests who enjoy together the hospitality given (Luke 14). And at the hour of the banquet a servant was sent out to the guests, saying: Come! For all is prepared. And the guests began, one after another, to give excuses. The first said, "I bought a field and have to go tend to it." The second said, "I don't have time. I bought five yokes of oxen and have to go tend to them." And a third said, "I have taken a wife and cannot come." He didn't want to separate from his wife. But the Lord was angry and said: I say to you, none of those people will have taste of my banquet! For so long as we place our love in useless and passing things which hold us back, the divine things can find no place in us. So if you give yourself to earthly things when heavenly things are there for you, just think, you are insulting the one who proffers you this, for you show contempt for the heavenly things and exchange them for what is earthly.

50.

"A great multitude went with Christ, and he turned and said to them, 'Anyone who comes to me and does not hate his father, mother, wife, child, brother, sister and even his own life, cannot be my disciple (Luke 14). Whoever does not carry the cross and follow me cannot be my disciple. And whoever among you does not forsake all that he has (note! all) cannot be my disciple.' " One can and must not himself be the lord, manager or ruler of his property and possessions. For that is not to forsake them. No one can have two kingdoms or inherit riches twice. If we want to obtain the one, we must shun the other. If we want to hold onto the one, we must let the other one go. If our desire is the heavenly, then we must despise the earthly. To have promise of the one, we must deny the other. *To have one, let the other one go.* As with sicknesses and terrible tumors, if one does not cleanse the wound of puss and dirt, it does not matter what kind of dressing you put on it. It is all for nothing if you don't first get rid of the cause of the sickness. The same is true with us. If our hearts are not prepared and yielded and our hands are not washed of and abstaining from greediness, we can never be the robust disciples of Christ we should be.

51.

"Use worldly wealth to gain friends for yourselves, so that when it is gone, you will be welcomed into eternal dwellings" (Luke 16:9). The true community of God is what is meant by these eternal dwellings

(Revelation 21). This community will always accept such people in need because of the commandment of love and accept them spiritually and temporally. These are the friends who offer each other their property in love and community as brothers. That is why Christ said to use your temporal goods and wealth, which he called unrighteous Mammon, to make friends for yourself.

52.

"Whoever can be trusted with very little can also be trusted with much, and whoever is dishonest with very little will also be dishonest with much" (Luke 16:10). If someone is faithful in his dealings in lesser and faulty things, that is, in temporal things, he also will be faithful and true in his dealings with great things, that is, spiritual things. For being faithful in great things, that is, spiritual things, is the source from which flows faithfulness in small, temporal things. What is the condition of the spring if there are no streams flowing from it? These two thing can be compared. If in dealing with temporal things and community one does not do what Christ willed and commanded, he will be like Ananias and be unfaithful in spiritual things. He will be unworthy before God.

53.

"So if you have not been trustworthy in handling worldly wealth, who will trust you with true riches? And if you have not been trustworthy with someone else's property, who will give you property of your own?" (Luke 16:11–12). Temporal wealth belongs to the stranger. Therefore, whoever takes it for his own and will hold and possess it is unrighteous and deals unfaithfully, as did the unrighteous steward. Who will now give him the heavenly wealth, that is, the true riches? That is why if one wills to serve God he must forsake his own Mammon. Likewise, if one wills to serve Mammon and cling to it, he must forsake God. For whoever clings to what is earthly shows thereby that he neither knows, seeks nor desires anything better. Rather, one always turns toward the better and more useful and gladly lets the worse (that which hinders from the better) go. It is simply absurd not to desire freely to give up that very thing which we will later receive back even more richly and much improved, something that will be taken from us unwillingly anyway, which we must leave behind us one day anyway, whether we want to or not.

157

54.

The greedy religious leaders heard all these things and were derisive, as if to say it would be nothing but foolish to give all your money away—what a shame if that kind of life were the only way to salvation. It was just the same as the world and its religious leaders say today! But Christ said to them, "You are the ones who justify yourselves" (Luke 16). That is, they keep possession of their worldly goods under the guise that they want to help their neighbors and say that their hearts are not bound to such possessions. They only want to be able to give alms to the poor. But Christ said to them, "God knows your hearts." That is, God knows that this is not really the case.

55.

Christ observed how the rich put money into the temple treasury and how much the rich gave. But then he saw also how a poor widow woman put in two small coins, and he said, "Truly I tell you, this poor widow woman has given more than any of them" (Luke 21:3; Mark 12). For they have given as an offering to God only from their excess. But this woman, in all her need, has given all that she has to live on (note! all that she had to live on). Therefore, the Lord demands that we come with all our possessions and all our heart to Christian community, whether that is with much wealth or with little. How can Christ be more clear in showing, teaching and commanding true yieldedness and community?

Through the rich young ruler he told the rich to give all that they have (Matthew 19). Now here he says to the poor (who say they have very little) to do the same thing. Therefore, we ought to practice Christian community, for there is nobody who can do more than this poor widow whose offering of two small coins in the temple box put the others to shame. For she gave all that she had. God does not pay attention to the amount you sacrifice. It is rather the heart and will of the giver which please God.

56.

The community and church of God is also compared to a vineyard in which a wine press has been built (Matthew 20; Luke 20). Christ is the vine and the Father is the gardener. We are the branches because we stand in unity and community in the same way that the grape vine does more than all other woods. We give and present all of our wealth, good fruits and gifts for the common use of the neighbor, just as the vineyard does not bear or hold its fruit or the branches their grapes for exclusive personal use. The scripture, in the same sense, also often compares us to good and fruitful trees who have been grafted onto the good olive tree of Christ, against the nature of greediness and selfishness (Matthew 7; Romans 11).

57.

"This is my commandment," said Christ, "that you love one another as I have loved you" (John 15). He loved us so much that he left behind his glory with the Father and for our sakes became poor and a servant, to share everything with his followers. This is how we should love each other, he said. Out of his great love he has made us inheritors of heaven. Therefore, we ought to make our brothers heirs to our earthly possessions with us. He has made us fellow subjects with the angels and companions with God. Therefore we ought also to take our brothers in under our roof and shelters, demonstrating love in both external as well as spiritual matters. That is why John said in his letter: If anyone has worldly possessions and sees a brother in need and closes his heart to him, how can the love of God be in him? (1 John 3).

58.

"A new commandment I give to you: Love one another. As I have loved you, so you must love one another. By this all men will know that you are my disciples, if you love one another" (John 13:34–35). Love is the special content of this new commandment, that we should have and demonstrate community with one another and set out for the common use all goods and gifts which we have received from God. It will be seen in you above all nations, that the branch of love blooms among you. If you have such love that you create a brotherly and Christian community, suffering together in body and soul, it will be seen that you are of one faith in Christ and are Christ's true disciples. For love is the foremost sign of holy and faithful people. That is why Paul admonished Titus to teach one should be sound in love (Titus 2). This love was not comprehensive among the people of the Old Covenant and did not lead to complete community. Therefore the new commandment is greater and more complete than in the Old Covenant. For Christ does not ask us to love one another as friends but rather as members of one body. Greater love and concern than this cannot be found.

159

59.

Christ completed and perfected the Law in saying, "It was said to our elders that you shall not kill. But I say to you that you should also not burn in anger. It was said to the elders that you shall not commit adultery. But I say to you that if you look on a woman with lust, you have broken your marriage vows. It was said to the elders that you shall not swear falsely. But I say to you that you should not swear at all. You have heard, an eye for an eye. But I say to you, resist not evil" (Matthew 5). In this way Christ brings love to perfection according to its practice and working. For it was said to the elders that you shall not harden your heart against a poor brother but be open-handed with him and lend to him according to his needs and help him from your possessions (Deuteronomy 15). Christ wills and commands in the New Testament that you should give all that you have to the poor and to have all things in common together. He said, "If your righteousness is not higher than that of the scribes and religious leaders you will not enter the kingdom of God" (Matthew 19; Luke 21; Luke 14).

60.

"Father, all I have is yours, and all you have is mine" (John 17:10). So it should be among the children of God. Where this is not the case, there one has perverted the way and the body has grown un-soundly cold, warmed in greed and yes, turned away from Christ.

61.

Christ desires that all who believe in him through his word should be as one, as the Father is one in him and he is one in the Father. Those who believe are one in him (John 17; Psalm 133; Ecclesiastes 25). For nothing can compare to the unity, community and amicability of will. One is many when ten or more unite and are in community. For then one is not alone but as ten and finds in ten one and in one ten. And then if the ten have a foe who attacks even one of them, it is as if it is attacking all ten. And thus is the foe conquered, because then he faces not one alone but is resisted by the ten together. If one is in need, that person actually is not in need. For his need overflows into the greater part (that is, the other nine) and the needs of the one, which is the smaller part, is covered by the abundance of the greater part. For then that one no longer sees only with his own eyes or walks with his own feet alone, but with all of those who are his friends. So Job could say, "I was eyes to the blind and feet to the lame" (Job 29).

He breaths now with ten souls, for he no longer cares for himself alone but for all the others, even if the number is a hundred. For then their strength multiplies. Such is the virtue of the chains and bonds of love and Christian unity and community. The preacher Solomon expressed this also when he said, "Two are better than one, because they have a good return for their work: If one falls down, his friend can help him up. But pity the man who falls and has no one to help him up! Also, if two lie down together, they will keep warm. But how can one keep warm alone? Though one may be overpowered, two can defend themselves. A cord of three strands is not quickly broken" (Ecclesiastes 4:9–12). Brothers standing beside each other are like a secure city and hold to one another like the tie bar on a castle door.

62.

Christ is the prince of the faith, our model and predecessor. When he came he instituted community among his disciples, for they had a common purse. Judas carried and was in charge of the purse and what was given out. But because he became possessed of greed, the mark of Belial and the devil, he betrayed Christ and hung himself. So then Matthew was appointed in his place for the same office. Therefore it ought to be the same in the community of God today; each ought not be master of his own purse. Rather, whoever is appointed for this purpose ought to divide out to both rich and poor. Where this is not done, the footsteps and model of Christ are thrown out and belittled.

63.

When the Holy Spirit was sent and came, the perfected Christian community was established (Acts 2 and 4). The three thousand and five thousand in Jerusalem, indeed, all who had come to the faith, were together and held all things in common. They sold their goods and possessions and divided it all with each among them who was in need. Therefore the apostle called this a community of the Holy Spirit. For where the Holy Spirit truly dwells, this community is worked and established (Philippians 2; 2 Corinthians 13).

64.

Luke wrote of this again in the fourth chapter of Acts. The great crowd who believed were of one heart and one mind. No one claimed that his possessions were his alone, but they shared all that they had in common. There were also none among them who were in need, for those who had fields or houses sold them and brought the money from the sales and laid it at the feet of the apostles. And it was given to each who was in need. It does not say that each took whatever he wanted. And so it should still be today, God willing and if God grants a place, that all things which serve to praise God should be held in common. Whoever does not do this betrays and mocks the footsteps of the earliest apostolic church.

65.

When Ananias and his wife Sapphira sold their possessions, they still had some of Belial in their hearts. Therefore, they held back part of the money. They laid only part of the money at the feet of the apostles, keeping the other part (Acts 5). This was doubtless so that they would still have something in case they would ever become poor or if the Christian cause came to nothing. For that reason they both died a sudden death. And Peter said, "Ananias, why has the devil filled your heart so that you would lie to the Holy Spirit and hold back part of the money? You have not lied to men but to God." And then Ananias fell down and died. Now if the Christian community of goods was not a foundational teaching of the Holy Spirit, just like other articles of the faith, Peter would have had to say to Ananias that he lied to men rather than to God.

66.

The story also tells of a man named Joseph, called Barnabas, a Levite from Cypress by birth (Acts 4). He sold a field and brought the money and laid it at the feet of the apostles. Luke wrote that nobody else dared to join them (Acts 5). Note this! They accepted no one unless he took upon himself the duty of the community of goods, to live with them and be one in spirit, soul and concern. Therefore you cannot ask if it can be otherwise. For each alike must give what he has and lay it before the community.

67.

Those who accepted his message with gladness were baptized, and about three thousand souls were added in one day. And they remained steadfast in the apostles' teaching, in community, in breaking of bread and in prayer (Acts 4). Who dares then, with honor and truth, to say that they did not participate in community? They were later persecuted and could not be together in such large numbers. But even though

162

the numbers together were later fewer, it is not correct at all to say that community dissolved among them. It was a commandment of Christ and one of the fundamentals of the teaching. It was not to be abandoned but to be fulfilled. Otherwise we would have to say that Ananias and his wife were dealt with too harshly.

68.

That community among them did not dissolve and was not abandoned is proven repeatedly. For Paul said there was community in the house of Priscilla and Aquila (Romans 16; 1 Corinthians 16). There was also community in Laodicea in the house of Nymphas, for Paul sent them greetings (Colossians 4). Archippus, the fellow worker with Paul, also had a community living in his house (Philemon 1). Did they live in community in these houses? Surely they did. They show that they did live communally, just as was done in Jerusalem. They did not do as the world today and the false brothers, who without shame sit at a separate table and eat, one better and the other less, according to the means of each.

69.

In the community at Antioch were prophets and teachers, namely Barnabas, Simon Niger and Luke of Cyrene and Manaen, who had been brought up with Herod the tetrarch (Acts 13). As it happened, they gathered together in community for a whole year. So who can say that it did not happen there as it happened in Jerusalem? For there were many there from Jerusalem, who had come because of the tribulation concerning the death of Stephen. They came to Antioch and gathered and taught a great number of people. It was there that they were first called "Christians." Likewise, there were many gathered in the house of Mary, mother of John Mark (Acts 12). Now, if they gathered together as they did in Jerusalem, then it follows that they conducted their household activities in community and continued to do so. Otherwise they would not have been steadfast in the teachings of the apostles.

70.

Fourteen years after his conversion, Paul went up to Jerusalem with Barnabas and Titus (Galatians 2). There Peter and John gave him the hand of fellowship and agreed that Paul and his helpers should preach among the Gentiles, while the others would preach among the Jews.

They only asked that Paul not forget the poor—"the very thing I was eager to do," said Paul. Paul also said to procurator Felix that after some years "I came to Jerusalem to bring my people alms and offerings" (Acts 24). So who can then say that community did not last long in Jerusalem and was soon abandoned?

71.

The apostle Paul, writing to the Romans, said of brother Gaius of Corinth that he hosted Paul and the entire community there (Romans 16). This also clearly shows that each was not his own house's steward, as it was with the world. Rather, there was a common household and Gaius was in charge of the economic matters.

72.

Also the group in Macedonia did the same and followed the model of community, as Paul showed when he wrote, praising them, that "they gave as much as they were able, and even beyond their ability. Entirely on their own, they urgently pleaded with us for the privilege of sharing in this service to the saints. And they did not do as we expected, but they gave themselves first to the Lord and then to us in keeping with God's will" (2 Corinthians 8:3–5). Now, is this not community as in Jerusalem? Nobody can deny it.

73.

The group at Thessalonica also lived in community of goods. For Paul wrote to them that those who live in disorderly fashion, do not work and go around as gossips, should eat their own bread, to their shame. Therefore, the others must have eaten the communal bread. For if everyone ate his own bread anyway (as false brothers and the world do now), Paul could not have said that such ones should eat their own bread.

74.

The apostle Peter said to the man who was lame from birth, "Silver and gold I do not have, but what I have I give to you. In the name of Jesus Christ of Nazareth, walk" (Acts 3:6). Peter had nothing that was his own. All things were common which people laid at the feet of the apostles.

75.

Paul, a prisoner coming to Rome, lived for two years in a house by himself with a soldier in charge of him (Acts 28). And there he received all who come to him. That is how we should receive others.

76.

"Therefore, I urge you, brothers, in view God's mercy, to offer your bodies as living sacrifices, holy and pleasing to God—this is your spiritual act of worship" (Romans 12:1). If we are to do that, how much more ought we to offer our possessions as a sacrifice to the community, just as the group in Macedonia did (2 Corinthians 8).

77.

"Do not conform any longer to the pattern of the world, but be transformed by the renewing of your mind" (Romans 12:2). The world possesses riches and treasures and the ungodly have riches. Each goes his own way and pursues his greed with all his strength (Psalm 73; Isaiah 56). They hang onto such things like dirt hangs onto the wheel. They tear and bite at each other over "mine and yours." Much for me, little for you. I'll take today, you take the future. That is the totality of what is in the hearts of children of this world. Each looks out only for his own welfare. This is exactly that to which we should not be conformed.

78.

"Just as each of us has one body with many members, and these members do not all have the same function, so in Christ we who are many form one body, and each member belongs to all the others. We have different gifts, according to the grace given us" (Romans 12:4–5). Here he admonishes each to think about what it means to be members of one body. You simply cannot find any greater teaching of Christian community than this. Love must be sincere and true, he says. Likewise, you should assume the needs of the saints and strive to be receptive to them, that is, to care for each other.

79.

"Accept one another, then, just as Christ has accepted you, in order to bring praise to God" (Romans 15:7). The apostle does not want that each should seek for a separate house, or that each should have a particular house or each should own and possess a separate house.

Rather, it should be as the prophet foretold when he said, "Draw together that I may sit among you."

80.
"Now, however, I am on my way to Jerusalem in the service of the saints there. For Macedonia and Achaia were pleased to make a contribution for the poor among the saints in Jerusalem. They were pleased to do it, and indeed they owe it to them. For if the Gentiles have shared in the Jews' spiritual blessings, they owe it to the Jews to share with them their material blessings" (Romans 15:25–27).

81.
"God, who is faithful in His promises, has called us to the community of His son, Jesus Christ our Lord." Note! It is to the community of Jesus Christ that we are called.

82.
The apostle said that for those who buy something, it should be as if they did not own it, to treat the things of this world as if they were not needed (1 Corinthians 7). David also said that if riches come to you, do not set your heart upon it (Psalm 62). Those who possess riches do not fulfill this. It is only done by those who live in community.

83.
"Those who compete in the games go into strict training. They do it to get a crown that will not last; but we do it to get a crown that will last forever" (1 Corinthians 9:25). Here the apostle points toward a model of authentic yieldedness in true community. Therefore, they that give themselves to God's struggle under the banner and flag of Christ and run toward a heavenly goal should themselves be empty, rid and free of property and temporal things.

84.
"Nobody should seek his own good, but the good of others . . . even as I try to please everybody in every way. For I am not seeking my own good but the good of many, that they might be saved" (1 Corinthians 10:24 and 33). Here the apostle illustrates in both teaching and example that nobody should seek his own good but should rather seek the good of the community, the common good. If we are to do that,

we must let go of our own good and our possessions, for the two cannot reside together in one heart.

85.

In the twelfth chapter of First Corinthians, Paul uses the parable of the body. There he says that God combined the parts of the body to give most honor to the most needy parts so that there should be no division in the body but that its parts should have equal concern for each other. Now think about what that means, "equal concern for each other."

86.

"Love is patient, love is kind. It does not envy, it does not boast, it is not proud" (1 Corinthians 13:4). Love does not seek its own good but surely only the good of the community. Those who have love and are vigorous in their love will follow the way of true community. Nothing is so ardently commanded as love, for it is community and seeks the common good. In love is the contents of the entire Law and the prophets. But there is no love in the one who seeks only his own good and his own profit. Indeed, where evil is in the heart and gains the upper hand, the branch of love there withers away.

87.

"Do everything in love. You know that the household of Stephanas were the first converts in Achaia, and they have devoted themselves to the service of the saints. I urge you, brothers, to submit to such as these and to everyone who joins in the work, and labors at it" (1 Corinthians 16:14–16). Notice then that they devoted themselves to the service of the saints and not to the service of possessions.

88.

"But just as you excel in everything—in faith, in speech, in knowledge, in complete earnestness and in your love for us—see that you also excel in this grace of giving. I am not commanding you, but I want to test the sincerity of your love by comparing it with the earnestness of others. For you know the grace of our Lord Jesus Christ, that though he was rich, yet for your sakes he became poor, so that you through his poverty might become rich" (2 Corinthians 8:7–9). Paul is here wanting that we would gladly also become poor for the sake of others, to love each other as Christ has loved us. This we would do if we put on Christ and put off the old human nature (Ephesians 4).

89.

"Now finish the work, so that your eager willingness to do it may be matched by your completion of it, according to your means. For if the willingness is there, the gift is acceptable according to what one has, not according to what he does not have. Our desire is not that others might be relieved while you are hard-pressed, but that there might be equality. At the present time your plenty will supply what they need, so that in turn their plenty will supply what you need. Then there will be equality, as it is written: He who gathered much did not have too much, and he who gathered little did not have too little" (2 Corinthians 8:11–15). Here the apostle desires that the rich have no more than the poor and the poor no more than the rich. Rather, there should be Christian community and equality.

90.

"There is no need for me to write to you about this service to the saints. For I know your eagerness to help and I have been boasting about it to the Macedonians, telling them that since last year you in Achaia were ready to give; and your enthusiasm has stirred most of them to action. But I am sending the brothers in order that our boasting about you in this matter should not prove hollow, but that you may be ready, as I said you would be. So I though it necessary to urge the brothers to visit you in advance and finish the arrangements for the generous gift you promised. Then it will be ready as a generous gift, not as one grudgingly given. Remember this: Whoever sows sparingly will reap sparingly, and whoever sows generously will reap generously. Each man should give what he has decided in his heart to give, not reluctantly or under compulsion, for God loves a cheerful giver" (2 Corinthians 9:1–7). It is as when, through Moses, the Lord commanded Israel to bring gifts for work on the Ark of the Covenant, that each should bring to the Lord gifts with a willing heart, of gold, silver, bronze, colored silks and the like (Exodus 25). Therefore, let us sow while there is yet time for harvest, for the winter will come. Then it will be too late to sow; the time to sow is now. When this time is over comes the harvest and cutting time. The one who does not sow in summer, but waits until the harvest time to sow, is foolish. Now is the seeding time, not time to harvest but to sow and scatter about. The seeding time calls us to scatter and not to gather, to give out and not to hold back, and in no way to be stingy with temporal goods, so that we will later reap a hundredfold. But whoever will not sow and in this way prepare for the harvest must go away empty-handed from the community.

91.

"This service that you perform is not only supplying the needs of God's people but is also overflowing in many expressions of thanks to God. Because of the service by which you have proved yourselves, men will praise God for the obedience that accompanies your confession of the gospel of Christ, and for your generosity in sharing with them and with everyone else" (2 Corinthians 9:12–13).

92.

And finally, after much teaching which the apostle gave to them, admonishing them to community, he wished them nothing other than the grace of our Lord Jesus Christ and the love of God and that the communion of the Holy Spirit be with them all. Amen (2 Corinthians 13).

93.

The mystery and meaning of baptism also teaches us true community. For Paul said that we are all baptized into one body, whether we are Jew or Gentile, slave or free (1 Corinthians 12). He said "into one body," for nothing is a higher figure or example of unity than the body.[9] Greater love and care than for the body cannot be found. The members of a sound and healthy body are needed for that body without distinction even if among themselves these parts are not the same. Although the hand is not the eye, both are given equal respect by the body. For all parts of the body are nourished in common and share commonly in the goods which God provides. Each part of the body does what it does for the use and benefit of the whole body. The eyes see, not for themselves; the ears hear, not for themselves; the hands work, not for themselves. Nor are these parts carried by themselves. In short, no part of the body is for itself but for the whole body. No part leaves the rest to suffer. If the eye is in danger, the hand is there for it. If one foot slips, the other is there to catch the fall. One helps the other as if it were itself. One suffers with the others, one rejoices with the others, and what happens to one happens to the others. The needs of the body are shared by the members in common. No part is happy without the others, and no part is of any use without the others. Here is true unity, love and service, and the parts agree with each other in marvelous fashion. No part can do without the others and each part is concerned for the care and provision of the others. The members of the body have nothing of their own. What each has is given for the good of the whole body. When the hand earns, it does not keep it all only for gloves. Where the feet go is not only for the sake of more shoes. It is for the common good. We are baptized into just such a spiritual body, that we may demonstrate just such community in spiritual graces and gifts, but also in the lesser things, in temporal gifts and possessions. Therefore, the scriptures often refer to us as one body and members of each other. And for the sake of such community we are baptized, as Paul said. What does it mean "into one body" except that we should not be divided, but have among us the highest unity and community?

94.

In the same way the communion bread and wine is a teaching for us, an admonition and witness, to Christian community. Christ used bread and wine exactly for this beautiful correspondence and comparison. For regardless of how many grains of corn there are, each is a separate entity. But as each is ground together, losing what was its own, the result is the loaf of bread. Any grain that is left stuck in the bread whole is plucked out and thrown away. This shows that although each believer is a special person and uniquely created, when ground by the word of God they make one loaf. They present all they have for the true community of the body of Christ, that is, Christ's church. That is why the believers are compared to the good wheat (Matthew 3; Matthew 13; Luke 3). In the same way, although there are many grapes and berries, they are crushed in the press and their juices all become one fluid. Therefore, the faithful should practice true unity and community, not only in the higher spiritual things but also in the simple temporal possessions, in honor of God and in service to the neighbor. Whoever does not stand within this community is yet a separated and unground piece of corn.

That is why Paul said that the bread we break is the common body of Christ (1 Corinthians 10). For since we eat the bread of the common body of Christ from one spiritual table, let us also share the communion of spiritual love. Even among the heathen it is enough for friendship that they live in the same city, to say nothing of eating together at one table. But we are also citizens of one city, of one house, one table, one way, one gate, one root and one life. We have but one head, Christ, our one shepherd, one king, one master, one judge. We have but one creator and one Father. Let us then not make ourselves unworthy of Him by divisions in our heart and lack of love for one another.

95.

Paul said to the Galatians, "You are all sons of God through faith in Christ Jesus, for all of you who were baptized into Christ have clothed yourselves with Christ. There is neither Jew nor Greek, slave nor free, male nor female, for you all one in Christ Jesus" (Galatians 3:26–28). If this is so, then surely our possessions must also be one.

96.

"Rather, serve one another in love. The entire law is summed up in a single command: Love your neighbor as yourself. If you keep on biting and devouring each other, watch out or you will be destroyed by each other" (Galatians 5:13–15). To serve one another in love is not to do so for money or payment. But if you really think about it, to love your neighbor as yourself, you arrive at nothing other than Christian community.[10]

97.

The apostle also clearly admonished the Ephesians when he said, "Instead, speaking the truth in love, we will in all things grow up into him who is the Head, that is, Christ. From him the whole body, joined and held together by every supporting ligament, grows and builds itself up in love, as each part does its work" (Ephesians 4:15–16; Colossians 2). And where this kind of love is found, there also most certainly is Christian community.

98.

"He who has been stealing must steal no longer, but must work, doing something useful with his own hands, that he may have something to share with those in need" (Ephesians 4:28). So here he admonishes not just that one work, but that one come to the aid of the needy.

171

99.

"But among you there must not be even a hint of sexual immorality, or of any kind of impurity, or of greed, because these are improper for God's holy people. Nor should there be obscenity, foolish talk or coarse joking, which are out of place, but rather thanksgiving. For of this you can be sure: No immoral, impure or greedy person—such a man is an idolater—has any inheritance in the kingdom of Christ and of God. Let no one deceive you with empty words, for because of such things God's wrath comes on those who are disobedient. Therefore do not be partners with them" (Ephesians 5:3–7). Now, who is the greedy person if not the one who wants, seeks and desires to have more than his brother, fellow member and neighbor. He is the one who always wants an advantage and possessions. Ananias was just such a server of idols, and the wrath of God came down upon him. For greediness is an idol which wants only possessions and money. In place of the temple, the greedy have a money box where they serve their idol. Of course they say they don't worship it. But then, others say they do not worship the icons either. No, but they worship the devil contained in it! In the same way, though you do not bow down to money and possessions, you pray to the devil in any case out of the love of these things, for it has possessed your heart. For you obey and do all that this greedy devil represents.

100.

Nobody hates his own flesh. Rather, he nourishes it and maintains it. And since we are all members of one another and one flesh of his flesh and of his bones, that is how we should treat each other. We cannot scorn each other, in the same sense that we cannot scorn or forsake our own self. For just as husband and wife are one body and have all goods in common, so it is with the Christian Church. Paul said that this is a great mystery, speaking of Christ and his community (Ephesians 5). We say that Paul saw in the clear words and teachings of Christ the divine unity and true community of the body of Christ, that this is to be practiced and held to in his church.

101.

To the Philippians Paul said, "If you have any encouragement from being united with Christ, if any comfort from his love, if any fellowship with the Spirit, if any tenderness and compassion, then make my joy complete by being like-minded, having the same love, being one in spirit and purpose. Do nothing out of selfish ambition or vain conceit, but in humility seek others better than yourselves. Each of you should look not only to your own interests, but also to the interests of others. Your attitude should be the same as that of Christ Jesus: Who, being in the very nature of God, did not consider equality with God something to be grasped, but made himself nothing, taking the very nature of a servant, being made in human likeness. And being found in appearance as a man, he humbled himself and became obedient to death— even death on a cross! Therefore God exalted him" (Philippians 2:1– 9). In this he shows that we also, even if we have been splendid and rich in this world, should empty ourselves and take the form of a servant in the house of God. Even if we were once lords of our own property, we should now become as any other believer and brother. We should humble ourselves and be obedient. Our obedience should extend not only to the communion of the Spirit, in the same love and emptying as his, but even to losing our own life. Only then have we put on Christ and become of like mind with him. And only then can we be exalted with him. Whoever does the opposite is not of like mind with Christ but with the devil. And like him, that person will end up in lowest hell.

102.

"But whatever was to my profit I now consider loss for the sake of Christ. What is more, I consider everything a loss compared to the surpassing greatness of knowing Christ Jesus my Lord, for whose sake I have lost all things. I consider them rubbish, that I may gain Christ and be found in him" (Philippians 3:7–9). Compared to the spiritual gains, the riches of this world are nothing but poverty, just as life in the absence of the heavenly things is actually death. Now, whoever cannot devalue temporal things and let them go for the sake of the truth cannot gain Christ. For according to the most holy teaching of the apostle there is no difference between accumulation of gold and accumulation of dirt. Therefore we should be careful of that upon which we set our hearts, and not be like the world. For as worms live in the dirt, so also do those who live only for the earthly and temporal things. The world takes its joy and pleasure in Mammon, wealth and riches just as insects take joy and pleasure in the dung heaps of strangers![11]

103.

"Brothers, I do not consider myself yet to have taken hold of it. But one thing I do: Forgetting what is behind and straining toward what is ahead, I press on toward the goal to win the prize for which God has called me heavenward in Christ Jesus. All of is who are mature should take such a view of things. And if on some point you think differently, that too God will make clear to you" (Philippians 3:13–15). Now notice what he is teaching about forgetting and renouncing the temporal, and he calls this the virtue of perfection. So how then can those who have not forgotten what is behind them—indeed, who struggle to hang on to their possessions—strive for that which is ahead?

104.

"Join with others in following my example, brothers, and take note of those who live according to the pattern we gave you. For, as I have often told you before and now say again even with tears, many live as enemies of the cross of Christ. Their destiny is destruction, their god is their stomach, and their glory is in their shame. Their mind is on earthly things" (Philippians 3:17–19). If they have sweet things to offer their bellies, they are well satisfied. They serve and care for this always. All of their plans and thoughts, day and night, are for the sake of their bellies. They tend to their bellies but not for their souls. They ornament the body and pursue gold pieces for clothing. They are like whores, for whom clothing is more important than the soul. They powder and stroke the body and let their souls lay about in all manner of filth. They make sure their bellies are full while their souls starve to death. Certainly then, the belly is their god.

105.

"I have received full payment and even more; I am amply supplied, now that I have received from Epaphroditus the gifts you sent. They are a fragrant offering, an acceptable sacrifice, pleasing to God. And my God will meet all your needs according to his glorious riches in Christ Jesus" (Philippians 4:18–19).

106.

Paul said to the Colossians, "Do not let anyone who delights in false humility and the worship of angels disqualify you for the prize. Such a person goes into great detail about what he has seen, and his unspiritual mind puffs him up with idle notions. He has lost connection with the Head, from whom the whole body, supported and held together by its ligaments and sinews, grows as God causes it to grow" (Colossians 2:18–19). Mark then what it means to say that the members care for one another and are held together. Do not be turned away by the enemy from the mind of Christ and his apostles.

107.
"Above all these virtues put on love, which binds them all together in perfect unity" (Colossians 3:14). That is, you are called to a true community and unity. This is the bond of perfection to which Christ called the rich young ruler when he said to sell all that you have and give to the poor.

108.
"Now about brotherly love we do not need to write to you, for you have yourselves been taught by God to love each other. And in fact, you do love all the brothers throughout Macedonia. Yet we urge you, brothers, to do so more and more. Make it your ambition to lead a quiet life, to mind your own business and to work with your hands, just as we told you" (1 Thessalonians 4:2–11).

109.
"But godliness with contentment is great gain. For we brought nothing into the world, and we can take nothing out of it. But if we have food and clothing, we will be content with that. People who want to get rich fall into temptation and a trap and into many foolish and harmful desires that plunge men into ruin and destruction" (1 Timothy 6:6–9). For greed is the root of all evil, the mother of all things evil, the fortress of all malice, a covering for all kinds of blasphemy, which grows and climbs to the heights of the ladder of evil. It leads to much sorrow. But you, people of God, flee from it! For just as you see a person tied hand and foot, held fast by his neck, know that this is how greed and lust for riches will tie you up. It puts a thousand chains around your neck and then makes you even love the chains.

110.
"Command those who are rich in this present world not to be arrogant or to put their hope in wealth, which is so uncertain, but to put their hope in God, who richly provides us with everything for our enjoy-

ment. Command them to do good, to be rich in good deeds, and to be generous and willing to share. In this way they will lay up treasure for themselves as a firm foundation for the coming age, so that they may take hold of the life that is truly life" (1 Timothy 6:17–19). See here how one should admonish, teach and lead the rich of this world to renunciation and community of goods.

111.

The apostle Peter said that we are to love each other deeply, with a pure heart. For we have been born again, not out of perishable seed but of imperishable seed—that is, the eternal and living word of God (1 Peter 1). We are called reborn people and new creatures because we hold together in love of true community, which is not the way of the old, fleshly human beings of this world. Think about this now. Would not those who have a deep, inner love for each other in their hearts share all that they have with the community and place their goods forward for the common use?

112.

"Offer hospitality to one another without grumbling. Each one should use whatever gift he has received to serve others, faithfully administering God's grace in its various forms" (1 Peter 4:9–10). This is totally contrary to holding private property.

113.

"For this reason, make every effort to add to your faith goodness; and to goodness, knowledge; and to knowledge, self-control; and to self-control, perseverance; and to perseverance, godliness; and to godliness, brotherly kindness; and to brotherly kindness, love. For if you possess these qualities in increasing measure, they will keep you from being ineffective and unproductive in your knowledge of our Lord Jesus Christ" (2 Peter 1:5–8).

114.

"But there were also false prophets among the people, just as there will be false teachers among you. They will secretly introduce destructive heresies, even denying the sovereign Lord who bought them— bringing swift destruction on themselves. Many will follow their shameful ways and will bring the way of truth into disrepute. In their greed (Look! Greed!) these teachers will exploit you with stories they have made up" (2 Peter 2:1–3). We find this even today, that there are such attackers, beguilers and ear ticklers, who like thieves and murderers would try to climb in, one at the window, another at the chimney, or at any place other than the narrow gate. They make fun of the narrow way, giving the flesh plenty of space. They speak from an unloving and greedy heart, saying that it is enough just to give some alms and to lend only as much as they want to, in accordance with the love which is common among the heathen, hypocrites and godless people of this world. These practice the same among themselves, teaching that one need not renounce all things, need not sell all and give to the poor, and that one may enter the kingdom of heaven without doing these things. They say, in effect, that you can keep your possessions, your own house and property, your own kitchen and cellar, your own money coffers and all that you have, just as the world does. And nevertheless, they say, you can be devoted and blessed, even though you do not give all that you have to the community. That is why the apostle said that through greed they will attack and try to win you through spurious words. Their condemnation has long been hanging over them and their destruction has not been sleeping (2 Peter 2).

115.

The apostle John, the most excellent teacher of love, said in his letter, "We proclaim to you that which we have seen and heard, so that you also may have fellowship with us. And our fellowship is with the Father and with His Son, Jesus Christ. If we claim to have fellowship with Him yet walk in darkness, we lie and do not live by the truth. But if we walk in the light, as He is in the light, we have fellowship with one another, and the blood of Jesus, His Son, purifies us from all sin" (1 John 1:3 and 6–7). Therefore, we may also conclude the opposite— that if we do not have community among us, then we must be walking in darkness. Think of this—when we are walking at night without a light, wood, lead, iron silver, gold, jewels and all other things look the same to us with no difference among them. It has not to do with the things themselves but rather with our own eyes. So it is with those people who love and possess earthly things. They do not understand that they are being deceived. They need to be delivered from their blindness and awakened from their dream and their darkness.

116.

"Yet I am writing you a new command; its truth is seen in him and you, because the darkness is passing and the true light is already shining. Whoever loves his brother lives in the light, and there is nothing in him to make him stumble. But whoever hates his brother is in the darkness and walks around in the darkness; he does not know where he is going, because darkness has blinded him" (1 John 2:7–11).

117.

"This is how we know who the children of God are and who the children of the devil are: Anyone who does not do what is right is not a child of God; nor is anyone who does not love his brother. This is the message you heard from the beginning: We should love one another. This is how we know what love is: Jesus Christ laid down his life for us. And we ought to lay down our lives for our brothers. If anyone has material possessions and sees his brother in need but has no pity on him, how can the love of God be in him? Dear children, let us not love with words or tongue but with actions and in truth" (1 John 3:10–11 and 16–18). Think here what is meant by deed and truth.

118.

"Dear friends, let us love one another, for love comes from God. Everyone who loves has been born of God and knows God. Whoever does not love does not know God, because God is love. This is how God showed His love among us: He sent His one and only Son into the world that we might live through him. This is love: not that we loved God, but that God loved us and sent His Son as an atoning sacrifice for our sins. Dear friends, since God so loved us, we also ought to love one another" (1 John 4:7–11). Here John is saying that because God, out of tender mercy for humanity and out of love for us, sent us the most inward treasure of His riches, the dearest of His jewels, His only Son, for our atonement, then we also should show love to one another. And how much more then should we place our temporal treasures before each other for the common use in common community. If one does not have that much love for the others, how can he be so shameless as to hope to enjoy the love of God, who gave His most precious son for us? If you want to have part in the love of God, so that He will give you part in the possessions of heaven along with all of His children, how then can you hang onto your own little

178

beggar's bag, which you will not here give over to the children of God, to have it in common with you and you with them? Are they not worth it to you? Then tell me, you coarse and shameless person, how can you expect God to give you part in the community of goods in heaven? It is as Job said. "What is this hope of the hypocrite, that he is so greedy? Do you think that God will hear your cries and come to you in your time of fear?"

119.

"God is love. Whoever lives in love lives in God, and God in him. In this way, love is made complete among us so that we will have confidence on the day of judgment, because in this world we are like Him. There is no fear in love. But perfect love drives out fear, because fear has to do with punishment. The one who fears is not made perfect in love. We love Him because He first loved us. If anyone says, 'I love God,' yet hates his brother, he is a liar. For anyone who does not love his brother, whom he has seen, cannot love God, whom he has not seen. And He has given us this command: Whoever loves God must also love his brother" (1 John 4:16–21). That which we would do for Christ if he were here among us we should do for other who are members of the body of Christ. For even though we do not have Christ bodily among us (since he was taken up into heaven) we do have the others by our side. If Christ did live here bodily among us, you would most gladly share all that you have with him, and even more. Then do this with others now. That is how people will know that what you do you do as to Christ.

120.

"Dear friend, you are faithful in what you are doing for the brothers, even though they are strangers to you. They have told the church about your love. You will do well to send them on their way in a manner worthy of God. I wrote to the church, but Diotrephes, who loves to be first, will have nothing to do with us. So if I come, I will call attention to what he is doing, gossiping maliciously about us. Not satisfied with that, he refuses to welcome the brothers. He also stops those who want to do so and puts them out of the church" (3 John 5–6 and 9–10). Now see here how the apostle reproves and will punish those who do the opposite of community.

179

HUTTERIAN ANABAPTISM

121.

The apostle said to the Hebrews, "God is not unjust; he will not forget your work and the love you have shown him as you have helped his people and continue to help them. We want each of you to show this same diligence to the very end, in order to make your hope sure" (Hebrews 6:10–11). Now look at this, how the believers in that time served the saints and worked for them, rather than for their own possessions and greed.

122.

"And let us consider how we may spur each one toward love and good deeds. Let us not give up meeting together, as some are in the habit of doing, but let us encourage one another—and all the more as you see the Day approaching" (Hebrews 10:24–25). This meeting together is what makes us different from animals. Not simply that we live together, but that we band together in love, one giving help to the other, one watching out for another, protecting the other from harm. For we have received from our Creator a weak nature which can do nothing for itself. But this is turned to our advantage when our weaknesses and needs are answered with brotherly aid, living together. In that way, the needs of one are helped by another, whether these needs are of body or of spirit. That is why Solomon said that a neighbor close by is better than a blood relative far away.

It would take us too long to recount all the advantages received from this inward and benevolent living together. For as Christ said, if your brother sins against you, go to him. For Christ certainly wanted them to live together in communion, just as did the three thousand and five thousand in Jerusalem. All were of one mind in the hall of Solomon, and shared one house, one table and were of one soul. This kind of gathering, unity and community was foretold often by the prophets, especially Isaiah, who said that it would happen in the time of the Messiah. See, they will come from afar—some from the north, some from the west, some from the region of Aswan. Lift up your eyes and look around; all your sons gather together (Note! Gather together!) and come to you. As surely as I live, declares the Lord, you will wear them all as ornaments; you will put them on, like a bride. Then the children born to you during your bereavement will yet say in your hearing, 'This place is too small for us; give is more space to live in.' See, I will beckon to the Gentiles, I will lift up my banner to the peoples; they will bring your sons in their arms and carry your daughters on their shoulders" (Isaiah 49:12, 18, 20 and 22).

123.

"Remember those earlier days after you received the light, when you stood your ground in a great contest in the face of suffering. Sometimes you were publicly exposed to insult and persecution; at other times you stood side by side with those who were so treated. You sympathized with those in prison and joyfully accepted the confiscation of your property, because you knew that you yourselves had better and lasting possessions. So do not throw away your confidence; it will be richly rewarded" (Hebrews 10:32–35). It is through our help and community of love which we practice with each other that we will obtain the joy of that which is to come. It is a great possession to have joy and freedom in the struggle of suffering and in yieldedness and community of the temporal. Out of hope for eternal life one freely puts what is heavenly before all other things. This is a great and wonderful good— not to be motivated by what is creaturely or some human thing but to have overcome the weak and grasping nature of the flesh by the fullness of the soul. And even greater still is the following, future reward. This no human tongue can express, no matter how articulate it is. Indeed, it has never entered the heart of a human being the unmeasurable glory which God has prepared for those who love Him. That means us, said Paul, who do not look toward the visible but rather the invisible. For what is visible is passing away, but what is invisible is eternal.

124.

Abraham, a father and archetype of all believers, when called by God was obedient to the one who called him. He went out from his home and his friends and fatherland and lived in tents with Isaac and Jacob, the fellow heirs of the promise. For he was looking forward to the city with foundations, whose builder and creator is God. These all died in faith. They did not receive the things promised. They saw them only from a distance and trusted and held to them, knowing that they were guests and strangers on this earth. People who say such things show that they are looking for a fatherland. Indeed, if they were thinking of the place from which they came they had the time and opportunity to return there. But their desire was for a better place. Therefore is

God not ashamed to be called their God, for he has prepared a city for them (Hebrews 11).

How much more are we of the New Covenant strangers and pilgrims on earth. We have nothing that is our own but are as guests and wanderers, taking only what is needed in these tents. We seek only the lasting eternal city which has been promised us in heaven. There we are citizens and there is our home, fatherland and possession. Let us say that one of noble birth and upstanding parents travels into a foreign country where no one knows him and must remain there. And he is there upbraided by someone. Would he consider this the same offence as he would if he were home? No, because he knows that he is a pilgrim in a foreign land. Therefore, it is better for him to yield in all things, whether scorn, hunger, thirst or any such thing. Let us say someone wants to take you to Persia with the idea of seeing the country and then returning immediately. And then he asks you to build a house there. Would you not call this senseless and say that he is laying on you an unnecessary expense? Well, that is just how it is in terms of our pilgrimage here in this world.

125.

By faith Moses, when he had grown up, refused to be known as the son of the Pharaoh's daughter. He much preferred to suffer evil with the people of God than to enjoy the fleeting pleasures of sin. He regarded disgrace for the sake of Christ as greater value than the treasures of Egypt. For he sought the reward (Hebrews 11). How much more then should we, who certainly do not have the goods and riches of Pharaoh's daughter, refuse and renounce these things, choosing to suffer evil and good with the church of Christ, rather than to have worldly prosperity and our own means. For we hold the poverty of the church of Christ as greater wealth than the pleasures of this world. And we have our eyes on the prize of the holy. And also on the ultimate end of the godless, who go to where their father is, that place where light is never seen. Of course, what they have in their houses may remain and even bear their name on earth. But they do not long remain honored. Rather, they die and lie in hell like sheep. They will be tormented by death and hell will be their dwelling place.

126.

"Keep on loving each other as brothers. Do not forget to entertain strangers, for by so doing some people have entertained angels without knowing it. Keep your lives free from the love of money and be content with what you have, because God has said, 'Never will I leave you; never will I forsake you.' And do not forget to do good and to share with others, for with such sacrifices God is pleased" (Hebrews 13:1–2, 5–6 and 16).

127.

"If you really keep the royal law found in scripture, 'Love your neighbor as yourself,' you are doing right. But if you show favoritism, you sin and are convicted by the law as lawbreakers. For whoever keeps the whole law and yet stumbles at just one point is guilty of breaking all of it" (James 2:8–10). Now see here what the apostle calls the royal law, that one should love his neighbor as himself. He does this particularly so that it will be especially observed, held dear and in earnest as one most prominently given. And they who love each other in truth will also surely give their temporal goods to each other for common use.

128.

"What good is it, my brothers, if a man claims to have faith but has no deeds? Can such a faith save him? Suppose a brother or sister is without clothes and daily food. If one of you says to him, 'Go, I wish you well; keep warm and well fed,' but does nothing about his physical needs, what good is it? In the same way, faith by itself, if it is not accompanied by action, is dead" (James 2:14–17). In the same way, if someone confesses and says that he believes in one holy Christian Church and the community of the saints, but there is no community in his church and he himself is against having things in common in deed and truth, then his faith is a dead faith. He himself is a liar and of Belial.

129.

In the book of Revelation, John wrote to the group at Laodicea, who were said to be neither hot nor cold, this commandment of God, "You say, 'I am rich; I have acquired wealth and do not need a thing.' But you do not realize that you are wretched, pitiful, poor, blind and naked. I counsel you to buy from me gold refined in the fire" (Revelation 3:17–18). This means that God wants them to buy or obtain from God the burning, divine and true love through eager and constant prayer. This love is not a creaturely love, but rather it burns and consumes all that is of the earthly nature. For no matter what a person may think he knows, if he has not conquered his love of the creaturely he does not yet know what he ought to know. As the Lord said of those who love the creature more than the Creator, "You are plenty lacking." A person cannot come to God so long as he is not free from and has not conquered all that is creaturely, but is held by and is trapped in his love for the creaturely. That is why it is greatly beneficial for a person to stand detached from what is temporal and to pay little attention to such needless things. You can take as an example the birds of the heavens. They snatch up their food from the earth and then quickly fly back to the peaks where they cannot be caught or captured. One who runs too far after the desires of the flesh and love of the creaturely (not to mention having wealth) will soon be imprisoned by Satan through his own lusts. For while poverty hurts no one, he makes a trap of riches. Nothing defeats and places a person under the power of the devil like love of the creaturely, the pursuit of money and the desire for wealth. For no matter how much you preach the truth to one whose heart is fastened on money and wealth, you can very seldom do him much good.

130.

The world and certain false brothers quote Paul (1 Corinthians 16), saying that he clearly wrote that, on the Sabbath, each should lay aside for the poor saints an amount in accordance with what he can and wants to give.[12] This is my answer. That is exactly why Paul saw a great failing among the Corinthians. For he said to them, "Brothers, I could not address you as spiritual but as worldly—mere infants in Christ. I gave you milk, not solid food, for you were still not ready. Indeed, you are still not ready. You are still worldly" (1 Corinthians 3:1–3). Because of the time, Paul had reason to be patient with them. He passed over certain things because he had to. But that does not mean he was drawing back from or done with true community. He uses the Macedonians to teach them. The Macedonians, according to and even beyond the abilities of their community, gave themselves to the service of the Lord and his servants. And Paul says they should follow them in this. As it was written, "He that gathered much did not have any left over, and he that gathered little lacked nothing," that there might be equality. Here he is trying to draw them away from a half-hearted community and a cold love toward a full and complete community of the saints. For as he said, "Because the others are so diligent, I want also to test the sincerity of your love." For Paul had not preached to them any other gospel than that preached by John and Peter to the three thousand and five thousand in Jerusalem and elsewhere, who remained steadfast in community. Now, because the Corinthians did this so badly, they should not be taken as a model to follow. It was certainly never in the mind or opinion of Paul, and surely not in his heart, that a Christian should possess and hold his goods only for himself to use as he pleases. All of his letters witness against this. Therefore, if even Peter or Paul or an angel from heaven should teach something different from community (as some false brothers are now doing) they would be bringing a different gospel, which would be a curse.

131.

They also say that one finds in the scriptures many who were living separately, and had children living with them. The widows had to provide for their own and administer their households, and children were to serve their parents. This is my answer. Those who live in community must and can do the same as those who live separately or with just a few households together. And just as happens today, it happened then that some lived separately for the sake of their marriage partners. We also believe that it was not always possible for the group to live together in large numbers because of persecution or other obstructions. Likewise, where they did have to live separately, it was ordered differently than in a community. But all that does not invalidate true community. They held the view that all goods should be held in common among the members, as is made clear by their initial actions. But in their particular situations they were not able to live together. The believer should show and hold to community, out of love for the neighbor, whether living with many or few, with few or many. In our time, when it is possible, we should not use these cases as a defense. There is nothing written by the apostles saying that true community should be given up or come into being. That was never their belief.

132.

They then say that Simon, the magician in Samaria, who was accepted as a brother in the community, still had his own money. For he offered the apostles money for the gift of God (Acts 8). This is my answer. Simon was the same kind of Christian as Ananias and Sapphira. Indeed, he was the same kind of disciple as Judas Iscariot, who betrayed the

Lord. All the false brothers of today are like him. That is why the apostle Peter preached to him saying his heart was not pure, but full of bitter gall, indeed, clogged with unrighteousness. Nothing is proven by a false Christian. The apostle Philip taught in Samaria no other doctrine than community, which was begun and furthered by Peter and the other apostles in Jerusalem.

133.

They also say that one reads of a woman in Joppa named Tabitha, who spent her life doing good works and giving alms (Acts 9). They say that if she did not have her own money and such that she would not have been able to help other and give alms. This is my answer. This in no way proves or maintains anything about private wealth. Luke wrote that among the believers, according to the preaching and teaching of the apostle Peter, nobody said of his goods that they were his own, but all was held in common. And there are also in the community today such Christian women and disciples (praise God!) who are full of good works and alms and demonstrate community without possessing private property. For they have this no longer, having given everything for the common and communal use. But daily work, their talents and produce, is a public alms. For they care only for the good of the neighbor.

134.

They also say that Onesimus, one of Philemon's slaves, stole something from his master and then ran away (Philemon 1). So Philemon must have had private property, for otherwise Onesimus could not have stolen it. This is my answer. That has neither twig nor shrub to do with private property and proves nothing about it. It would be possible even today that someone might abscond with something from one of our elders or other person. But it does not follow from this that anyone among us has private property or money. Paul wrote to Philemon that he should receive Onesimus back into the community in love, to accept him as a brother and hold nothing back from him. He owed it to Paul to do this, for Paul had given Philemon the fundamental teaching of the Holy Spirit. For he said to Philemon, "So if you consider me a partner, welcome [Onesimus] as you would welcome me. I will pay it back—not to mention that you owe me your very self" (Philemon 1:17 and 19). (See, it is a debt!) Now, anyone who does not see that here Paul is actually fostering the community of the saints must be blinded by the god of this world.

135.

Another argument they give is to say that Paul and Peter do not write to the rich to tell them they should make all their wealth common, but only that they should not be proud, should give freely and use their riches wisely (1 Timothy 6). This is my answer. This was not written concerning the rich in the community but rather concerning the rich of the world. This is, therefore, above all else a command to teach the rich people of the world that they should become rich in good works and in that way strive toward community. But to the members of the community they wrote that nobody should seek his own welfare but the welfare of the others; that they should live as members of one body, having this same concern for each other (1 Corinthians 12); about loving one another (Philippians 2); about brotherly love (1 Thessalonians 4); about showing communal love (2 Peter 1); about loving your neighbor as yourself (Galatians 5; James 2; Matthew 22); about the right kind of love (2 Corinthians 8); about not seeking one's own good (1 Corinthians 13) but having all equal (2 Corinthians 8). Likewise, that they should receive one another as Christ received us (Romans 15) and serve one another with those gifts which have been received from God (1 Peter 4). All of this wholly and completely opposes and contradicts the idea of private property. Now, if we want to speak of "using one's wealth correctly," then this can mean nothing other than using it according to the way it was used in the first apostolic church—that is, the way it was used among the three thousand and five thousand in Jerusalem, and according to the clear teaching of Christ and his apostles. And this is clearly taught and shown to be community.

136.

Here is yet another fig leaf with which the world and these false comrades try to cover themselves. They say they are but stewards of temporal goods—it does not belong to them but only has been lent by God to be used for the good of the neighbor. Here is my answer. What you say is true—that it is not yours. And yet you use it as if it were yours, even quarreling with each other concerning what should be seen as "mine" and "yours," and you possess what ought to be shared, holding as your own property what should be communal property. You are the master, ruling over it, and you do with it what you will. You act with it according to your own desires and not as one bought by Christ. You present yourself outwardly as one full of renunciation and life, yet greed and death has pierced through your heart. You gloat of your faith in Christ, who did not even have anything to lay his head on. You become religious only so that you can obtain wealth from it. Put yourself on the same scales as your servants, neighbors and peers and let us just see how much you have for their good!

137.

These greedy ones whose love has grown cold and who squirm around like a worm on the ground also say that to speak of spiritual communion and aid means one doctrine, faith and knowledge of the Son of God. Here is my answer. One should know that where there is true spiritual community there will also be an external community of goods. One cannot exist without the other and remain without the other. Otherwise we would have to conclude that the inner baptism of the Spirit is sufficient and the external verification of this in the baptism of water is totally unnecessary. But we cannot have one without the other. If you want to make these kinds of separations and disturbances it would also follow that there is no need to use bread and wine in the Lord's Supper. For one may inwardly and spiritually remember Christ's death, shedding of blood and glorious redemption and give him thanks. No, one cannot be without the other. One should be done, but not without the other. For it is written not only that they were of one heart and soul but also that they shared one purse. For whoever in unfaithful in the little things, that is, the temporal things, will also be untrue and unworthy in the greater things, that is, the spiritual things. If someone does not have love enough to place his possessions and wealth in community for common and equal use, who will believe that he will love others enough to lose his life for them, as Christ and the apostles taught us to do?

138.

They also say that it is written in Sirach (Ecclesiasticus 33) that we should not give our goods to another, for we may regret it and want it back. Here is my answer. That is truly said by Sirach, particularly for his time but also for our time. For we also teach that if one is not firmly grounded and secure in the truth and might later regret it, then he should hold onto his possessions and goods. We say exactly that to all candidates before we take them in.[13] Indeed, we accept nobody before we warn him about this matter. He must know, think about and ponder it before he surrenders himself and his possessions in the community. This way he will not cheat himself. For if later he falls away, we owe him nothing and give him nothing back.

Why? Because what today one gives as a gift—of his own free will, without coercion, with full understanding and reason, unhurried and in full knowledge of what he is doing—tomorrow no longer belongs to him. So even if they should break their word, given during their Christian baptism, we can never break our word, weaken it or deny it. It is not in our power to return that which was freely given to the Lord and his people. For this is the Lord's business, and they made this covenant and surrender to the Lord. Heaven and earth and all saints of God present at the time were taken as witnesses. It was not simply lent, or given for safe keeping, which the community then would have to repay later. We cannot make of the community and house of God some kind of false lending house. We immediately use what is given for the common needs and use it directly for all manner of food and clothing. There is most often not a coin or penny left of it. It simply would not be possible for the community to return what was given. For there are many who have nothing at all to bring to the community, many more than there are of those who bring something or much to the community.[14] If you want a reckoning to be given for those who have brought something, then take as your reckoning all those who bring nothing with them, often with children, widows and orphans, those who have been weak and sick for years, all of which costs plenty. So who will pay the community back for that?

There is no scripture or command of Christ or of the apostles which says that such temporal things should be given back to the one who leaves. If the apostles were going to give it all back anyway, then Ananias would not have needed to hold back a part of his money. In case he could not continue, it simply would have been given back to him. Therefore, those who do not have confidence in their ability to endure, with God's help, it would be a thousand times better if they would leave us alone. For we seek not their wealth but rather their salvation. Also, we never accept people because they have money. If someone had hundreds of thousands of gold coins, but his heart and confidence were not right, and we know this or perceive it, we do not want him or his money. But if someone does have a right heart, enthusiasm and perceives divine knowledge, we accept him with joy,

189

even if he does not have a single penny. But even so, if one who has fallen away does ask us for some food money or other help, and he does not behave himself wantonly, we certainly do not send him away empty or without food, even if he is one who came to us with nothing.

139.

We are all called to one hope and common inheritance. For when a father has many children—excepting those who are bastards and disobedient, disinheriting themselves—they are equally heirs to his goods and inheritance. Therefore, if we say that we have communion in spiritual things such as faith, God, gospel, Christ, gifts of the Holy Spirit, and want to inherit the goods of heaven equally with each other, then we should show this here in temporal things all the more. Therefore we are children and not slaves, as it would be if each had only his own. We will be called the children of God.

140.

We are also brothers because we have and show brotherhood. As Christ said, you shall not be called Master, for you have only one Master, Christ. But you are all brothers. Now, to be like brothers, all things are shared with each other—the more evenly, the more brotherly it is. Those who do not divide things evenly, but rather each one seeks his own advantage and fate, and who cheat one another, do not treat each other as brothers. Even if they call themselves brothers, they are false brothers. Therefore, act according to the truth in the brotherhood of Christ, which alone proves that one is a fellow heir to the kingdom of heaven. So should we also be fellow inheritors here.

141.

God does not want His children to live here on earth like cattle, like cows, like donkeys, like buffalo, where each one only seeks to fill his own belly. To do so is to be less than dogs, who never know when they have had enough.[15] Or like a sow, who wants the feeding trough all to herself and will give to the others only what is left over. Rather, God wants His own to live here on earth as a new humanity and as members of one body.

142.

Community means nothing else than to have all things in common out of love for one's neighbor, to have everything equal and for no one to have private property. There is nothing higher, better or more perfect than someone presenting himself and his wealth for the common good and from that point on sharing with each other both sickness and health, love and suffering, each one wanting to be the others' neighbor, debtor, fellow member and loyal comrade. That is the Christian Church and the community of the saints, which is neither forced nor unnatural, nor impossible to do, so long as love is there. Earthly fathers will live sparingly and do without food themselves in order to help their children. Likewise, a mother will take something from her own hungry belly to give to her child. So should believers not be able to hold their temporal goods in common with each others? It would be unchristian not to do so, because we are to love our neighbors and fellows members as ourselves, to have together, to want together, to suffer together, to experience ups and downs together. No matter what you say, it is no community, no unity, no common use, when each has his own house, his own field and goods, his own kitchen, his own cellar and his own table.

143.

Private property does not belong in the Christian Church. Private property is a thing of the world, of the heathen, of those without divine love, of those who will have their own way. For there would be no property if it were not for selfish will. But the true community of goods belongs among believers. For by divine law all things should be held in common and nobody should take for himself what is God's any more than the air, rain, snow or water, the sun or other elements. Just as these cannot be divided up, so it is with temporal goods, which God has given in the same portion and measure for the common good. These should not be made private, and surely this cannot be done according to divine or Christian law. For owning private property is contrary to the nature and conditions of His creation. Whoever encloses and holds privately that which is and should be free, sins and goes against the One who created it free and made it free. The writer of the *German Theology* says this as well.[16] But because of the wickedness humanity has taken on, out of envy and greed, each one stashes away in his own sack. One says, "that is mine," while another says, "that is mine." And so there is in any case a dividing of goods among humans, but it has become in this life one of great inequality. It has unfortunately gone so far that if they could reach the sun and moon and contain the elements, they would call them their private possessions and then sell them for money.

144.

Some desires are necessary. For example, an animal must eat, drink
and sleep. Other desires are natural, even if they cannot be said to be
necessary—for example physical love. But the desire for and love of
money is neither natural nor necessary. It is simply excessive. For gold
and silver were for a long time hidden. Therefore, it is an acquired
corruption, a result of the advice of the snake. The devil once led Eve
astray with the apple. Now the whole world is led astray with gold
and money. Concerning being a eunuch for the kingdom, Christ said
that whoever can accept it should accept it. But of money he said that
whoever does not renounce all that he has cannot be his disciple. For
one single soul is not able to handle too many desire. One will subdue
the others. Whoever has only one child loves that child without measure. But whoever has many children has his affections divided. That
is why it is impossible for a person to give full enthusiasm and exertion
to both things at once. For the same reason it is very dangerous for a
child to have a knife in his hand or for a lunatic to have a sword. That
is just how harmful property and wealth are to humans. In fact, it is
more dangerous, for if the lunatic sticks himself with the sword, his
lunacy leaves him and he has peace. But as for the greedy and selfish
person it is not so. He receives his wounds a thousand times a day,
for the desire for money and wealth is a thing which includes countless
wounds. Therefore we must rid our hearts of these desires.

145.

Greed is a serious and evil sickness which blinds a person's eyes and
stops up his ears. Nothing is more wretched and vexing to such a one
than to hear about community and yieldedness. The disease of greed
withers the hand so that it is useless in helping others. The greedy
lose their reason and do not know what or why they are here on this
earth. Greed allows neither the self, the conscience, nor the soul to
know salvation. For the most corrupt kind of metal commands them
and rules them. All the while they think they are commanding and
ruling over others. Therefore, there is nothing more senseless and
more adverse than to serve and cling to money and greed. Their joy
is to be tangled up in bondage, and they are happy and jubilant to see
themselves be pressed under by a greedy dog. They give that dog all
the more to gorge on so that it becomes even stronger and in this way
make for themselves countless roads into hell. For greed is like putting
more wood on the fire to make it greater. The more a person brings

to it, the more it rises up. The greedy do not care what they already have. They put it behind them and snap after more in front of them. And finally they come to the same fate as Aesop's dog.

That is why we should ponder this and flee from it with highest diligence. We should search out the antidote for this disease with which we may kill this terrible beast and pull all greed out by the roots. This pestilent disease has spoiled the earth. This sin has mixed things all up so that while one dies of hunger, another bursts from being too full. One must go around naked while another piles clothes upon clothes, only to be eaten by moths. That is why there are so many vagrants and beggars on all the streets, knocking on doors and crying for alms. This affliction of Belial has filled the streets with blood and the towns with weeping and wailing. It has taken us away from the most holy service of Christ and eats away our hearts from the word and seed of God. Even when we do something good, greed comes along and spoils it, the longer the more wicked. Greed is such a hateful affliction before God that if "anyone calls himself a brother, but is greedy, have nothing to do with him and do not even eat with him," said Paul (1 Corinthians 5). Greed is counted as one of the cursed, deadly afflictions that separates a person from the kingdom of God. It has spoiled the glorious image of God in humans, who made us of honorable standing, so that we could look up toward the heavens. Greed strikes human beings down to the earth so that they cannot get up, but rather like a sow are drawn toward the mud by the devil, choosing to live like worms. This craving made Judas into a betrayer, ruined Ananias and his wife and covered Gehazi, who could have been a disciple and prophet, with leprosy. Indeed, it is a general plague in the world, which allows no one to be satisfied with what he has. All eyes and hearts are set on nothing other than greed, caring for nothing else than how much money they can get. And they never even think about how they may justly invest it. They dress their mules and horses with gold and let Christ and his own go unclothed.

146.

God so loved the world that he gave (did not spare) his only begotten son for our sakes (John 3). It is to our shame that we are unworthy of such a great love. And it is our pain that we wanted to spare our money for ourselves and did not want to give even a little to his own. How can we repay this, when we see that another person suffered for our sake? We can entrust all we have to him and still not think we have done enough for him. Well, how much more then do we owe to Christ and his own!

147.

The old church histories, such as Eusebius (Hyst. Eclia. 2. lib. 17. cap.) show and witness to the fact that the believers held to community, not only in Jerusalem but in many other places. He quotes from Philo's little book, titled *The Contemplative Life* or *The Life of Prayer*, which reports that the believers among men and women were called physicians and nurses of God. The reason for this is that when souls came to the Christians which were in a grossly irrational state, they lifted them up aright and like a physician they healed them of their illnesses and made them well. Or another reason was that because they sincerely served God with good conscience, they earned this name on account of their lives. But whether Philo first gave the Christians this name because of their works, or whether it was given by those who from the beginning lived according to the gospel before the Christians were spread throughout the world, is not significant. It is only important that the reading shows to whom this name fairly belonged. But Philo said that those who dedicate themselves to the teaching or philosophy of the Christians give over all their goods and possessions and escape from all the cares of this life. They avoid the cities and live in gardens and small farms and flee from unnecessary company. For they know that these things hinder those who desire to walk the narrow path of virtuous understanding.

Therefore it was said that those ones lived as those who first had that burning and glowing faith lived, that is (as we read in the book of Acts), as they lived in Jerusalem and according to apostolic faith. They sold their possessions and laid the money at the feet of the apostles to be divided up and given to those in need. And they had no poverty among them. Philo wrote that this was also the case with the believers in Alexandria. He also said that there were many places on earth where people of this kind could be found, in Greece and elsewhere. So there must have been many places where this use of possessions was practiced. There were especially many in such places as Egypt and the surrounding territory, above all in Alexandria. There are many faithful people there who came from many places and directions, just as the farmer goes to where he finds good land.

Clement wrote in the year 92 to his brother James in Jerusalem, the Lord's brother, saying that the common life is necessary for everyone, but particularly for those who without reproach struggle for God and desire to follow the life of the apostles and their disciples. For things should be held in common by all people in this world. But because of sin one says, "that is mine," while another says, "that is mine." And so dividing up does take place among people, but not according to the counsel of God. And that is why the wisest person among the Greeks recognized that this was how it should be, for he said that just as the sunshine cannot be divided up, or the air, so people should share all things in this life in common and not divide it up. Psalm 133 is an allegory of this, as is the practice of the first church in Jerusalem, that all things are given for the common use.

The old teacher Augustine (who lived some 370 years after Christ) heard also that there were to be found in his time those who held community. He wrote that a Christian is a distributor or manager of his possessions, not a lord over them. According to divine law all things should be held in common (Augustine Epist. 48). And elsewhere he wrote that only by human law, not by divine law, could one say, "this village is mine!"

John Chrysostomus, who lived some 390 years after the birth of Christ, in his book on the Gospel of John wrote concerning the various sayings and teachings in the first chapter, "In what way may we become disciples of Christ? In that we use all things for the common good and not only for our private good. For Christ did not only gratify himself." And he said a number of such things. But they finally gave in to what is human and erred from the works of perfection. Again, concerning the first chapter of the Gospel of John he said, among other things, "We must labor with all our power to be disciples of Christ where he said that foxes have holes and birds their nests, but the Son of Man has nothing on which to lay his head." This I would demand of you, he said. Now perhaps many think this very difficult, which is why, on account of our short-sightedness, we have forsaken this perfection. But I do admonish you not to have your eyes on money, but rather do as I do in my own short-sightedness, to strive toward this as highest virtue. Therefore it is seemly for you that you also draw back from this greatest of evil—that you possess your wealth not as a servant but as a lord—and not be possessed by it.

The *German Theology* says in Chapter 51, "Were there no selfishness, there would be no private property. In heaven there is no private property and that is why there is contentment, joy and blessedness. And if anyone in heaven took something to be held privately, he would have to be thrown out into hell with the devil. Where one is selfishly willed, there is misfortune and misery." And so it is also with us. Again, where one possesses something for himself, or would like to possess something for himself, he is in fact himself a possession, that is, a possession of his own desires or longings. And the one who possesses nothing and has no desire to possess anything is free and liberated and the possession of no one.

Again, Christ said, "Follow me!" But whoever will follow him must leave everything behind just as he also left all behind. That is why he said: "Whoever will not renounce all that he has and take up the cross is not worthy of me; he is not my disciple and does not follow me."

148.

Paul the apostle said, "I no longer live, but Christ lives in me" (Galatians 2:20); and elsewhere, "Christ is my life." Now, whoever does not live himself, but Christ lives in him, will demonstrate Christ in him by doing that which Christ did, namely, that Christ had community with his disciples. The one in whom Christ lives will have nothing on which to lay his head. The one in whom Christ lives will say, "All that I have is yours and all that you have is mine." Indeed, the one in whom Christ lives will share the little loaves and few fishes he has and hold them in common with the four and five thousand.

Part IV:
Dutch Anabaptism

Dirk Philips

Dirk Philips was born in 1504 in Holland. It is not clear what sort of education he had, but he did know Latin and Greek and became a Franciscan monk. Along with his brother Obbe, Dirk joined the Anabaptist movement in 1533. Although Obbe later left the movement, Dirk became an elder and leader. He initially worked in the Netherlands, but when Dutch Anabaptists began to move to North Germany and Prussia, Dirk moved with them. From 1550 he considered Danzig his home. The Dutch Anabaptist movement had its beginnings in the chiliastic and visionary teaching of Melchior Hofmann in about 1530. Although only as small minority of Dutch Anabaptists took part in the "kingdom" in Münster, the whole movement was deeply compromised and affected by this debacle. The task which serious-minded leaders such as Dirk Philips and Menno Simons had before them was to rescue and revive the evangelical wing of Anabaptism among the Dutch. The skills of Dirk Philips as a theologian and dogmatician were very needed for accomplishing this goal. Dirk Philips has been criticized for being extremely severe and close-minded in his dealings with opponents, especially those from within the Anabaptist circles. Yet in the situation in which he worked, it is not difficult to understand that a man of this character would rise to the position of leadership. His final years were spent in writing and adjudicating splits and divisions which were taking place within the movement. He died in 1568.

The major doctrinal writings of Dirk Philips were collected in his Enchiridion, *which has gone through numerous editions. The chapters presented here, "Concerning the New Birth," and "Concerning the Spiritual Restitution," are taken from the 1564 edition of* Enchiridion oft Hantboecxken van de Christelijke Leere ende Religion.

"Concerning the New Birth and the New Creature: Brief Admonition and Teaching From the Holy Bible" (1556)
Dirk Philips

> I tell you the truth, no one can see the kingdom of God unless he is born again (John 3:3).

> If anyone is in Christ, he is a new creation; the old has gone, the new has come! (2 Corinthians 5:17).

Greetings! May the eternal, almighty and merciful God give you his grace through Jesus Christ his only son, our Lord and Savior. May God strengthen, confirm and renew your inner self through his Holy Spirit, to praise his name and for your salvation. Amen.

Loving brothers and sisters in the Lord! In our time there are many people who claim the new birth. They prattle on about the new creature and Paul's statement, "[In Christ] neither circumcision nor uncircumcision means anything; what counts is a new creation" (Galatians 6:15). But in very few are found the true rebirth and the character of the new creature.[1] What is found is the guile and deception of Satan, who "masquerades as an angel of light" (2 Corinthians 11:14). He shows himself in great power in his servants, who make a fine show of themselves and speak with elevated and arrogant words concerning godly and spiritual things (though it is all hypocrisy.) They speak glowingly of the new birth and the new creature and the true inner self. Indeed, some people are dazzled by this display, for they enchant them and blind their eyes with fine and affected language and a beautiful appearance of false piety.

Therefore, out of Christian love I must warn you against such false Christians and messengers of Satan.[2] Through the grace of God I write for you this short admonition concerning the new birth and the new creature. I want to show that not everyone who claims the new birth and prattles on about the new creature is in fact a person reborn from God. It is only the person who has taken on a godly character and the nature of Jesus Christ, who has part in the power and character of the Holy Spirit, is conformed to the image of Jesus Christ and serves God in submission, obedience and righteousness. In short, a true Christian is a new person and a new creation in Jesus

Christ. Therefore, we must observe how the new birth happens, from where it comes, through what it happens, how powerful it is, and what fruits it brings.

In the first place we note that God originally created humans in God's own image and likeness. Holy scripture says this in many places. God originally created human beings for eternal life, as honest, immortal and divine beings. Indeed, they were created in the image and likeness of his only son, Jesus Christ. For he is the radiance of the eternal Light, the radiance of God's honor, the image of God's essence, a reflection of God's purity and the image of the invisible God. That is why, when Philip asked Christ to see the Father, Christ answered him saying, "Don't you know me, Philip, even after I have been among you such a long time? Anyone who has seen me has seen the Father" (John 14:9).

So then, Jesus Christ is the image of God, and Adam was created by God in that image. But human beings did not remain in the state of original creation. They transgressed the commandments of God. Therefore, they entered into death and corruption. But God, rich in mercy, had compassion for fallen and corrupt human beings, according to his great mercy. He therefore gave them a comforting promise concerning the seed of woman—concerning his only son, Jesus Christ, who would become the redeemer and savior of the human race. Jesus Christ would free all those who believe from the devil and all powers of tyranny.

Through this promise, through this gracious gospel of Jesus Christ, human beings are again comforted. Indeed, they are renewed in the image of God and reborn to eternal life. From the beginning God willed, and wills even now, to have human beings in his own likeness. That is why God originally created them in his own image and likeness. As it is written, "Yet God did make man imperishable; he made him in the image of his own (that is, God's own) nature" (Wisdom 2:23).

After human beings were created in the image and likeness of God the Father (that is, in the image and likeness of Christ) they were restored from the fall from grace through the obedience and righteousness of God's son. Therefore, each person who has reached the age of understanding and knows the difference between good and evil must be transformed into a new, godly being through the enlightenment, work and transfiguration of the Holy Spirit. Indeed, each must be reborn into the communion and likeness of Jesus Christ, transformed into his image, from glory to glory (all by the Spirit of the Lord—2 Corinthians 3:18), and thereby be renewed according to the image of God and created in God's likeness, through Jesus Christ and the Holy Spirit.

Therefore Christ said to Nicodemus, "I tell you the truth, no one can see the kingdom of God unless he is born again" (John 3:3). And further, "I tell you the truth, no one can enter the kingdom of God unless he is born of water and the Spirit" (John 3:5).

Take these words of Christ to heart. For here Christ plainly and publicly denies the kingdom of heaven to anyone who has not been born again—that is, to those who have not put off the works of the old man and put on the new man. This new man was created in the image of God in righteousness and truth. This new man is renewed in the knowledge and likeness of the creator.

Just how this new birth and renewal happens is shown in the testimony of the apostle Peter, who wrote, "For you have been born again, not of perishable seed, but of imperishable, through the living and enduring word of God" (1 Peter 1:23). James is in full agreement; he said, "Every good and perfect gift is from above, coming down from the Father of the heavenly lights, who does not change like shifting shadows. He chose to give us birth through the word of truth, that we might be a kind of firstfruits of all he created" (James 1:17–18). And Paul wrote to Titus, saying that God "saved us, not because of the righteous things we had done, but because of his mercy. He saved us through the washing of rebirth and renewal by the Holy Spirit, whom he poured out on us generously through Jesus Christ our Savior, so that, having been justified by his grace, we might become heirs having hope of eternal life" (Titus 3:5–7).

In these passages we see that the new birth happens in human beings through the word of truth. Renewal happens through the Holy Spirit. All who hear the gospel, and who, through cooperation with the Holy Spirit, believe in Christ Jesus the only son of the living God, who is our Lord and Savior, are born of God, enlightened and taught by the Holy Spirit and are children of God.[3]

Paul confessed this same teaching when he said, "You are all sons of God through faith in Christ Jesus" (Galatians 3:26). And John said, "Yet to all who received him, to those who believed in his name, he gave the right to become children of God—children born not of natural descent, nor of human decision or a husband's will, but born of God" (John 1:12–13). And further John said, "Everyone who believes that Jesus is the Christ is born of God and everyone who loves the father loves his child as well" (1 John 5:1). And again, "For everyone born of God overcomes the world. This is the victory that has overcome the world, even our faith. Who is it that overcomes the world? Only he who believes that Jesus is the Son of God" (1 John 5:4–5).

From all this it is clear that the new birth is actually a work of God in human beings by which one is born again from God through faith in Jesus Christ in the Holy Spirit. For the heavenly Father bears or brings forth a new creature. The word of the heavenly Father is the seed by which the new creature is born. The Holy Spirit renews, heals and keeps this new creature in a godly character. Therefore, this new birth is a mighty and fruitful work of God, coming from the almighty and most high God, through Jesus Christ, in the Holy Spirit.

The apostle James said of the power and fruit of this new birth, "Every good and perfect gift is from above, coming down from the Father of the heavenly lights, who does not change like shifting shadows. He chose to give us birth through the word of truth, that we might be a kind of firstfruits of all he created" (James 1:17–18). What is meant by the firstfruits of his creatures is given us in the figure or symbol of the firstfruits as offerings to the Lord in the Old Testament. For just as in Israel the firstfruits were sanctified and offered to the Lord, so also were the apostles the first ones called to faith and apostolic office by Christ Jesus. Therefore, beyond all doubt they possessed the greatest and most glorious gifts of the Holy Spirit. As Paul wrote to the Romans, "Not only so, but we ourselves, who have the firstfruits of the Spirit, groan inwardly as we wait eagerly for our adoption as sons, the redemption of our bodies" (Romans 8:23).

Therefore, all Christians are also a peculiar people of God, gathered from among all human beings. They are bought with the precious blood of the Lamb, Jesus Christ, and sanctified by the Holy Spirit as a sweet-smelling and worthy offering to God. That is why they are called the firstfruits of God's creation. As John said it in his Revelation, "Then I looked, and there before me was the Lamb, standing on Mount Zion, and with him 144,000 who had his name and his Father's name written on their foreheads. And I heard a sound from heaven like the roar of rushing waters and like a loud peal of thunder. The sound I heard was like that of harpists playing their harps. And they sang a new song before the throne and before the four living creatures and the elders. No one could learn the song except the 144,000 who had been redeemed from the earth. These are those who did not defile themselves with women, for they kept themselves pure. They follow the Lamb wherever he goes. They were purchased from among men and offered as firstfruits to God and the Lamb. No lie was found in their mouths. They are blameless" (Revelation 14:1–5).

From this passage it is clear what the firstfruits of the creation are. They are those who stand on Mount Zion with Christ Jesus the Lamb of God. They are the community of God, marked on their foreheads with the name of the heavenly Father. In true faith they confess the one whose name they bear. They praise God without ceasing and sing to God a new song. For they speak with new tongues and have a new spirit. They are virgins and maidens, a pure bride of the Lamb come down from heaven, enlightened by the radiance of God. They are gathered from among all human beings to be a particular and holy people. In short, they stand blameless before the throne of God, by pure grace alone, by the service of our Lord Jesus Christ.[4]

The new birth, by which such firstfruits are born of God, is a powerful and effective work of God. Through the new birth, a person becomes a new creature in Christ Jesus. Now, for this very reason, the new birth cannot be for innocent children who are without understanding. To those who think this, one must speak in the same manner as the Lord spoke to the Sadducees. "You are in error because you do not know the scriptures or the power of God" (Matthew 22:29). For the only way one could say such things as that the new birth, faith and baptism are for infants is by a total misunderstanding of what the new birth, faith, and baptism are and what they mean. Indeed, if anything may be applied to such people, it is what is written in the book of Wisdom, that they "have less understanding and are more miserable than a child" (Wisdom 15:14). Those who insist that children can have faith, when they do not even know the difference between good and evil, must lack all understanding. For faith and true knowledge of God the Father and his only son Jesus Christ are taught and learned in people by the Holy Spirit. Faith comes by hearing God's word.

As the apostle said, "Faith comes from hearing the message, and the message is heard through the word of Christ" (Romans 10:17). "Now faith is being sure of what we hope for and certain of what we do not see" (Hebrews 11:1). That is, faith is a living hope and sure trust in the grace of God and stretches toward invisible, eternal and heavenly things.

Now, children are without understanding and therefore cannot be taught the word of God. For the scriptures speak only to those who have ears to hear and the heart to understand. Therefore, I must ask with the apostle, "How, then, can they call on the one they have not believed in? And how can they believe in the one of whom they have not heard? And how can they hear without someone preaching to them?" (Romans 10:14). But then if children do not believe and are without faith, how can they be born again from God? True faith in Christ Jesus actually is a work of God in human beings. Through this faith a person is changed and reborn of God. The person comes to recognize his own sin and acts of injustice, which causes him shame and grief. He prays for grace and trusts in the grace of God. He loves God as the highest and noblest good and places all trust in God. Then, through the grace of the Lord, he avoids evil and does what is good, in gratitude to God. He begins to work the fruits of repentance, showing love for God and his neighbor, and bears the fruits of the Spirit.

Children simply do not have this kind of faith. Anyone who has been taught by God knows this well. For both scripture and common experience clearly witness to and prove the fact that children do not have faith. They are saved by grace through Jesus Christ. Understanding adults are made pleasing to God by their faith. But children are pleasing to God in their childish and simple innocence. That is why both Christ and Paul used children as a symbol and an example. Not, of course, that we should become as children in terms of a lack of understanding. We should be as children in their lack of viciousness, but be as adults in terms of understanding. We should always keep in mind this simplicity and humility of children, so that we may strive for the same conduct.

The new birth is of God the heavenly Father. Through Jesus Christ and through the Holy Spirit, a person is changed and made new. This is proper for reasoning adults. They must be born again from on high, in water and the blood, from imperishable seed, through the word of the living God. They must be washed with the word in the bath of the reborn and be changed by renewal of the Holy Spirit. They must put off the Old Adam, be renewed in the spirit of their minds, and then put on the new man, which is the Lord Jesus Christ.

All of this points toward the fact that as a person comes to the age of understanding and can recognize good and evil, he must then hear God's word, better his way of living and believe the gospel. He must be baptized in the name of the Lord upon his confession of faith

205

and receive the gifts of the Holy Spirit for the renewal of his mind according to the image of God. That is, according to the explicit likeness of the invisible God, which is Christ Jesus. He is an example to all Christians and a beginning of God's creation. All true, believing Christians are born of God the heavenly Father in the Holy Spirit. Therefore, they ought to be conformed to the image of his only son Jesus Christ, who is the firstborn of many brothers.

Therefore, we must keep well in mind the whole life of Christ. He was totally obedient to his Father and faithfully carried out his Father's will. He spoke the words of his Father and fulfilled these in all righteousness. He was circumcised according to the Law and made offerings in the temple. Indeed, there was not one letter of the Law which he did not hold in accord with the intention and will of the Father. As he said himself, "Do not think that I have come to abolish the Law or the Prophets; I have not come to abolish them but to fulfill them. I tell you the truth, until heaven and earth disappear, not the smallest letter, not the least stroke of a pen, will by any means disappear from the Law until everything is accomplished" (Matthew 5:17–18).

As our true mediator in the New Testament, Christ showed us the way to follow. He came to John the Baptist and was baptized by him, saying, "Let it be so now; it is proper for us to do this to fulfill all righteousness" (Matthew 3:15).

So if it was proper for Christ to be baptized with the baptism of John, how much more proper is it for us to be baptized with the baptism of Christ? The baptism of Christ means that we are baptized internally with the Holy Spirit and fire and externally baptized by Christ's true representative on our confession of faith, in the name of the Father, Son and Holy Spirit. Therefore, both those who say that only the inner baptism is important, as well as those who baptize externally but forget the true, internal essence of baptism, err and miss the true path. For without faith, the new birth, the Holy Spirit and true Christian character, externals do not matter before God. But also the external rites, such as baptism and the Lord's Supper and other ordinances of the Lord (which are called sacraments), must not be diminished or neglected in any way. For the external wisdom of Christ Jesus was not spoken for nothing, and we humans should live according to every word which came from his mouth. The only son of the Almighty did nothing other than what his Father commanded him to do. Indeed, all that Christ Jesus taught and commanded is without doubt the perfect will and counsel of God. It is the will of the eternal and all-wise God, revealed to us through Christ Jesus the wonderful counselor, and through his Holy Spirit.

Therefore also we ought not to begin or conclude anything other than what Christ Jesus taught us and for which he was the example. He is the beginning and end of all things. He is the leader of our faith and we look to him. He is the true light which has come into the world and we are his disciples. He is the one way to the Father. He is the true gate for the sheep. Whoever comes through that gate comes to the true fold and finds there the pastures of eternal life. But whoever tries to sneak in by another way is a thief and murderer, as Christ himself said. They do not want to enter by the way of Christ but, like thieves and murderers, search for some other way of entry. They want to be saved some other way than through Christ Jesus alone. They want to serve God some other way than that which was commanded, taught and exemplified by Christ Jesus and his apostles. But outside of Christ there is no wisdom, righteousness, holiness, salvation, truth or life. That is why John said, "Whoever believes in the Son has eternal life, but whoever rejects the Son will not see life, for God's wrath remains on him" (John 3:36). And again, "Anyone who runs ahead and does not continue in the teaching of Christ does not have God; whoever continues in the teaching has both the Father and the Son" (2 John 1:9).

I have written here briefly concerning Christ Jesus, in part for the comfort and assurance of my brothers and sisters—to show that we stand in the true grace of God and walk in the right way so long as we follow Christ—and in part to warn the brothers and sisters of frivolous types who have appeared lately. They say much about the new creature and yet really are themselves only hypocrites, self-inflated people and despisers of the word and commandments of Christ. They have left the true way for the way of apostasy. They serve Baal to please Jezebel. And for the sake of their bellies, they run with the world and play the hypocrite. They have no respect for the baptism which Christ Jesus himself instituted, which was practiced by the apostles and which the Bible holds dear. The Lord's Supper, which is done in memory of Christ's suffering and death and which is a spiritual sign of communion in his body and blood, means nothing to them. Footwashing, which was practiced by Jesus Christ himself and which his disciples earnestly practiced, following his example, is seen by them as little more than foolishness. The gospel method of church discipline, without which the community of God could not stand, is to them a disgrace and mockery.[5]

What more can I say? They make light of every saving teaching and ordinance of the Lord Jesus Christ. They see themselves as so wise, so understanding and intelligent, so full of the internal essence of truth, that they claim to have no need of these "external ceremonies," as they call the institutions and ordinance of the Lord.

In saying such things they err. They are blinded by their evil so that they do not know God's divine wisdom, a treasure which is hidden from the ungodly. They do not see that they have been deceived by the devil. Indeed, they are full of pride, drowning in unbelief and gross ingratitude toward God. The gospel for them has become stale and boring. They want to hear something new to tickle their ears. They must think of themselves as the judges and masters of Christ Jesus and the Holy Spirit, for they scorn his teaching and claim no need to follow his ordinances.

Oh! To what end have these poor miserable creatures come that they set themselves up above God the Lord? What will they do and where will they go when the Lord comes after them? They think that they are among the wise virgins, with plenty of oil for their lamps. But when the bridegroom comes, they will be standing with the foolish maidens who had no oil left and were therefore not permitted into the wedding celebration by the groom.

As is the way of lazy servants, they think they are being very clever when they bury the Lord's talents in the ground. But when the Lord comes for an accounting, they will hear a terrible judgment and suffer an awful punishment, for they have hidden the Lord's talents, gaining nothing, rather than putting them to good use.

They are like the church at Laodicea, of which it was written, "You say, 'I am rich; I have acquired wealth and do not need a thing.' But you do not realize that you are wretched, pitiful, poor, blind and naked. I counsel you to buy from me gold refined in the fire, so you can become rich; and white clothes to wear, so that you can cover your shameful nakedness; and salve to put on your eyes, so you can see" (Revelations 3:17–18).

They should take these words truly and earnestly to heart, these ones who are so rich in the Spirit that they think they need nothing— all the while not recognizing what poor and miserable creatures they really are. Let them hear the counsel of the Lord to buy the pure and refined gold of God's word, the noble and precious pearls of gospel truth, that they might become rich in the faith. Let them put off the old Adam, the world and all that belongs to the world. Let them become conquerors in the faith, so that the Lord might clothe them in white garments. Then, at the Lord's coming, they will not be ashamed. Let them salve their eyes well so that they might see clearly that the kingdom of God does not consist merely of words. It consists of power and deeds.

Therefore, all of their high sounding words and lovely chatter about the new creature and inner character means nothing to the Lord so long as they remain and walk in the old character, according to the flesh. Hypocrites also boasted to Christ that they were of the seed of Abraham and had God as their father. But Christ answered them, saying, "If you were Abraham's children then you would do the things Abraham did. If God were your Father, you would love me, for I came from God and now am here. I have not come on my own; but he sent me" (John 8:39 and 42).

So it is useless—indeed, an offense before God—that these despisers of Christ and his word talk about inner character and the new birth. For in fact, they refuse to do what Christ taught, commanded and did himself. So all of their talk is useless and false. If they were genuinely new creatures in Christ Jesus, they would hold to his character from beginning to end. But the character of Christ is of a godly nature and the new character (of righteousness, holiness, truth, faith, love, kindness, friendliness and all good virtues) is worked in us by the Holy Spirit. The true beginning of the Christian life in us is that we truly reform our way of living, show the works and fruits of this reform, believe the gospel and are then baptized on our confession of faith in the name of the Father, Son and Holy Spirit.

This was the beginning of the teachings of Christ himself. "Repent, for the kingdom of heaven is near" (Matthew 4:17). His parting message to his apostles was also like this. "Therefore go and make disciples of all nations, baptizing them in the name of the Father and of the Son and of the Holy Spirit, teaching them to obey everything I have commanded you" (Matthew 28: 19–20).

Because these people do not do this, or even want to, all of their talk about the new birth, the new creature, and all that they profess about the inner character is nothing but idle chatter. For if they were born of God, they would never make fun of the bath of the new birth. If they were really baptized inwardly by Christ Jesus with the Holy

Spirit and with fire, they would never forsake the external baptism, which was commanded by Jesus Christ as a sign and example.

The apostle Paul was specially chosen by God and filled with the Holy Spirit. And then Ananias said to him, "And now what are you waiting for? Get up, be baptized and wash your sins away, calling on his name" (Acts 22:16). Likewise, when Peter preached in the house of Cornelius, the Holy Spirit fell upon all who heard the word. When Peter saw this, he said, "Can anyone keep these people from being baptized with water? They have received the Holy Spirit just as we have. So he ordered that they be baptized in the name of Jesus Christ" (Acts 10:47–48).

From these and other such examples it is clear that the Holy Spirit (which begins the new, Christian character in a person) does not hinder one from water baptism. To the contrary, one is compelled and incited to water baptism. For it is actually the role of the Holy Spirit, as Christ himself taught, to lead believers into all truth and obedience and to glorify Christ. "He will bring glory to me by taking what is mine and making it known to you" (John 16:14).

This glorifying or praising of Christ through the Holy Spirit actually takes place in his followers who accept and keep his word in true faith. As he said himself, "And glory has come to me through them (that is, his disciples)" (John 17:10). Christ is glorified in his followers just as the Father is glorified in Christ. The Father was glorified in Christ in that Christ revealed the name of the Father to his disciples, he spoke his Father's word, did his Father's will and fulfilled his Father's work. As he said himself, "I have brought you glory on earth by completing the work you gave me to do" (John 17:4).

Therefore, all followers of Christ must keep his teachings, do his will and fulfill his work. It is in this way that Christ will be glorified. And it is the beginning and end of Christ's work that we truly reform our lives, believe the gospel and be baptized on our faith in the name of the holy Trinity—the Father, Son and Holy Spirit. And then, through the Lord's grace, we must strive to hold all that Christ commanded us.

Therefore, anyone who refuses to follow Christ Jesus and is disobedient to his word, or who practices the ordinances and truth of Christ differently than Christ himself taught and practiced, does not fear God. He is being unfaithful and in opposition to his word. He shall not escape the punishment of God. Whoever despises Christ and does not accept his word will be judged on that final day by the words of his own mouth.

Now here, some of these big-talking despisers raise a protest, using Paul's saying, "Neither circumcision nor uncircumcision means anything; what counts is a new creation" (Galatians 6:15).

In the first place, I answer that the apostle who wrote these words was never himself of the opinion that the word or ordinances of the Lord should be changed or altered. It never occurred to him! What he meant to say by this was that in the New Covenant, the circumcised and uncircumcised—that is, Jews and Gentiles—were the same before God. This is just as the apostle Peter said when he saw that the gift of the Holy Spirit was poured out by God on the Gentiles. "I now realize how true it is that God does not show favoritism, but accepts men from every nation who fear him and do what is right" (Acts 10:34–35).

These words of Peter are in unity with those of Paul. Namely, that whether one is Jew or Gentile, circumcised or uncircumcised, if one fears God, believes in Jesus Christ and does what is right, one is a child of God, pleasing to God and an heir of his kingdom. This is according to the promise God made to Abraham. "And through your offspring (which is Christ) all nations on earth will be blessed" (Genesis 22:18; Galatians 3:16–18).

Secondly, it is wrong and false exegesis of these words of Paul to compare the ordinances and institutions of the Lord with circumcision or uncircumcision of the flesh. The reason is this. Circumcision of the flesh was a symbol of spiritual circumcision. Uncircumcision represented the uncircumcised, unbelieving heathen, who lived as heathen. That is why both those who were circumcised and uncircumcised in the flesh have to undergo spiritual circumcision, a circumcision of the heart. This circumcision is not by hands, but through the word of God, by putting off the sinful life of the flesh. But what our Lord Christ Jesus taught and commanded in the New Testament is and remains eternal, unchanging truth. That is why Christ said, "Heaven and earth will pass away, but my words will never pass away" (Matthew 24:35).

Thirdly, Paul himself more than sufficiently explained these words, that in Christ Jesus there is neither circumcision nor uncircumcision but a new creature, when he said immediately following, "Peace and mercy to all who follow this rule, (that is, the rule, measure and ordinances of Jesus Christ) even to the Israel of God" (Galatians 6:16).

211

And in the preceding chapter he said, "For in Christ Jesus neither circumcision nor uncircumcision has any value. The only thing that counts is faith expressing itself through love" (Galatians 5:6). And to the Corinthians he said, "Circumcision is nothing and uncircumcision is nothing. Keeping God's commandments is what counts" (1 Corinthians 7:19).

If we are to keep God's commandments and if in Christ Jesus faith works in acts of love, and if God's peace is given to those who live according to the rule of Jesus Christ, then what must be said of those who pay no attention to the commandments of God or the institutions of the Lord Jesus Christ? Indeed, of those who act just as the hypocrites, to whom Christ said, "And why do you break the command of God for the sake of your tradition?" (Matthew 15:3).

Therefore, these simple despisers transgress and reject all of the saving teachings and ordinances of the Lord Jesus Christ. In doing so, they help to strengthen the sacraments and ceremonies of men which God neither willed nor which serve him, just as he said through Isaiah and as Christ himself stated and confirmed in the gospel. They do this hypocritically so that they will please the world. For they are enemies of the cross of Christ and would rather have the honor of men than the honor of God. Furthermore, they make fun of us, they mock us and call us names because we hold to the true institutions of the Lord concerning baptism and the Lord's Supper and willingly suffer persecution for this.[6]

Well, so be it. Some make fun of us, other persecute us. But it is all done for no other reason (thank God!) than because of our faith and for the truth of Jesus Christ. We plead our case to God, the true judge. We take it as an honor to be mocked by those who, holding themselves so wise in their own eyes, reject the counsel of God along with all other hypocrites. We gladly let each one hold himself as wise and clever according to his own view, will and opinion. We would rather be as humble people, so that it will not be said of us what was spoken through the prophet: "Woe to those who are wise in their own eyes and clever in their own sight" (Isaiah 5:21). Again, "Do you see a man wise in his own eyes? There is more hope for a fool than for him" (Proverbs 26:12). Again, "For everyone who exalts himself will be humbled" (Luke 18:14).

So we desire to be humble under the powerful hand of God, to walk upright in righteousness. We know well that by doing this, we will not be deceived. For it is written, "The man of integrity walks securely" (Proverbs 10:9). Which is why the prophet called to the Lord, saying, "May integrity and uprightness protect me, because my hope is in you" (Psalm 25:21).

Therefore, we ask of the Lord that he preserve us in humility, simplicity and devotion and guard us against a self-wisdom and cleverness. Indeed, let him give us a mind willing to be fools for Christ's sake. Just as Paul said, "Do not deceive yourselves. If any one of you thinks he is wise by the standards of this age, he should become a 'fool' so that he may become wise. For the wisdom of this world is foolishness in God's sight" (1 Corinthians 3:18–19).

We would rather be persecuted for the sake of righteousness and be saved than play the hypocrite for the world and be damned. For we know that hypocrites will have no place in the kingdom of God and Christ. We know that the Lord God has no use for the commandments and ceremonies of men, no matter how good they might seem (for what seems great to human beings is, as Christ said, useless to God.) Therefore, we will not play hypocrites to the world. We will not honor their commands and ceremonies and have no intention of participating in them or in any other way helping to strengthen them. But we do desire, through his grace, to hold all that was commanded us by Christ Jesus, the son of the living God, our Lord and Savior, who secured us through the precious blood of his innocent death. Indeed, we will live and die by that, and if people therefore hate us, mock us and persecute us, we take comfort in God, our Savior and Aide.

We seek by God's grace to do his will as poor and humble servants. But never let it be said or thought of us that we seek our salvation in anything other than God's grace and the work of Christ alone.[7] For we believe firmly and confess openly that we are saved only by the grace of our Lord Jesus Christ, exactly as the apostle Peter confessed before the church in Jerusalem. Therefore, in accord with the teaching of this apostle, from our deepest inner being we set our hope on the grace of God which was shown to us in Christ Jesus, a grace which Paul called a saving grace. For it brings to us and works in us our eternal salvation through Christ.

We also fully know and confess that the holy scriptures teach that all people are under sin. In his prayer to God, Solomon said that there is no person who does not sin. And in Job it is written, "Can a mortal be more righteous then God? Can a man be more pure than his Maker? God places no trust in his servants, he charges his angels with error"

213

(Job 4:17–18). Elsewhere he says, "What is man, that he could be pure, or one born of woman, that he could be righteous? If God places no trust in his holy ones, if even the heavens are not pure in his eyes, how much less man, who is vile and corrupt, who drinks up evil like water!" (Job 15:14–16). And David the prophet said, "O Lord, hear my prayer, listen to my cry for mercy; in your faithfulness and righteousness come to my relief. Do not bring your servant into judgment, for no one living is righteous before you" (Psalm 143:1–2).

We confess ourselves to be poor sinners and unworthy servants of the Lord. We lament with the prophets that we are drowning in sin and that our sin is a burden too great for us to bear. Indeed, our sins are more than the number of hairs on our heads! If the grace of God had not taken the upper hand, as it does daily through Christ Jesus, we would be totally lost. But just as it is written in the book of Wisdom, when the children of Israel sinned and God sent the plague of poisonous snakes among them, they were also given a healing sign. God gave them this because of his grace. The sign was the serpent which Moses was commanded by the Lord to erect among the people. Anyone who looked upon this sign was healed—not by what met his eyes but by the Lord, the savior of all people.

Therefore, we also confess that we are poor sinners. We are born according to Adam's flesh, bitten and poisoned by the snake. All who come after him take part in that sinful nature.[8] But countering this poison of the snake and this sinful nature is the merciful heavenly Father. He has given us a true and healing sign—his only beloved son Jesus Christ, who was lifted up from the earth. Whoever looks upon him in true faith will not die but live eternally. Just as among the Israelites no medicine or remedy could cure or heal someone bitten by the snakes—they had to be healed or made well by the word of the Lord alone, which heals all things—so Jesus Christ alone heals and makes us well. There is no other way to salvation. There is no other name given under heaven whereby we may be saved.

But if Christ Jesus is to heal us and save us, we must believe in him and be obedient. For anyone who does not believe will be damned. Indeed, he is already condemned. Disobedience is like the sin of sorcery. Obstinacy is like the blasphemy of idol worship. If Noah had not believed the word of God and built the ark according to the Lord's command, he would have died right along with the rest of the world in the flood waters. If the Israelites in the wilderness had not looked upon the healing sign which, by his grace, God gave them, they would

214

never have become well. If the leper Naaman of Syria had not believed the word of the prophet and washed himself seven times in the river Jordan, he would not have been cleansed of his leprosy, because in refusing to do so he would have been despising the Lord's word. He had to believe and obey in order to be healed. Had the blind man not gone to the pool of Siloam and washed himself, he would have remained blind. The scripture is full of such examples.

Now, in none of these examples did the healing come from any outward thing. It came through God's word, which they believed. That is why the Lord said, "Man does not live on bread alone, but on every word that comes from the mouth of God" (Matthew 4:4). Human life comes from faith in the word of God. As it is written, "The just shall live by faith" (Hebrews 10:38). Another passage says the same thing. "It is not ripened fruit which nourishes a man. Those who put their trust and faith in God are sustained by the word of the Lord" (Wisdom of Solomon 16:26).

Christ spoke of this power of the divine word in the gospels. "Blessed rather are those who hear the word of God and obey it" (Luke 11:28). Again, "I tell you the truth, if anyone keeps my word, he shall never see death" (John 8:51). And to his disciples he said, "You are already clean because of the word I have spoken to you" (John 15:3). And Paul said, "I am not ashamed of the gospel, because it is the power of God for the salvation of everyone who believes" (Romans 1:16). And James said, "Therefore, get rid of all moral filth and the evil that is so prevalent and humbly accept the word planted in you, which can save you" (James 1:21).

In summary, God's word sustains people, but only those who trust in the Lord. God's word is spirit and life, giving life to us, but only if we believe it. God's word purifies the soul, but only of those who obey God's word. Yes, God's word is a healing power, but only for those who hear it and keep it. But whoever despises the word despises God himself. He rejects Christ Jesus and rebels against the Holy Spirit who testifies to the word.

So then, in returning to my original proposition and intention concerning the new birth and new creature, let me say here in conclusion that the newborn children of God are new creatures in Christ Jesus. They are born again from God the heavenly Father through Christ Jesus and are renewed and healed through the Holy Spirit. They take part in the divine nature and character of Jesus Christ and the virtues of the Holy Spirit.[9] They have died to sin and do so die more each day. They live for righteousness. They exalt in nothing but the cross of Christ our Lord, through which the world is crucified to them and they to the world. They walk in true faith according to the rule of Christ, following in his footsteps. They know no one according to the flesh and seek not what is worldly but only what is godly. In short, they are just and do justice, even as God is just, from whom they are born. They are motivated by the Holy Spirit. And where that happens, there one sees the kingdom of God. There one comes into the kingdom of heaven. There one is a new creature in Christ Jesus.

From the beginning the holy people of God have been new creatures. Abel, Seth and Noah, from faith and a free heart made their offerings to God. They walked the path of righteousness and were submissive and obedient to God.

Abraham, Isaac and Jacob were such new men. Following the command and will of God they went on faith and willingly left the land of their fathers. They went out and lived in tents and were happy with that. They acknowledged that they were strangers and guests on this earth, in search of a homeland—namely, heaven—and a city whose foundation is built and laid by God. Therefore, as the apostle said, God was not ashamed to be called their God and has prepared a city for them.

The great prophet Moses had this same character. When he was grown, he no longer wanted to be called the son of Pharaoh's daughter. He chose to suffer injustice with the people of God rather than the temporal pleasures of sin. He held the humiliation of Jesus Christ to be of more worth than all the treasures of Egypt, for he looked for a different reward.

This character was also found in the apostle Paul. Those things he once valued he now counted as nothing for the sake of Christ. "But whatever was to my profit I now consider loss for the sake of Christ. What is more, I consider everything a loss compared to the surpassing greatness of knowing Christ Jesus my Lord, for whose sake I have lost all things. I consider them rubbish, that I may gain Christ and be found in him, not having a righteousness of my own that comes from the law, but that which is through faith in Christ—the righteousness that comes from God and is by faith" (Philippians 3:7–9).

In such faithful and holy men of God and in all faithful believers before us we can clearly see the character of the new birth and the power of faith. For they knew and served God in Spirit. They feared and trusted God. They loved God above all else, forsaking temporal things and seeking heavenly things, for they are fully satisfied by the Lord and his grace. They know well that the Lord is part or portion of the holy ones and their reward is and will be the Most High. This was also known by the prophet, who said, "Whom have I in heaven but you? And earth has nothing I desire besides you. My flesh and my heart may fail, but God is the strength of my heart and my portion forever" (Psalm 73:25–26).

These are the words of a man who has been reborn. It is the fruit of the new creature. Let us take this as our model and follow it by the grace of God. Let us be like-minded and find our trust in God. If we are born of God, we are new creatures in Christ Jesus and will make this same confession.

As I said above and say again, Jesus Christ, the only son of God, a reflection of God's glory and an image of God's being, is the example to all Christians, ordained by the Father that we might be conformed to him. For godly character, which is to be our pattern, is perfectly reflected and shown in him. Therefore, all those who claim to know the new birth should have the character and nature of Christ and hold firmly to his character from beginning to end.

These are the reborn children of God. They are born again into eternal life and renewed in the image of God. They are made holy through the Holy Spirit, for God the heavenly Father is holy and desires that his children also be holy. Jesus Christ, the son of the Most High, is holy and therefore desires his brothers and sisters to be holy. The Holy Spirit is holy and therefore desires also that the temple within which he dwells also be holy.

Therefore, Paul said, "Praise be to the God and Father of our Lord Jesus Christ, who has blessed us in the heavenly realms with every spiritual blessing in Christ. For he chose us in him before the creation of the world to be holy and blameless in his sight. In love he predestined us to be adopted as his sons through Jesus Christ, in accordance with his pleasure and will—to the praise of his glorious grace, which he has freely given us in the One he loves" (Ephesians 1:3–6).

In this passage we see just how holy and blameless the children of God must be. As the Lord said to his disciples, "Consecrate yourselves and be holy, because I am holy" (Leviticus 11:44). And again, "Be perfect, therefore, as your heavenly Father is perfect" (Matthew 5:48).

And John said, "No one who is born of God will continue to

sin, because God's seed remains in him; he cannot go on sinning, because he has been born of God" (1 John 3:9). The reborn of God takes part in the character and nature of the holy stock. According to Christ's word, "The Spirit gives birth to spirit" (John 3:6). Therefore, "We know that anyone born of God does not continue to sin; the one who was born of God keeps him safe, and the evil one cannot harm him" (1 John 5:18).

"Concerning Spiritual Restitution" (1559)
Dirk Philips

That is, how what was done from the beginning is spiritually fulfilled and restored in Christ Jesus. A Christian and scriptural meditation compiled from the Holy Bible in the service of all who love the truth by D.P.

> This is what I told you while I was still with you: Everything must be fulfilled that is written about me in the Law of Moses, the prophets and the psalms (Luke 24:44).

> He must remain in heaven until the time comes for God to restore everything, as he promised long ago through his holy prophets (Acts 3:21).

> The old has gone, the new has come! (2 Corinthians 5:17).

Introduction

The holy and divine scriptures speak and testify often of the restitution or restoration in Christ Jesus of all things which have happened since the beginning of the world. As Peter said, the heavens must receive Christ "until the time comes for God to restore everything, as he promised long ago through his holy prophets."

Many errors have arisen concerning these matters.[10] For each person has falsely interpreted this restoration according to his own wisdom and worldly understanding. Therefore, I have attempted here by the grace of God to deal briefly with all that has happened since the beginning of the world and how in Christ and his kingdom these things have been spiritually restored. Simple people may be instructed in these things and not be deceived by false prophets. These false

218

prophets adorn and mask their dishonest teachings with the old characters of the letter as shadows and symbols. All that which they cannot maintain from the New Testament they try to prove by using the Old Testament and the letter of the prophets. That is why so many sects have sprung up. That is also why so many false forms of worship have been instituted. In fact, from this same fountain flows both the idolatrous ceremonies and pomp of the papal church and the lamentable errors of those fanatical sects who in our time have done much evil and caused much ill-will in the name of the holy gospel, faith and the Christian religion.

Therefore, with the Lord's help, we will here clarify the spiritual meaning of the tabernacle of Moses. We desire through assistance of Christ's Spirit to explain this restoration, or at least to offer our simple understanding of it to all Christians for their consideration. By this the simple people may be shown direction as to how the scriptures ought to be understood, reflecting on all things according to the Spirit and not the flesh.

For the kingdom of God is not of this world. It dwells among all true and upright Christians. The flesh is oriented toward death, but the spirit is oriented toward life and peace. The flesh is useless, but the spirit brings life. The words of Christ are spirit and life. May the eternal, almighty and wise God give us, through Christ Jesus, a true and scriptural understanding of all things. To his praise, for the joy and animation of our consciences and for the building up of his community. Amen.

The Spiritual Restitution

Christ Jesus is the spirit and truth of all figures of the past, the end and fulfillment of the law of types. He is the beginning of the eternal and true character and comprehensiveness. As the apostle said, in Christ Jesus is the true essence, in him is found all the hidden treasures of wisdom and knowledge of God. In him dwells the fullness of the essence of God and all shadows and types are brought to an end in him. He is the bright morning star, the sun of righteousness which enlightens all things. The gloriousness in the face of Moses (meaning the Law) is nothing like the gloriousness of Jesus Christ and his holy gospel. As Paul said, the veil over the face of Moses, which prevented the people from understanding Moses and the prophets, is taken away by Christ. All things are changed, transformed and made

219

new in Christ. The letter is transformed into spirit, the flesh is transformed into true essence, the old is made new, what was figurative is
given true and lasting substance and clear truth, and that which was
passing away is transformed into what is eternal and divine. One must
know these things so as to seek only in Christ and nowhere else all
truth, righteousness, holiness, salvation and all godly wisdom, gifts of
virtue, power and action. This brings to shame all those who in these
last and dangerous times have brazenly and arrogantly presumed to
set up a kingdom to restore all things. For nobody can do this other
than the Lord Jesus Christ, who is the completion of wisdom, truth
and righteousness. His name is above all other names in this world
and the coming world. He is the head of all principalities and powers.
In short, he is the one through whom all things were created and are
sustained, who works all things in God and apart from whom nothing
of God can be accomplished.

First of all, in Christ the creation of heaven and earth is renewed,
for God has made a new heaven. That is, God now dwells in the
believers, and especially in the apostles and upright teachers. In these
Christ Jesus, the sun of righteousness, shines forth and brings light
everywhere, making fruitful all of the fruits of the spirit. The hearts
of Christians are the new earth. For there the seed of the divine word
is sown and they are renewed through the grace of God and the power
of the Holy Spirit.

This is clearly seen in the words of the prophet, who said, "The
heavens declare the glory of God; the skies proclaim the work of his
hands. Day after day they pour forth speech; night after night they
display knowledge. There is no speech or language where their voice
is not heard. Their voice goes out into all the earth, their words to
the ends of the world. In the heavens he has pitched a tent for the
sun, which is like a bridegroom coming forth from his pavilion, like a
champion rejoicing to run his course. It rises at one end of the heavens
and makes its circuit to the other; nothing is hidden from its heat"
(Psalm 19:1–6).

As Paul testified, this is a prophecy of the gospel which went out
from the apostles and was preached throughout the world. Therefore,
the heavens which declare the glory of God and are the dwelling place
of the Son, which shines on all things, are the apostles and all upright
teachers and Christians who preach the word of God and in whom
God dwells.

Here is also the new moon which lights the heavens. It is namely the sure word of prophecy which shines in the darkness. Here are also the new stars. They are the righteous ones who show to others the way of godliness. They shine as the brightness of heaven, as eternal stars, through the glory of the divine word and through the radiance of Christ in the heavenly state.

That is why the community of God is described as a pregnant woman who is clothed with the radiance of Christ and his word. She is compared to and illustrated by the sun, with the moon under foot. For the community of God is planted on the sure word of prophecy, which, through the Holy Spirit, was the testimony of Moses and the prophets. She has a golden crown with twelve stars on her head. These stars signify the pure, unspotted and true teaching of the holy apostles, which is the adornment of the community of God. She is also pregnant or fruitful with the seed of God. That is, with the word of the heavenly Father which she has received. And she will bear in great distress and fear, for she is powerfully persecuted by the dragon.

In this the creation of heaven and earth is spiritually fulfilled in Christ, until that time when complete changing occurs from the corruptible to the incorruptible. Then all believers shall inherit and possess forever the new heaven and new earth, wherein righteousness dwells. It is this, which God shall make, for which we wait.[11]

The creation of human beings is also renewed in Christ Jesus. For Adam sinned and the image of God in him and according to which he was created was shattered. Therefore a renewal of human beings, indeed, a new creation, had to occur. This happened also through Jesus Christ, through whom God works all things. But the image of God is a spiritual essence of the invisible God. It is his eternal wisdom, power, righteousness and eternal life. This is Jesus Christ, who is the pure image of his heavenly Father. He is the splendor of God's majesty and the undefiled mirror of God's divine glory. This was seen by Abraham, not with eyes of flesh but with spiritual eyes. It must also be seen in and acknowledged by all believers.

The first human beings, Adam and Eve, were created according to this image of God. They were made in God's own likeness, given great understanding and recognition of God and all creatures. They also had great righteousness and holiness. They loved God and were blessed with a godly and innocent life in Paradise and eternal life in heaven.

But because human beings did not remain in this original state of creation and lost the image of God through their disobedience,

221

human beings had to be recreated by God through Jesus Christ. That is why the son of God was promised to Adam. This son appeared to all people and destroyed the work of the devil. Then the lost image of God in humanity was renewed, for the sins of the world were taken away. Death was consumed and humanity won eternal life through his triumphant resurrection. By his word and spirit human beings are made new in this life and at his radiant appearance in the resurrection he prepares completed human beings according to his image and righteousness. They will be glorified and shine as the sun in the kingdom of the Father. They will be conformed in their nature to the angels and will take part in divine majesty. [12] Thus has a new creation or new birth of human beings occurred through Jesus Christ.

Jesus Christ also renewed marriage and restored it to its proper place. According to God's original ordering in Paradise, marriage was between one man and woman, both of whom were created in the image of God and brought together by God. But this order did not endure. It was totally abused by God's children in the original world because of their corrupted nature and lust of the flesh. For that reason the Lord and his servant Moses, partly in becoming a symbol, as was the case with Abraham and others, and partly because of the hardheartedness of the people of Israel, allowed marriage to fall into foreign customs and practices. But Christ came to remind us of the original intention of God as it was in the beginning, in the Garden of Paradise. "Haven't you read, he replied, that at the beginning the Creator made them male and female, and said, For this reason a man will leave his father and mother and be united to his wife, and the two will become one flesh? So they are no longer two, but one. Therefore what God has joined together, let man not separate" (Matthew 19:4–6).

So marriage was restored by Christ as it was in the beginning, according to the divine order, namely, that marriage is a bringing together by God of two persons, one man and one woman, into one flesh. They must both be people created by God in his image. That is, they must be born of God, conformed to Christ Jesus and renewed internally by the Holy Spirit. They must be united by God in Paradise—that is, in the gathering of the community of the Lord. That is a true marriage before God, in his will and his name, in which God himself takes part. This Paul called a marriage in the Lord. It is in this manner that Christ restored marriage, and anything other than this or contrary to this is erroneous before God, regardless of how fancy and flowery you make it. [13]

222

Even in this way the symbolic marriage between Adam and Eve was spiritually restored in Christ Jesus. For he is the New Adam and the bride which was taken from his side, which is flesh of his flesh and bone of his bone, is the spiritual Eve. She (the church) is mother to all believing Christians and from her will issue and be born a new world, a new generation. These born-again children of God are of his incorruptible seed, which is his living and powerful word. They are born anew and brought forth from his bride.

But among the children of the first Adam, defection happened because of envy, evil and promiscuity, in that the murderous Cain killed the righteous Abel. Evil gained the upper hand and all flesh was turned away from the Lord and his way. The children of God looked upon the daughters of men and, seeing that they were attractive in appearance, took each to wife according to his own desires. That is just what happened also with the children of the second and spiritual Adam. For the righteous children of God were strangled by the seed of Cain, that is, by the godless and unfaithful. The children of God were deceived by the attractive appearance of the daughters of men, by the evil lusts of the flesh, by the external, glorious beauty of the idolatrous church, by the great whore of Babylon and the false prophets of Jezebel. They were led into idolatry and the world was totally given to evil under the Antichrist. And all things were laid to waste through this child of debauchery. Yet there remained among them a remnant of the righteous children of God who found grace in God's eyes. They entered into the ark of Noah and their souls were preserved in eternity.

Now in Christ Jesus there is fulfillment of the bargain of Noah and his ark, the flood and the saving of a few souls. For Christ Jesus is the true and spiritual Noah, the preacher of righteousness, and the children of God, the true Christians, are his household. He has preached to the corrupt world the coming wrath of God and threatened the unconverted and unbelievers with the judgment of damnation. But he also has built an ark, that is, the holy Christian Church, for the purpose of protecting and preserving all believing souls. All who stubbornly despise the word of God and reject the offer of mercy in Jesus Christ, closing their eyes to the light of the gospel, will remain outside of this ark and be destroyed by the punishment of the Lord. Indeed, upon them will fall the wrath and ruthlessness of heaven on that day when God will judge the world through Jesus Christ.

But as many as have received Christ with a true faith and entered into his spiritual ark will be preserved to eternal life. The covenant of

God was renewed with them and was signified by the rainbow which is Jesus Christ. He is the true symbol of heavenly grace, the right hand of the almighty Father. They were blessed by God with a heavenly blessing for spiritual growth. They increased and won many children through the gospel of Jesus Christ, just as was done by the apostles, who converted many thousands to God through the preaching of the divine word and the working of the Holy Spirit.

Then once again an evil seed grew up and sprouted through the ridiculing Ham, who was the symbol of these false brothers. The Antichrist, an evil seed left over from Canaan which in the time of the apostles went out from the community of God, despised and mocked Jesus Christ and caused the pious much suffering. For where the children of God are, Satan also soon mixes among them.[14] That is why Paul said that schisms will appear among Christians, so that those who have God's approval might be known publicly. It has been so since the beginning, in the time of Adam, Noah, Lot, in Israel of the flesh and in the community of the apostles and everywhere.

In Christ Jesus there is a repetition in true and spiritual essence of the dealing of God with Abraham, Isaac, Jacob and the whole of Israel. For the spiritual Abraham is God the heavenly Father himself. His two wives are the two testaments. The first of these was for many years unfruitful, up until the time of the promise. In the meantime the slave woman Hagar (that is, the literal, subservient synagogue) produced her fruit and issuance, namely, the Hebrew people and the Levitical priesthood, with all of its imperfect ceremonies and offerings which could make no one either perfect or righteous. But then the free child Isaac (Jesus Christ) was born outside of the normal workings of nature. God's word became flesh and the one Son of the Father came into the world. He was the first of God's new creation, the firstborn among brothers. He was born of the free woman Sarah, the heavenly Jerusalem. And as Isaac was reckoned the seed of the promise, Ishmael quarreled with him and mocked him, and was therefore cast out and not given part in the inheritance. Likewise, some people rejected, mocked and persecuted Christ and his people and would not accept them. Therefore, the kingdom of God was taken from them and given to the heathen, and they will not take part in the inheritance so long as they remain unbelievers.

But between Abraham and Isaac comes the king and priest of the most high God, Melchizedek, a beautiful symbol of Jesus Christ, his eternal kingdom and priesthood. For Melchizedek was described by the apostle as a king of righteousness and peace, a priest of the most high, who was greater than Abraham or Levi. For the blessed Abraham and Levi gave him tithes. Indeed, as a symbol of Christ, he is described as having neither father nor mother, nor offspring, without a beginning or end of life and is compared to the son of God.

All this is found in Christ Jesus. For he is the king of eternal righteousness and all godly peace. He is himself the peace and righteousness of all believers. He is greater than Abraham, for he is prior to Abraham. He took away the Levitical priesthood and became himself our one high priest, ordained and seated with a high and precious oath and sitting on the right hand of God in heaven. He had neither father nor mother, nor earthly offspring, for he came from God his heavenly Father. He was conceived in Mary through the Holy Spirit by a reflection of divine power. He became human and a son of the most high was born of her, the first and the last, the firstborn of all creation, indeed, eternal life itself.

Item. Here also is a repetition of the dealing with Sodom, the angels with Lot and his wife. For the spiritual Sodom, full of pride, cruelty and inhuman impurity, is the evil world which crucified the Lord. Out of this Sodom, the angels of God will lead all those who, with Lot, desire to fear God, who love God and are ordained for eternal life. But the world, with all of its evil lusts, wickedness and works, will pass away, just as Sodom and Gomorrah passed away. And the unbelievers, who look back like Lot's wife and are therefore not fit for the kingdom of God, will remain there. They will be blinded and hardened by God and given over to their backward senses. They will not escape the punishment of God. That is why Christ said in the gospel, "Remember Lot's wife!" (Luke 17:32).

In Christ Jesus there is also a renewal and fulfillment of the symbolic sacrifice of Isaac. Isaac carried the wood up the mountain to where his father would offer him up on the altar. Yet he did not die. A goat or ram was killed and offered in his place. That is a sign to us that Jesus Christ was obedient to his heavenly Father even unto death. He carried with his own body the wood of the cross because of the burning love he had for us. He was offered for us on the altar of the cross. Yet he was not killed in Spirit, though he died in flesh. Just as Abraham received Isaac before the altar as one who returned from the dead (a symbol of the resurrection) so also Jesus Christ, after he offered himself as a sweet-smelling offering, rose up from the dead and became, with all of his eternal seed, that is, all true Christians, an heir to all of the goods of his heavenly Father Abraham.

Item. In Christ, the symbol of Isaac and Rebecca is spiritually fulfilled and repeated. Abraham made his servant take an oath and swear that he would not allow his son Isaac to marry a wife from among any other people than his own relatives. The servant did this and brought to his master Isaac the willing Rebecca as a wife. Thus is it with the spiritual courtship of the bride of Christ through John the Baptist, the apostles and other true servants of the Lord. These true servants of the most high God are sent out, bound by a high oath, to seek out and bring to Christ Jesus (the true Isaac) the true heirs of all the goods of his heavenly Father, a willing Rebecca who by faith and the new birth have become his relatives, of his own nature and kind. This is, namely, the community which he loves and adorns with radiant spiritual gifts. It is with this community that he sires the children of the kingdom, those born again from God's word and who are therefore also his brothers and companions in grace through the acceptance of adoptive status under God.

Item. Isaac had his servants dig out and purify the springs of living water which the servant of his father Abraham dug, but which the envious Philistines had stopped up with dirt. That is why the shepherds of Gerar quarreled with the servants of Isaac. In the same way God the heavenly Father gave us the springs of living water, that is, his pure, divine word, through his true messengers, the good prophets. But false prophets stopped it up with impure teachings of man and mundane wisdom, falsifying the clear word of God. The prophets also lamented this fact, saying that the false prophets trampled under foot the good pastures in which the sheep should be fed and polluted the clear waters which the sheep drink. Therefore the sheep eat and drink that which has been made impure and trampled under foot. That is, they have accepted the impure, human teaching they have heard from false prophets instead of the divine word, and so are led astray.

But Christ Jesus, the true Isaac, has again opened the clogged springs through the Holy Spirit. The word of God, once obscure, is again brought into the light of day and the clear and lucid gospel is again preached everywhere by his servants and apostles. But the uncircumcised Philistines (the scholars and hypocrites who are uncircumcised in their hearts, the Antichrist and false teachers) set themselves against it and quarrel with the servants of Isaac, the servants of

226

Jesus Christ, concerning the living water, which they presume is only for themselves. For they alone presume to be interpreters of the scriptures, saying proudly, "We will triumph with our tongues; we own our lips—who is our master?" (Psalm 12:4). That is why the quarrel between the servants of Jesus Christ and the false teachers, who are true Philistines, enemies of the gospel and spiritual Israel, will continue.

In Christ are also repeated many beautiful symbols concerning the patriarch Jacob. Some of these have already been explained in my book on the tabernacle of Moses, [15] for I wrote much there concerning Esau and Jacob. But here I will just say briefly that Jacob was sent by his father Isaac to Laban, the brother of his mother Rebecca. Along the way, as the sun was sinking, the Lord appeared to him at Bethel and he fell into a deep sleep. He saw in a dream a ladder which reached right up into heaven. God stood there and said, " 'I am the Lord, the God of your father Abraham and the God of Isaac. I will give you and your descendants the land on which you are lying. Your descendants will be like the dust of the earth, and you will spread out to the west and to the east, to the north and to the south. All peoples on earth will be blessed through you and your offspring. I am with you and will watch over you wherever you go, and I will bring you back to this land. I will not leave you until I have done what I have promised you.' When Jacob awoke from his sleep, he thought, 'Surely the Lord is in this place, and I was not aware of it.' He was afraid and said, 'How awesome is this place! This is none other than the house of God; this is the gate of heaven' " (Genesis 28:13–17).

This ladder signifies Jesus Christ, who is the one way to the Father and into the kingdom of heaven. Through him believers come to God. Here is also the promise of the gospel, symbolized by the angels on the ladder, for the angels also preach the gospel from the heavens. Here is the renewal of the divine covenant through Jesus Christ, the promised seed, in whom all who follow in the footsteps of the faith of Abraham will be blessed, not only the Hebrews but also the heathen who believe on Jesus Christ. Here certainly the Lord is among his community and here is the house of God, the gates of heaven, for here through Jesus Christ is given the new and comforting promise concerning the glorious and spiritual kingdom and inheritance of blessed rest in the truly promised land of Canaan—that is, in the eternal and incorruptible kingdom with God in heaven. It is there to which the Lord Jesus Christ ascended to prepare a dwelling place for us, a tabernacle, a different kind of building not made by hands. God is the master builder and creator of this building. The Lord Jesus Christ will come again to take us to him, so that where he is we will also be. We will see his glory and take part in it for eternity.

Of Jacob were born the twelve patriarchs from whom stemmed the twelve tribes of Israel. These twelve patriarchs symbolize for us the twelve apostles, who were born again in the Spirit and given power from on high. These are the spiritual fathers who through the gospel and faith in Jesus Christ have begotten the Israel of God. Such faithful Christians are the true spiritual Israelites and seeds of Abraham, who are won to Christ through God's word. These are the fathers, as the apostles themselves testified when they called themselves "fathers" and called the believers "children." And this is all of God, for he is, as Paul said, the true Father of all who are called children in heaven and on earth.

The figure of Joseph is also spiritually fulfilled in Christ Jesus. Joseph was sent out by his father Jacob. His twelve brothers were so jealous that they sold him and he was brought to Egypt. There, because of his piety and innocence, he was thrown into prison. But through God's foresight and for the sake of God's will he was again set free and placed before the king Pharaoh. After interpreting the king's dreams, he was set up and exalted as Lord over all of Egypt.

In the Spirit, the same things happened to Christ. He was sent by God, his heavenly Father, to his brothers, that is, to the Hebrew people, for he was born a Hebrew according to the flesh. But they would neither receive him nor accept him as their Lord. He was hated, persecuted, betrayed, sold, arrested, crucified and killed. But even so, the Lord Jesus has been exalted by the right hand of God over all principalities, powers, thrones, authorities and any name given, both in this world and the world to come. He is given all power in heaven and on earth to portion out spiritual gifts. He has received from his heavenly Father all judgment over the living and the dead that they may honor the Son just as they honor the Father. They fall before him and worship him, for he sits at the right hand of his heavenly Father, in heavenly splendor, a Lord over all with his Father and the Holy Spirit.

Here we also see a renewal of the divine covenant with Abraham, Isaac and Jacob which was made through Jesus Christ. For he is the promised seed in whom all are blessed who walk in the footsteps of the faith of Abraham. Not only Hebrew people, but also heathens believe on Jesus Christ. They are circumcised, not in the flesh but in the heart. This is the circumcision of Christ, which takes place in the Spirit through the repudiation of the sinful body, killing of the old person, burial of sin and resurrection into a new way of living. To these people Jesus Christ also has given a new and comforting promise of a glorious, spiritual kingdom and inheritance, of a blessed rest in the land of Canaan, the eternal, imperishable kingdom of God in heaven. Christ has gone there to prepare for us a dwelling place, a temple. It is not a building made by human hands, but one whose builder is the creator God. Christ will come again and take us to him, that we may be where he is. We shall see his glory and take part in it in eternity.

Here we see clearly also the spiritual Egypt, the land of darkness, just as the physical Egypt of long ago. For the people of God, the children of Israel, were plagued by Pharaoh and his servants. God used miracles by the hand of Moses, many signs and wonders. With his mighty hand and outstretched arm he saved them from Egyptian slavery. He led them through the Red Sea in the wilderness by a pillar of cloud by day and a pillar of fire by night. He fed them with bread from heaven and water from the rock to drink. He finally led a remnant into the promised land. In the same way, we are plagued with slavery to sin, with injustice and death in the hell of Pharaoh, of Satan. But through the true Moses, Jesus Christ, we are delivered. We are baptized into his death in the cloud and the sea; that is, with his precious blood, which was shed and with which our consciences are baptized and our sins are washed away, and with the Holy Spirit which God poured out on us through Jesus Christ. But Pharaoh, with all his servants, riders and chariots, our enemies and persecutors (that is, the devil, hell, sin and death) are all defeated by the blood of the cross of Christ and by our faith in his name. For we are also brought into the wilderness on our way to the promised land in heaven.

In Christ Jesus, the symbol of the Passover Lamb is also fulfilled. The children of Israel roasted the lamb in the fire and ate it and sprinkled their doorposts with its blood. They did this so that the avenging angel of the Lord, seeing the blood of the lamb, would pass over and not kill the firstborn of that house, as he did in all of Egypt. Jesus Christ is our Passover Lamb. He was roasted by his burning love for us on the wood of the cross. We spiritually eat this Passover Lamb in faith and we are sprinkled with his blood in defence against the coming wrath of God which is coming upon this blind world. Whoever desires to learn more about this can read of it in our confession concerning the Lord's Supper.

Item. In Christ the symbol of manna from heaven, with which the Lord God fed Israel in the wilderness, is also fulfilled. It is also called the bread of angels in the scriptures. For Jesus Christ is the true living bread come from heaven. He is the bread of God which gives life to the world. He is the food for all hungry souls. Indeed, he is eternal life by which both the angels of heaven and the faithful on earth are sustained.

Likewise, the symbol of the rock which gave water to Israel is repeated in Christ. This is the rock which Moses, his staff in hand, struck. For Jesus is the precious cornerstone which God laid in Zion, the living stone on which the community is built. It is also the stone from which flows, by the power of God (represented by the staff of Moses), the living water of the Holy Spirit for the filling of all thirsty souls.

The symbol of the angel of the Lord who was placed in front of Israel and led them with a pillar of fire by night and a pillar of cloud by day is also fulfilled in Christ. Jesus Christ is our guide who shows us the way through the darkness of this world with his divine word. With the filling of his Holy Spirit we are protected, comforted and refreshed from the heat of tribulation, so that we are not burned up. He teaches us always what to do and what not to do. Therefore, we should not begin anything unless Jesus Christ is before us, guiding us by his teaching, example and spirit. To do otherwise would be to err in darkness, to leave the proper path in the wilderness of this world and to come to no good.

The bitter waters of Marah, the waters of sorrow, affliction and persecution, are made sweet by the tree of life in the Paradise of God. That is the comforting gospel of Jesus Christ. He is always with his followers, through all kinds of perils. His word is sweet and comforting. Spiritual struggle begins here against Amalek and Israel's surrounding enemies. One must put on the armor of God and take up the weapons of the Spirit against the princes of this world, against the spirits of evil, and struggle against and overcome Satan. The uplifted hands of Jesus Christ do not become weary, as did the hands of Moses (this may be understood as the weakness and imperfection of the Law). This is the eternal sacrifice and holy perfection of Christ's prayers, for he sits on the right hand of the almighty God, praying for us. Indeed, he has already overcome our enemies. Our faith in his name is victory over the world, just as John said.

But many people transgress and sin against the Lord. Therefore, just as happened symbolically in Israel as an example to us, they are struck down in the wilderness. That is, many who were at one time enlightened in a recognition of the truth and were delivered from Egypt, later fell away from the living God. That can happen in various ways. Some are overcome with lust for the meat of Egypt and become dissatisfied and weary of the heavenly manna. That is to say, they are carnally minded and follow after false, human teachings which tickle their ears. They forsake God's word, the living heavenly bread of Jesus Christ, and perish for it, punished by God.

Others, desiring idols they can see, pray to the Golden Calf, deserting Moses who lingers on the mountain. That is, they turn away from the living God and from the Lord Jesus Christ, who having ascended to heaven, delays in his return (so they think). So they fall into worship of strange gods and choose for themselves idols which they can see, playing and jumping around the Golden Calf.[16]

Whoever loves or honors the creation more than the creator, or who values human teaching equal to or above God's teaching, or hopes for righteousness and salvation in a false form of worship which God did not expressly command, without any doubt is worshipping the Golden Calf and is an idolater in the eyes of the Lord. No matter how much he dresses up his idolatry with an outward appearance of holiness and calls it true worship, it is nothing but idolatry in the eyes of the Lord. God alone will be God and Lord and confessed as such. He is not to be served according to our good intentions but according to his word alone.

Some fornicate with the daughters of the Moabites. That is, they become deceived by false prophets and idolatrous groups and are overcome with a promiscuous spirit and fall into a carnal, ungodly way of living. Like Zimri, they show no concern that the community mourns over such sins and offenses and are repentant before the Lord. Instead, they willfully continue in their evil. They will also be punished by the Lord for this. They will be excluded from the community of God so that affliction is not brought upon the whole of Israel because of them.

These new Balaamites were there in the time of the apostles and we find them in our time as well. They are the false teachers who seek the wages of injustice. They are therefore unable to see the angel of the Lord blocking their way with a fiery sword. They will not turn from their ways or be reproved by the ass, whose mouth is opened by God. That is, they will not accept the Lord's rebuke from the simple and humble people through which God speaks and works. They are happy to proclaim judgment and denunciations on Israel. But God refuses to listen to them and blesses his people even more, so that even their enemies wonder at the glorious dwellings of Jacob and the camp of Israel.

Some side with Korah, Dathan and Abiram against Moses and Aaron and are swallowed alive by the earth. These are the ones who cause discord in the community of God. They are malicious despisers, mockers and violators of the blessed teachings of Jesus Christ. They create dissention and splinter groups and presume to leadership when this has not been entrusted to them.[17] They will therefore be judged harshly by the Lord. Indeed, unless they repent, which hardly ever happens, they will receive eternal death instead of eternal life, hell instead of the kingdom of God. For the apostle said that the person who is divisive and splintering "is warped and sinful; he is self-condemned" (Titus 3:11). These people crucify the Son of God all over again by mocking him and hold the blood of the covenant by which we are saved as unholy. They bring shame to the Spirit of grace, as now unfortunately we see some doing.

Some become anxious during trials they must endure and murmur against the Lord when they might better praise the Lord for it. They will be destroyed by the Destroyer. Others tempt Christ and are bitten by snakes and mortally poisoned with sin. They will perish unless they repent and again look with eyes of faith upon the sign of grace, Jesus Christ. The symbolic, metal serpent in the wilderness looked like a serpent but was not poisonous. It was rather a sign of blessing, so that all who looked upon it were healed by the Lord, who is the healer of all. Jesus Christ was also sent by God in the form of sinful flesh. But he did not know sin. He is the innocent and perfect Lamb of God who takes away the sins of the world. He is the true sign of blessing of grace and eternal life. He was lifted up from the earth on the cross so that those who believe in him are healed from the bite of evil sin and are given eternal life by God.

Item. Let us now consider the twelve men whom Moses sent to spy out the land. They were all frightened and scared by the strong people of that land, the children of Anak and the great walls of the cities. Only Joshua and Caleb remained bold in the Lord and encouraged the community of Israel. For that reason, the others said they should be stoned. The Lord grew angry at Israel and said, "Not one of you [who have complained and been unfaithful] will enter the land I swore with uplifted hand to make your home, except Caleb son of Jephunneh and Joshua son of Nun [who have remained strong in faith]" (Numbers 14:30).

These spies are a symbol of the teachers and leaders of the community who fall away and do not trust the Lord. They rather fear human beings and cause others to fear as well. God-fearing servants set themselves against this and comfort the community with God's word. For this they must often endure suffering from their own brothers. But the Lord knows not only how to deliver his own, but also how to punish those who fall away, the unbelieving and disobedient, just as he did as an example in Israel. That is why the apostle said, "And with whom was he angry for forty years? Was it not with those who sinned, whose bodies fell in the desert? And to whom did God swear that they would never enter his rest if not to those who disobeyed? So we see that they were not able to enter, because of their unbelief" (Hebrews 3:17–19). "Therefore, since the promise of entering his rest still stands, let us be careful that none of you be found to have fallen short of it. For we also have had the gospel preached to us, just as they did; but the message they heard was of no value to them, because those who heard did not combine it with faith. Now we who have believed enter that rest" (Hebrews 4:1–3).

Item. The way God dealt with Moses concerning preparation and ornamentation of the Tabernacle or tent is a symbol from the time of the Law until the time of grace and truth which appeared in Jesus Christ, as we see from both the Letter to the Hebrews and in our own book concerning the Tabernacle of Moses.

Here it is seen that both Moses and Aaron died in the wilderness. They did not enter into the promised land because they provoked the Lord. Joshua led the people and divided up the land. That shows us that both the Law and the Levitical priesthood and its ceremonies ended and were fulfilled in Christ Jesus. These could neither bring anyone to perfection nor take away sins, nor bring justice nor blessings. But the spiritual Joshua, Jesus Christ, the prince of our faith and finisher of our salvation, leads us into the true promised land, the kingdom of God. This kingdom is here already in the Spirit, in the power of the new birth and abundance of spiritual gifts. And it is present in the hereafter in eternal, heavenly majesty and possession of all eternal things. For we shall be like Christ and see him face to face in this coming and perfect nature.

Therefore, let us look at how the promised land and rest are to be obtained. Namely, one must go through the Jordan River, where the waves of water are high and fearful to see. That shows us that we must enter into the kingdom of God with much tribulation, suffering and temporal death. The righteous must endure much and suffer death daily, which is fearful to our human nature. But the priests walk ahead in the Jordan River with the Ark of God. They comfort us with its holiness, that is, with God's word. For that is our comfort and power of life in the midst of death until that time in which we come out of this world into the city of the heavenly rest, where we shall rest with God eternally from all of our working, cares and labors.

We first come out of Egypt, through the sea and into the wilderness. That is, from darkness into the light, freed from the kingdom of Satan, delivered from sin, hell and death, we turn to the true way which leads to eternal life. We go through the Jordan River into the promised land when we leave this life and enter into the blessed rest. But Joshua was commanded by God to take a stone knife and circumcise all those children of Israel who were born in the wilderness and were not yet circumcised. This means for us that all true Israelites must be circumcised of heart by Christ, renouncing the sinful life of the flesh, before they can enter into eternal blessings in the kingdom of the heavenly Father. Furthermore, there follows a symbolic period of rulership by Judges. These Judges often had to deliver Israel from the hands of the Philistines and other enemies, keep peace in the land and judge for the people. All of this is spiritually restored in Christ Jesus. For he is the strong warrior and conqueror who delivers his people from all enemies and brings peace to the conscience. He is the righteous judge of his community. With his word and spirit he will judge the living and the dead on that final day.

Item. The figure of Samson is also restored in Christ Jesus. Samson was the Nazarite of God, a Judge of Israel who took a daughter of the Philistines as his wife. His father and mother could not understand this and did not know that it was part of God's plan when the young man tore the lion apart, slew a thousand Philistines with the jawbone of an ass, or took the city gates of Gaza on his shoulders and carried them up the Hebron mountain. He also won the love of other foreign women and lost his power for their sakes. He fell into the hands of his enemies, who plucked out his eyes and mocked him. But then his hair grew back and he regained his power. The princes of the Philistines gathered together to make offerings to their god, Dagon, and to celebrate that their enemy, Samson, was their prisoner. But Samson took hold of the pillars on which the house sat, one in his right hand and one in his left hand, and pushed so powerfully that the house fell down. So in his death he killed more of his enemies than he had during his life.

This is spiritually fulfilled in Christ. He is the true Nazarene, the holy son of the almighty. He is the Judge of God's Israel who takes the heathens unto himself and makes a community of them. He gathers them by preaching the gospel and they are betrothed to him by faith. The people cannot understand that this was foreseen and ordained by the Lord. He conquered the young lion, that is, Satan, the antagonist of Christians. And through this victory has come all of the sweetness of divine grace, all comfort and renewal of the soul. With the jawbone of an ass, that is, with his unlearned apostles who were reckoned as asses in the eyes of the world, he slew those uncircumcised of heart, the worldly wise and scholars, the enemies of the gospel. From the simple word of the cross God gives to all true supplicators the living water of the Holy Spirit, by which the thirsting soul is filled.

He destroys the gates of hell and frees the captives. With his own body he carries the sins of the world on the wood of the cross. He put aside his divine nature and abandoned his eternal majesty, humbling himself in love for us heathen people, who were lost in idol worship. In accord with the plan of his heavenly Father, for the sake of our salvation, he fell into the hands of the enemy, who took him prisoner, mocked and persecuted him and made fun of his suffering. But the Lord Jesus Christ, the true redeemer, was victorious through his suffering and death over all. He took away the power of the devil, conquered death and brought life and eternal salvation to us.

. . . .

Next comes the symbol of the kingdom of David, son of Jesse. He was the smallest of the brothers and a shepherd of his father's sheep. He was taken from the flocks and anointed by the prophet Samuel to be king over Israel. He killed a lion and a bear, rescued lost sheep and with his own sword he killed Goliath, a hero of the Philistines and an enemy, a mocker and blasphemer of Israel. This caused great rejoicing in Israel, for its greatest enemy was killed. God was praised for this on the harp, drums and psalters. Then David was persecuted by Saul because of Saul's anger and jealousy. He had to hide for a long time in the mountains and caverns. Finally, he became a powerful king over all of Israel.

All of this was spiritually restored in Christ Jesus. For he is the true root of Jesse, a branch of David, a plant of righteousness who was the least in the view of human beings. He is the one true shepherd of his heavenly Father's sheep. He has saved the lost sheep of the human race from the mouth of the lion and the claws of the bear. He was anointed by God with the oil of joy above all others. With his death and the blood of the cross, he defeated Satan, the great Goliath. Therefore, the Israel of God rejoices in the conquering of this great enemy of Christians, the evil Satan, the adversary of the children of God. Our spiritual David, Jesus Christ, in his divine righteousness has taken away our sin and slew death with his eternal life. With his healing grace all condemnation has been removed. That is the joyous gospel with which the Holy Spirit comforts all repentant and troubled hearts. For this God is thanked and we sing and play praises to the Lord in our hearts with great rejoicing in the Spirit.

Item. Christ also was persecuted by unbelieving and godless people and often had to escape from Judea and hide himself in the wilderness. But after this he received his kingdom and was established and inaugurated by God his Father as the mighty king on Mount Zion. God gave him the throne of David to rule in the house of Jacob for eternity, a kingdom without end.

He also comes forward as the peaceful Solomon. He is our peace and hope before God the Father. Through his apostles, who received power from on high during Pentecost, he built the temple in Jerusalem. That is the Christian church. He has adorned it with many spiritual gifts. As was the case with the church of the apostles and is clearly shown in scripture, the apostles apply the promises of Solomon to Christ. What God promised to David, that the fruit of his loins would sit on the throne, was literally fulfilled. Solomon replaced his father as king over Israel, as is clearly shown in scripture and as Solomon himself witnessed. But spiritually this is to be understood as the true Solomon, Jesus Christ. His throne will remain in eternity and he is the king of his community, over the whole of spiritual Israel.

Item. The consecration of the symbolic temple of Solomon in Jerusalem shows us that the community of the Lord is consecrated by God through Jesus Christ with his Holy Spirit. It is a holy temple, a house of the living God, a pillar and foundation of truth. God wills to be worshipped in spirit and in truth in this temple. Here God receives offerings. Here are the true priests and Levites, the children and descendants of the spiritual Aaron, our one high priest Jesus Christ. Here is the tabernacle of our God, the Ark of the Covenant, the pure and holy word of the gospel with all of God's promises of grace concerning forgiveness of sins, reconciliation with God and of eternal life through Jesus Christ. Here is the holy mystery of the signs of sacrament, of baptism and the Lord's Supper, which were given by Christ to all believers.

We must come to this temple to celebrate spiritually unto the Lord the feast of Passover, of Pentecost and of Tabernacles. We celebrate the Passover by preaching that Jesus Christ is our Passover Lamb who was slain for us. By faith in him, we are cleansed of the old yeast of ill will and evil and become a new bread. So we spiritually eat our Passover Lamb with the unleavened bread of integrity. We meditate on our terrible captivity in Egypt, which was under Satan and the rule of darkness, and on how we were delivered from this by the mighty hand of God. The precious blood of the perfect Passover Lamb Jesus Christ is sprinkled on our conscience, protecting us from the coming judgment of this blind world.

We celebrate the feast of Pentecost by coming before God, confessing that we were once captives in Egypt under the terrible Pharaoh. But God marvelously delivered us from that and chose and accepted us as the firstfruits of his creation and as heirs of his eternal kingdom in heaven. He has generously given to us the gifts of heaven and blessed us. For this we praise and thank God and offer him the fruits of justice and thanksgiving from the lips of those who confess his name. It is very important that we truly confess our ignorance, blindness and the weight of sin which weighed us down, but which is countered by the riches of the grace of God which is poured out upon us through Jesus Christ. We meditate on this and praise and thank God for the inexpressible gift of his benevolence which we have received.

We celebrate the feast of Tabernacles by confessing that we are pilgrims in this world and have no abiding place in it. We are under way toward the promised land. We long for entrance into that blessed rest, the heavenly Jerusalem, the city of the living God. There Jesus Christ has prepared a place for us. There we have a tabernacle not made by hands. It is eternal and heavenly and we shall put it on when our earthly tabernacles are broken. That is, when we lay aside this corruptible and mortal flesh and put on a body which is incorruptible, immortal and magnified.

Christ Jesus also spiritually restores the glory of Solomon's kingship, the riches and plenty of gold and silver, the generous peace, the great wisdom and many other gifts, so that even the servants were called blessed who could stand before him and hear the words of wisdom which came from his mouth. All of this is spiritually restored in Christ Jesus. For in him the riches of divine grace are poured out on us. Through him we have the clear and pure word of God, which is better than gold and silver. Through him we have peace with God in our minds. He is our wisdom, justice, holiness and salvation, and the servants who serve him are blessed, those who stand before him, hear his word and obey.

There are also twelve officials or rulers in the royal house of Christ. These are the twelve apostles of the Lord. They are given spiritual authority and rulership over all nations. And there is the household of the king, the members of the Christian church, who are nourished with the food of God's word. At the suitable time the food of the soul is given out. This happens when the gospel is preached to all creatures, the repentant believers are baptized and the bread of the Lord is broken among the baptized. This happens when hungry souls are fed with the word of Christ. As spiritual victors, armed with the weapons of justice, they have destroyed all powers and taken captive all pride and understanding. With the two-edged sword of the Spirit they have slain all enemies and opposition. With the sharp arrows of divine wrath they have shot through the hearts of those seeking repentance. With the chain of the righteous judgment of God they have secured the disobedient, the stubborn and obdurate people to eternal corruption and strife. They have assumed spiritual dominion and serve the royal and priestly offices over the Israel of God in the peace and power of the Spirit, even to the end of the world.

The peace-loving Jesus Christ had such princes, priests and servants in his administration, as well as many Israelite men, soldiers and fathers of that time. These are namely the esteemed group of pastors, shepherds and leaders who are assistants and builders of the holy temple. The cities and towns of the country which make up this good land and kingdom are the spiritual congregations. The land which brings forth good fruit, overflowing with honey and milk, is the people of renewal, who bear all sorts of sweet things in the Spirit. The good trees of the land are the teachers of righteousness, adorned with many gifts. There is great comfort and fruit in Zion, not of the flesh but of the Holy Spirit. There people play on harps, drums and trumpets and the true Israel praises the Lord in truth and in spirit. There people are prepared and adorned in purple and finery in honor of Jesus Christ the king—with spiritual virtues and gifts in the power of faith. There people are salved with the oil of peace, eating the bread of heaven and drinking the wine of holiness for the strengthening of their hearts. There are also the daughters of Pharaoh and other foreigners, and in fact a large crowd of princes and princesses who have come to the royal throne in Zion. These are those who make up the church of Jesus Christ, which the apostles assembled and united in him from among all heathen nations.

In Christ and his community is also a spiritual restoration of the Song of Solomon, of the king and his bride. Christ, the bridegroom, kisses his bride with the holy kiss of peace and takes joy in her beauty and the aroma of her perfumes. These refer to the internal gifts, virtues and anointing of the Holy Spirit with which she is adorned. The full power of this spirituality is in these words of the groom to the bride. "Arise, my darling, my beautiful one, and come with me. See! The winter is past; the rains are over and gone. Flowers appear on the earth; the season of singing has come, the cooing of doves is heard in our land. The fig tree forms its early fruit; the blossoming vines spread their fragrance" (Song of Songs 2:10–13). This means that the time of the Law is gone, the wrath of God is stilled, the punishment of God is taken away. The time of grace has come and the comforting gospel is heard. The sweet fruits of justice are in blooming and the land is fruitful in faith and recognition of God. The flora of the Lord springs forth and the branches of the true vine, Jesus Christ, are full of buds. They give off the sweet smell of life through the power of Christ within them. So it was in the time of the apostolic church and continues even today among all believers.

There is also, spiritually speaking, the sixty strong men of Israel standing around Solomon's bed. Each had a sword at his side to protect against fear in the night. That is, they stand around the bed of Christ and his bride, where they sweetly sleep in the friendship and love of the Spirit. These are the servants of the word, the preachers of the gospel. They are chosen from among those with strong faith in Israel to protect the flock of Christ. They are armed with the sword of the Spirit against the wiles of Satan and against the pestilence that hides in darkness and the arrows which are shot in the night by the spirit of darkness. In short, the entire Song of Songs is spiritually restored in Christ and his community.

We see here also the eternal, spiritual and heavenly kingdom of Christ in the power of God and the Holy Spirit. Here the true Solomon, the prince and king of peace Jesus Christ, rules with all of authority in heaven and on earth and sits on the throne of glory on the right hand of God. He rules on Mount Zion, his church, with the invincible scepter of his divine word. With it he defeats the hearts of the heathen and breaks them to pieces. But he judges and punishes the unbelievers. In this glorious kingdom, justice and faith are triumphant. They have rest in the true peace of Jesus Christ and joy in the Holy Spirit. As conquerors in faith, they are filled with all manner of heavenly goods and riches.

But then, because of Jeroboam, there was also a falling away from the kingdom of Solomon. He left behind the true worship of God and chose a false kind of worship. He erected two calves at Bethel and Dan and installed priests and Levites from among the worst of the people. He filled their hands and erected an altar for offerings. And so he led Israel into error and sin, until they were finally taken into captivity by the Assyrian kings. Likewise, because of the Antichrist, there was a spiritual falling away from true doctrine in the kingdom of Christ. He left behind the true worship of God in Jerusalem and erected for himself a false worship. In a hypocritical way, he copied all that Christ taught and commanded, with all of his priests, altars, offerings, church services and pomp and his terrible defilement of the sacraments of Jesus Christ. All of this he adorned with passages from scripture, just as if it were the true service of God, as if it were in service of the almighty God in heaven. But it is finally nothing but terrible idolatry and blasphemy against God. For it is all so obviously contrary to the gospel of Christ, just as clearly as what was done by Jeroboam, doing what he thought was right, was contrary to the Law of Moses. Therefore, God-fearing people should not go to these calves to pray. Rather, with the pious Israelites, they must shun this false worship of the spiritual Jeroboam, the Antichrist. They must come to the heavenly Jerusalem, to the community of the Lord, to honor and pray to the Most High in his temple, according to his command.

Item. Among the earthly and fallen Israel, besides the false worship of the golden calves of Jeroboam, there were other incidents of idolatry with Baal and other heathen gods. Even though some prophets and kings admonished against such practices and partly purified them, both calves remained right up until the captivity of Israel. In the same way, under the rule of the Antichrist, various terrible forms of idolatry and divisions were introduced over time. Although these were opposed and interrupted by some, the two golden calves of Jeroboam, that is, the shameful manipulation of the holy baptism and holy supper of Jesus Christ remained. Salvation itself was tied to them and people sought righteousness in them, to the extent of forsaking the grace of the precious blood of Jesus Christ.

Item. The falling away of Israel happened because of Jeroboam. But there was also a falling away in Judah. Likewise, in the first falling away many good Christians remained with God and his word, for falling away was already evident in the time of the apostles. There were many antichrists and apostates at work then, but many more held fast to the house and temple of Jerusalem, that is, to the kingdom of Christ and his true worship. But in time many more fell away and their children were led astray, erecting more and various forms of idolatry, until finally they were all carried into a Babylonian captivity among the Antichrist. Just as in the time of Israel and Judah there were faithful prophets, God-fearing priests, Israelites and Jewish people who would have nothing to do with the false forms of worship, there were doubtless those who in the time of the spiritual falling away also remained and did not follow the Antichrist. We can see this from the Revelation of John.

And so the splendid kingdom of the spiritual Solomon, the divine church of Jesus Christ as it was in the time of the apostles, was miserably destroyed. The Holy City was given to the heathen, the Antichrist and his power. This is just as happened literally with Israel and Judah, for after building the temple and the long reign of kings, many sins, impurities and evil emerged over time. And so God gave his people into the hands of the Babylonians and the Holy City and temple were ruined and laid to waste.

This devastation of the Holy City and the temple happened through the Antichrist, the whore of Babylon, who, decked in purple, silks, scarlet and gold, inverted the divine order.[18] This whore holds the golden chalice in her hand and is drunk with the blood of the saints and the martyrs of Jesus Christ. She has also made the heathens drunk with the wine of harlotry and magical arts. Her merchants have become rich by the power of her favors, her possessions and fashions. The kings and princes of this earth trafficked with this whore and do so even today. In short, she is the mother of all ignominy on this earth. All of those whose souls she possesses, and who want to be saved, must renounce this whore and come out of Babylon. As the scripture says, "Flee from Babylon! Flee to the land of the Chaldeans! Come out of her, my people, so that you will not share in her sins, so that you will not receive any of her plagues; for her sins are piled up to heaven, and God has remembered her crimes" (Revelation 18:4–5).

Now, we ought to note here that Israel was in captivity twice. It was delivered twice and twice entered into the kingdom of glory. The temple was built twice on the same form and foundation. We have already spoken about the first captivity and deliverance from Egypt, of the kingdom of David and Solomon and of the glorious building of the temple. We speak now of the second deliverance out of Babylon, of the second building of the temple and the city of Jerusalem. For God now wondrously delivers his people each day out of captivity in Babylon. God delivers his elect from the clutches of the Babylonian whore with steadfast admonition from the holy scriptures and his messengers to come out of Babylon, leave that which is impure alone and to go with joy to Jerusalem, there to rebuild the temple and the city. This is the church of Christ, as can be clearly seen (praise God!)

We ought to consider that those of the people and children of Israel who married heathen wives in Babylon, which was contrary to God's Law, had to leave them behind, purifying themselves of that which was heathen. This means and teaches us two things. One, that all true Christians must separate themselves from all manner of Babylonian idolatry and communion, cleansing themselves in body and spirit as a holy people of the Lord and worthy servants of God. This cannot happen unless and until a person leaves behind all of the offenses of the heathens and Babylonians. Secondly, marriage between people of God and heathen wives, which is contrary to the Law, will not be tolerated by God. Therefore, Ezra broke it off, because such marriages were impure in the eyes of the Lord. The sons of God were severely punished by God for this in the original world and it was strictly forbidden by Moses. If such marriages and mixing of the children of God with unbelievers was so strongly forbidden in the time of the Law, a time of imperfection, how could it possibly be allowed now in this time of Christian perfection, according to the gospel and in the eyes of the community? Each of you may ponder that in your heart.[19]

The temple of our Lord and the city of the living God is being rebuilt. As it was literally in the second building of the temple in Jerusalem, so it is now figuratively, being built on the same form and foundation, which is the Spirit. The enemies of Judah and Benjamin wanted to build with Zerubbabel and the others, but Zerubbabel and other elders of Israel said to them, "You have no part with us in building a temple to our God. We alone will build it for the Lord, the God of Israel, as King Cyrus, the king of Persia, commanded us" (Ezra 4:3). The heathen ridiculed Nehemiah and his brothers concerning the rebuilding of the city. They wanted to oppose them with violence and tear down the city walls. But Nehemiah and the rest of the people worked even harder on the walls of the city, some keeping watch and others working, but all with swords ready to defend against intruders.

We see the same thing today in the Spirit. For now the temple of the Lord, the community of God, is being built on the original foundation, on the foundation of the prophets and the apostles, with Christ as the cornerstone. Those living stones which were scattered here and there are now being gathered as building materials for the house of the Lord. We now have true servants of the word, true preachers of the gospel of Jesus Christ. The divine order and teachings of the apostles are being restored and renewed. These are genuine repentance, belief in God, true recognition of Jesus Christ and the Holy Spirit, true observance of Christian baptism and the Lord's Supper, a reverent life of brotherly love and trust among all saints, employment of gospel separation or the ban and all institutions of God, through the power of the Spirit. We now sing praises to the Lord with great joy in the Spirit. We now offer to the Lord living, holy and acceptable sacrifices, which are reasonable and true worship of God by which God wills to be served. We bring to the Lord urgent prayer as a sweet perfume and lift up holy hands for the evening offering. So the temple of the Lord, the house of the living God, stands on the original foundation, in its original form, visage and glory.

But the enemies of Judah and Benjamin who want to build the house of the Lord along with Zerubbabel are those who falsely and hypocritically declare the gospel. It is as if they want to serve God, but their hearts are divided. They are not the true builders and laborers in Israel. Therefore, true Christians cannot build with them. No person except the true Israelites, descendants of Abraham and Isaac, are suited to this task, that is, the reborn person of God, born anew from the heavenly Father through Jesus Christ and the Holy Spirit.

243

The heathen come and mock the elders who are building this Holy City of Jerusalem. They consider them too weak. They speak of them mockingly and with blasphemy. To the powerful of this world, the educated and perverted, it is craziness that such a poor and forsaken people would undertake to rebuild the devastated Jerusalem, the community of Christ, and to strengthen its walls. They seem not to remember that Christ established his church through simple, unlearned apostles and gave glory to such as these. They also take no notice that in the gospels, Christ said, "I praise you, Father, Lord of heaven and earth, because you have hidden these things from the wise and learned, and revealed them to little children. Yes, Father, for this was your good pleasure" (Matthew 11:25–26).

God gave witness to this through Isaiah with these words, "The wisdom of the wise will perish, the intelligence of the intelligent will vanish" (Isaiah 29:14). And again, Paul said to the Corinthians, "Where is the wise man? Where is the scholar? Where is the philosopher of this age? Has not God made foolish the wisdom of the world?" (1 Corinthians 1:20). And another passage says, "Look, you scoffers, wonder and perish, for I am going to do something in your days that you would never believe, even if someone told you" (Acts 13:41).

When these scoffers of Israel see that their mocking remains unnoticed and that the work of the Lord in building the Holy City is not slowed one bit by it, they become angry and conspire together against the Lord and his community, for they do not want this Jerusalem to be built. These are the tyrants, with their severe edicts, with water, fire and sword. These are the learned scholars, who would weaken the scriptures with their philosophies, arguments and sharp reasoning, trying through their preaching and writing to arouse the rulers into persecution of the people who are building the city of Jerusalem, to root them out and kill them, and in that way hinder the work of the Lord.[20]

But the people of the Lord are armed against such as these, not with weapons of the flesh (as some—unfortunately—lacking in all understanding, have done)[21] but with the armor of God. They have the sword of righteousness in their hands, the breastplate of salvation and the shield of faith to help them survive the fiery arrows of Satan. Their souls possess the mighty, two-edged sword of God and Christian patience. With these they can be victorious over their enemies. They will rebuild the walls of Jerusalem with such armor. Their hearts are brave and courageous, for they know that God in heaven is their aide in times of peril. They know that the hand of Christ is with them and that even with all their power, the heathen, who have no place in the house of the Lord or in the city of Jerusalem, cannot prevent them from rebuilding this city and temple. The Lord is with his people and faithfully helps his servants. Amen.

Item. The second temple and the rebuilt city of Jerusalem stood and lasted until the first coming of Christ. During that time the people had to endure many afflictions and persecutions. They were cruelly plagued and murdered by Antiochus and other tyrants because they would not break the Law of God and would not worship or honor the idols of the heathen. Even so, many did fall away. As hypocrites seeking their own benefit, they served these godless tyrants and lords. These very ones often became the archenemies, traitors and persecutors of the God-fearing people, as we read in the book of Maccabees and in other history books.

Likewise, the second spiritual temple and city of Jerusalem will stand and last until the second coming and revelation of our lord Jesus Christ. For an eternal kingdom is given under heaven to the people of God, and the kingdom of Christ has no end. But this does not change the fact that all who live godly lives in Christ Jesus will suffer persecution. These Christians will be robbed and their houses will be burned down. They are considered to be crazy by the heathen. They are ridiculed as foolish. They are reckoned as fanatics. The bodies of these servants of God are given as food to the birds of the air. Flesh of the saints is given as food to the wild animals of the field. Their innocent blood flows like water and there is no one to bury the dead. In short, Antiochus is insane, mad without measure, in being against these pious people who believe the gospel and attempt to live by it. But those who honor and follow in worship of his idols he glorifies and makes rich, as we see every day.

Now from all that has been said it is clear that all things are spiritually restored and fulfilled in Christ Jesus, from the time of his authority until his future return and revelation, just as the apostle Peter said. Therefore, we may expect no sort of restitution or restoration of things other than as spiritually done in Christ Jesus. He is the Alpha and Omega, the first of all creatures, the perfection of all works of God, both now in the Spirit and hereafter in finished perfection. There all things will be renewed and restored, changed and clarified into that which is eternal. The final reward and rulership of all believers and saints will be in that place where God the Father and the Lord Jesus

Christ, along with the Holy Spirit and the angels exist forever and ever. All that the prophets announced and promised concerning the rebuilding of the tabernacle of David, of the kingdom of Christ in glory and of the revenge of God against the Babylonians—in summary, all that is to be restored—must be understood according to the rule of interpretation that the literal is changed into the spiritual. That way, the structure of our most holy Christian faith is greatly strengthened. For then we see and understand clearly that what we believe and confess was originally prefigured by many beautiful symbols and was subsequently clarified, witnessed to and confirmed by Jesus Christ, the eternal truth.

Now may the eternal, almighty God, who from the beginning created and worked in all things, first in symbolic form and then true essence through his eternal word, his only son Jesus Christ, guard us in his truth through his unspeakable mercy. May he renew in us the inner person and keep us in his true way until the end. May we stand with joy before the judgment seat of Jesus Christ, when he comes again in power with the angels with the flaming sword of wrath, raised against those who have not believed in God nor were obedient to the gospel. May this gospel be clarified in his saints and marvelously revealed in all believers, in the resurrection and revelation of heavenly adoration. May we be clothed in the power of Christ and be with him in eternal glory, accepting and possessing with him eternal and incorruptible honor in perfection. Amen. *Soli Sapienti Deo Gloria.*

Menno Simons

Menno Simons was born in 1496 in Witmarsum, Friesland. Little is known of his background. His parents were dairy farmers, and he entered the priesthood in 1524 at the age of 28. He said that during his first year of the priesthood, he began to have doubts concerning the doctrine of transubstantiation of the eucharist. Of course, Holland had for generations been a breeding ground for Sacramentarianism, whose adherents denied the Roman teaching on the nature of the bread and wine. This history of Sacramentarianism probably explains why the Calvinist rather than Lutheran version of Protestantism took such a strong hold in Holland. The earliest Dutch Anabaptists also emerged from among Sacramentarian circles. But in spite of his doubts, Menno remained a Roman Catholic priest until 1536, when he left the priesthood to join the Anabaptist movement. What prompted Menno to join the Anabaptists was the defeat of the Münsterite Anabaptist "kingdom." His own brother was killed in that fiasco. Because of his own Bible study, Menno was personally convinced of the rightness not only of the Anabaptist view of the sacraments, but also of adult baptism. Yet he held these convictions in silence. It was only when he saw that the Anabaptists were being deceived by unscrupulous leaders such as those in Münster that he decided that he had to publicly join the movement. Because the largest denomination whose historical roots date back to the Anabaptists, the Mennonites, bears Menno's name, it is often assumed that Menno was the founder of the Anabaptists. But the movement was already more than a decade old in Switzerland, and in its sixth year in Holland, before Menno joined. His real significance lies in the fact that he assumed leadership among the Dutch Anabaptists at a crisis point in their history, following the Münsterite debacle. From that point until his death, Menno became a central organizer of the scattered congregations and a chief opponent of the politically chiliastic trends on the one hand and the airy "spiritu-

alist" trends on the other. *Menno supported a sober biblicist version of Anabaptism in which a disciplined community of believers sought to follow the simple teachings of Christ and the doctrines of the apostles. His motto, which appeared on most of his writings, was taken from 1 Corinthians 3:11, "For no one can lay any foundation other than the one already laid, which is Jesus Christ." Menno spent the rest of his life as a fugitive with a price on his head. Many stories have circulated concerning his narrow escapes from the law. He traveled extensively among the congregations. Although crippled during the final years of his life, he continued his activities and writing up to the end. He died in January of 1561, twenty-five years after becoming an Anabaptist.*

The writing presented here, "Meditation on the Twenty-fifth Psalm," written in 1537, is rendered in the form of a prayer to God. It reveals the spiritual depths of Menno's early Anabaptist career and the deep shame he felt for having remained a part of the Roman church long after his personal convictions should have dictated his leaving that institution. Yet Menno decided that the love and forgiveness of God would cover all of his sins. He approached his God, therefore, in a repentant but assured manner. There have been many editions of Menno's works. The translation here is taken from the 1681 edition of his Opera omnia theologica, of alle de godtgeleerde wercken.

"A Meditation on the Twenty-fifth Psalm" (1537)
Menno Simons

1. *To you, O Lord, I lift my soul; in you I trust, O My God. Do not let me be put to shame.* Lord and king, sovereign of heaven and earth! I call you my Lord, though I am not worthy to be called your servant. For I have not served only you from my youth, but your enemy, the devil. Even so, I do not doubt your grace, for I find in your word of truth that you are an abundant and good Lord to all who call on you. Therefore, Lord, I do call on you. Hear me, Lord, hear me! I lift up my soul to you with a sure heart and in full confidence—not my head or my hands, as the hypocrites do. I lift up my soul to you alone, I say, not to Abraham, who never knew us, nor to Israel, who never knew us. But you are our Lord and Father. You are our redeemer. As the prophet said, this has been your name since ancient times. Loving Father, that is why I trust in you. For I know without a doubt that you are a faithful God for all those who put their trust in you. When

I am in darkness, you are my light. When I am in prison, you are there with me. When I am deserted, you are my comfort. In death, you are my life. When people curse me, you bless me. When people cause me sorrow, you bring me joy. When people kill me, you bring resurrection. When I walk through the valley of darkness, you are always with me. Lord, it is right that I raise my troubled and miserable soul to you, trusting in your promises without shame.

2. *Nor let my enemies triumph over me. No one whose hope is in you will ever be put to shame.* Lord of hosts, Lord of lords! My flesh is weak, my affliction and need is great. Even so, I do not fear the physical mocking of my enemies. But this I do fear more and more, that I would deny your great and praise-worthy name and fall away from your truth. Then my enemies would revel in my weakness and disobedience, mocking me, saying, "Now where is your God? Now where is your Christ?" Your divine honor would be blasphemed because of me. Lord, protect me! Protect me, Lord! My enemies are powerful and numerous, more than the hairs on my head and the grass of the field. My corrupt flesh finds no peace. Satan stalks me like a bellowing lion, looking to devour me. The murderous world seeks to kill me, just as all those who seek your honor have been hated, persecuted, burned and murdered. Miserable human being that I am, I do not know where to turn. There is oppression, tribulation, distress and fear everywhere. There is fighting within and persecution outside. Even so, I say with King Jehoshaphat that if I do not know where to go, I will lift my eyes to you and trust in your grace and goodness, just as Abraham did at Gerar, as Jacob did in Mesopotamia, as Joseph did in Egypt, as Moses did in Midian, as Israel did in the wilderness, as David did in the mountains, as Hezekiah did in Jerusalem, as the young men did in the fiery furnace and as Daniel did in the den of lions. These godfearing ancestors all placed their hope in you, waited on you. And they were not put to shame.

3. *But they will be put to shame who are treacherous without excuse.* Sovereign Lord, just as all who fear you are covered by your merciful grace, so also does your solemn wrath go out toward all those who scorn you, who walk according to their own desires and who say, with foolishness in their hearts, "There is no God. We have made an agreement with death and a covenant with hell. God knows nothing of our dealings. Thick clouds cover over the works of human beings.

We eat and drink, and tomorrow we die. Life is short and full of troubles and hard work and there is no revival when it is all over. We will live as we want to for as long as it lasts, and use the creation as it pleases us. We will oppress the poor and deceive the righteous. We will condemn them to a most shameful death." Beloved Lord, that is the error of the world. It is nothing other than the lusts of the flesh, lusts of the eyes and prideful living. There is nothing but idle falsehood, injustice and tyranny wherever you look. Very few are those who truly fear your name. Paul said, "The mind of sinful man is death" (Romans 8:6). That judgment is true. He who lives according to the flesh will die, as the whole of scripture teaches. If people do not repent, nothing is more sure than your stern wrath. Therefore, beloved Lord, threaten, punish, admonish and teach them. Then perhaps they will regret their ways, recognize the truth and be saved. They are, after all, the work of your hand, created in your image and purchased at a great price. Let them not, therefore, come to a shameful end, as did Cain, Sodom, Pharaoh and Antiochus and all others who unjustly scorned you.

4. *Show me your ways, O Lord, teach me your paths.* Lord of hosts, I know your grace through your word. There is but one way which leads to life. For the flesh, it is too small and narrow—but a foot wide, as Esdras says it. It is ringed on all sides by thorns and other dangers. Few find it, and even fewer walk along it. It is like a gem hidden in a field which nobody can find unless the Spirit shows it to him. Beloved Lord, there is no other way than you alone. All who walk in you will find the portals of life. But the other way seems attractive to the flesh. Its appearance is pleasing. It is wide and straight. But it leads to death. The whole world walks along this way without fear or even a second thought. Along this way, that which is corruptible is valued above that which is incorruptible, evil is valued above what is good, and darkness is valued above the light of the world. They walk along this reversed and twisted way. They weary themselves in the ways of injustice and do not acknowledge to way of the Lord. It is clearly true that the way of error seems right in the eyes of the fool. But I know through your Spirit and your word that it is the way which leads to certain hell. Therefore, I pray, beloved Lord, be gracious toward this miserable sinner. Show me your pathway and teach me your ways. For your way is the true path, the way of blessing and love, humility, chastity, full of peace and goodness, and will lead my soul into eternal life.

5. *Guide me in your truth and teach me, for you are God my Savior, and my hope is in you all day long.* Lord, Lord! As David said, "My tears have been my food day and night" (Psalm 42:3). My heart moves within my body. My strength has left me. The light of my eyes is almost gone because of the many perils and entanglements set for my soul. I fear constantly that I might be lured from your truth by human fallacies or Satan's trickery.

Lord, the guile of the learned is sharp and cunning. Satan masterfully uses his subtlety. There are those who teach nothing but human doctrines and commandments, which are fruitless and foul trees. Others constantly speak of grace, Spirit and Christ. But at the same time they daily trample on your grace, betray your Holy Spirit and crucify your son with their idle and worldly lives, as is well known. There are those who at one time came out from Sodom, Egypt and Babylonia and accepted the yoke of the cross of Christ. Yet now they are again devoured by the devil, led astray by false prophets, just as if they had never known your word and your will. They are possessed of seven spirits worse than before and their present errors are worse than that which they left behind. They bedeck themselves with your holy word and ordinances, imagining that what you never contemplated, much less commanded, is now your preference, word and will. This is why I am troubled and full of sadness and heartache. For I know that your true word is not the deceitful lies which they teach. It is the upright truth to which your perfect mouth witnesses here on earth and is taught in this troubled world. All who are in the truth hear your voice, the voice of the one true shepherd and bridegroom. They flee from the voice of strangers, fearing they will be deceived.

Lord! Consider your troubled and poor servants. You examine every heart. You know me. You know that I seek and desire nothing but your will. Loving Lord, direct and teach me in your truth. For you alone are my God and Lord, my salvation. Apart from you I know no other. You alone are my hope, my comfort, my shield, fortress and protection. I place my trust in you and in my fear, tribulation and suffering I daily wait on you.

6. *Remember, O Lord, your great mercy and love, for they are from of old.* Lord of hosts! When I swim in the merciful waters of your grace I find that I can neither plumb nor measure the depths. Your compassion is the greatest of all your works. Lord, who ever came to you with a devout heart and was turned away? Who ever sought you

and did not find you? Who ever desired aid from you and was not given help. Who ever prayed for your grace and did not receive it? Who ever called upon you and was not heard? Yes, beloved Lord, how many you have received in grace when according to your strict sense of justice they would have deserved something else. Adam departed from you and believed the counsel of the serpent. He transgressed your covenant became for you a child of death. But your fatherly love would not allow him to be thrown aside. In grace you sought after him, you called and admonished him and covered his nakedness with pelts of fur. You mercifully comforted him with a promise concerning his seed. Paul, your chosen vessel, was at one time like a roaring lion and a ravaging wolf against your holy mountain. Yet you shone your grace upon him and enlightened his blindness. You called him from heaven and chose him to be an apostle and servant in your house.

Beloved Lord, I am the greatest of sinners and the least among the saints. I am unworthy to be called your child or servant, for I have sinned against heaven and before you. There was a time when I opposed your glorious word and your holy will with all my power. With open eyes and understanding heart I disputed against your clear truth. I taught and lived according to the flesh and sought my own selfish honor rather than your justice, honor, truth and word. Yet this miserable sinner was never abandoned by your fatherly grace. You accepted me in love and converted me to a new understanding. You led me with your right hand and taught me through your Holy Spirit. Then by my own free will I began also to strive against the world, the flesh and the devil. I renounced all my comforts, serenity, honor and easy living and willingly took upon myself the heavy cross of the Lord Jesus Christ. Now I also am an inheritor of that promised kingdom with all servants of God and disciples of Christ. So again I say, your mercy is the greatest of all your works. Therefore, beloved Lord, come to my aid. Stand by me and comfort me. Comfort this miserable sinner.

My soul is in mortal need and I am surrounded by the danger of hell. Lord, help me, protect me and do not scorn me. Consider your great goodness in which all take part who have placed their hope in your holy name and gracious mercy since the beginning of the world.

7. *Remember not the sins of my youth and my rebellious ways; according to your love remember me, for you are good, O Lord.* Sovereign Lord! I was born of sinful seed and was conceived in sin. I am born of sinful flesh. The evil seed of Adam is sown in my heart and much sorrow

has flowed from it. Miserable sinner that I am, I did not recognize my transgressions until your Spirit showed them to me. I thought I was a Christian. But when I saw myself truly, what I found was wholly earthly, of the flesh, and outside of your word. What was light to me is darkness. What was truth to me is falsehood. What was righteousness to me is sinful. My worship of God was idolatry and my life was surely death. Loving God, I did not recognize who I was until I saw myself mirrored in your holy word. Then I recognized my blindness, nakedness and inborn sinfulness. As Paul, I saw that nothing good was in my flesh. All was ulcerous and blisterous from head to toe. My gold was filth, my wheat was chaff, my deeds were deceptions and lies. I walked before you according to the flesh. My thoughts were of the flesh and my words and works were without reverence to God. I was impure whether waking or sleeping, my praying was hypocrisy and nothing I did was without sin. Lord, think not on the sins of my youth which I committed in such great number, both knowingly and unknowingly, before you. Also, do not remember the transgressions I commit daily because of my extreme weakness. But consider me according to your great mercy. Where I am blind, enlighten me. Where I am naked, clothe me. Where I am injured, heal me. Where I am dead, raise me up. I know of no other light, life and healing balm apart from you. Accept me in grace and give me your mercy, blessing and confidence, Lord, for the sake of your own goodness.

8. *Good and upright is the Lord; therefore he instructs sinners in his ways.* Lord of hosts! I have walked before you in unrighteousness since my youth. I am ashamed to turn my eyes toward heaven. Yet I do come before your throne of mercy, for I know that you are gracious and good. You do not desire that sinners should die but that they repent and have life. You sent your faithful servant Moses and through this messenger you imparted to Israel the service of the Law. Also your servants, the prophets, preached the way of repentance and brought the bread of life to the people. They sternly admonished sin, proclaimed your grace and taught the way of justice. Your sharp and dividing word was in their mouths. Their lives shone out like lamps of gold. They were as blossoming olive trees, as the aroma of expensive incense, indeed, as a beautiful hillside covered with roses and lilies. But people did not heed them. In their anger they threw them out, mocked them and persecuted them, even killing them. Even so, the fountains of your goodness were not stopped up. You sent your beloved son, the most

precious guarantee of your grace. He preached your word and fulfilled your righteousness. He completed your will and bore our sins, extinguishing them with his blood and bringing reconciliation. He overcame the devil, hell, sin and death. He secured grace, mercy, approval and peace for all those who believe in him with a true heart. Obedience to him is eternal life. He sent out his apostles as messengers and preachers of peace and they spread this grace throughout the entire world. They shone like bright beacons for all people to see and erring sinners like me could be led to the path of justice. Lord, praise and honor is due, not to me, but to your name. I love their words and follow their example. I believe in your beloved son, whom they preached to me. I seek your will and way. I confess your great love, not in myself but through you. For you, Lord, are good and I am evil. You are truth and I am falsehood. You are just and I am unjust. Teach me, beloved Lord, in your ways of justice. Teach me, for I am a lamb of your fold. Take me into your care, under the shelter of your wing. Cover me, for I am greatly troubled, miserable and sorrowful unto death.

9. *He guides the humble in what is right and teaches them his way.* Sovereign Lord! Your blessed grace has shined on me, your divine word has taught me and your Holy Spirit has led me. Now I have left behind the seat of mockery, the counsel of the godless and the way of the sinful. I was one of the godless and carried the standard of unrighteousness for many years. I was the first among the foolish. Useless words, idleness, gambling and drinking and gluttony was how I spent the time each day. Fear of God was never before my eyes. I was a prince and lord of Babylon. I was sought and liked by everyone. I loved the world and the world loved me. I had the most prominent place among the guests in the places of worship and was most celebrated among all people—even among the elders of many years. I was honored by everyone. When I spoke, they were silent. When I called, they came. When I dismissed them, they left. They did what I wanted. My word triumphed in all matters. Every wish of my heart was fulfilled. But like Solomon, I saw that all is vanity. And like Paul, I held everything as nothing. I left behind the haughty, godless living of this world and sought you and your kingdom. Then I found that everything was reversed. Where I was once honored, now I am dishonored. Where I was once loved, now I am hated. Those who once were friends are now enemies. Where I was once held to be wise, now I am considered a fool. Where I was once thought to be pious, now I am thought evil.

Where I was once considered to be a Christian, now I am considered to be a heretic. Indeed, everyone now sees me as wicked and an evil person. Lord, comfort me, protect your suffering servant, for I am immensely poor and miserable. My sins rise up against me and the whole world hates and mocks me. Lords and princes persecute me. The learned curse and mock me. My best friends have left me and those who once stood with me now hold me at a distance. Who will show me mercy and accept me? I am miserable, beloved Lord. Have mercy on me and accept me with honor. There is nobody who can protect me but you alone. So I pray, beloved Lord, incline your ear to my request, lead me by your right hand, guide me on the right path so that my feet do not stumble on the dark hills. I see that the human race neither teaches nor does what is right. Hypocrisy and deceit is in all flesh. The fraudulent sects are great and many in number, each one claiming to be building on the foundation. But they do not have your truth. Beloved Lord, beloved Lord, teach me and do not cast me out from before you. For I am miserable and walk among lions and bears who seek to devour my soul and lead me away from the way of truth. Lord, strengthen me! Lord, protect me, so that I remain in your way. For I know surely that you are the perfect and pure truth and the sure way of peace.

10. *All the ways of the Lord are loving and faithful for those who keep the demands of his covenant.* Lord of hosts! People boast of your grace and goodness despite the fact that in all of their conduct they are seen to be children of disgrace. They lie and deceive, eat and drink with gluttony, fornicate and commit adultery. They are greedy and quarrelsome, they curse and swear without restraint. And then they cover all of this with your grace and the blood of Christ. They all sing and shout, "The Lord's mercy is great, Christ died for our sins, all of our works are but sin and unrighteousness." This is certainly true, beloved Lord, but yet I know that they have no part in you. Their hope is shallow, their labors bear no fruit and their works are useless. Indeed, their hope is like a dry thistle flower blowing in the wind. They will have no part in your kingdom, for they remain unrepentant and do not believe in your truth. They do not acknowledge that your grace is eternally over those who fear you and hold to your covenant. As David said, your goodness is for the saints and your concern is for your chosen ones. Your eye is on the righteous and your ear is inclined for those who pray. But you turn your face from evildoers. Their

memory will be rooted out from the earth. I am your friend, for I do what you have commanded. It is true, beloved Lord, that Christ was given for us and that he died for us. But not so that we may simply go on living according to our lusts and sinful will, but so that we may live according to your good will and word, according to your commandments. I know, beloved Lord, that you are no less just than good, that you hate evil. You love the faithful people and the good people are your friends. But the time will come when you will be a righteous judge of the wicked. Of what benefit was the pure blood of the eternal covenant to Cain and Judas, who despised your grace and, by their own murder, excluded themselves from the virtues of your son? Of what benefit was it to Pilate, Herod, Annas and Caiaphas to have seen with their eyes the gracious wellsprings of your goodness, Jesus Christ, and to have touched him, when they condemned this innocent, spotless lamb, the king of glory, to death on the cross? But to those who have kept your covenant and heeded your witnesses, as Abel, Enoch, Noah, Abraham, Isaac and Jacob did in their time, your ways are peace and joy, great mercy, goodness and trust.

11. *For the sake of your name, O Lord, forgive my iniquity, though it is great.* Lord, Lord! With the holy David I pray to you, do not punish me in your anger and do not chastise me in your indignation. For I know that my wounds are many, infected and stinking. My sins weigh on me like a heavy weight and there is no peace in my bones. As the beloved David did, I humble myself before you from the depths of my heart. Beloved Lord! You are a great and terrible God! I have sinned, done injustice before you. I have been godless and fallen away from you. I have not walked according to your commandments and laws. I have scorned your grace and cast away your holy word. I have crucified your beloved son, grieved your Holy Spirit and done injustice in all of my works. Lord, I am frightened by the measure of my sins, for I know of no evil which I have not done. As Cain, I have been greedy. As Sodom, I have been proud and impure. As the Pharaoh, I have been hard-hearted. As Korah, I have been rebellious. As Shimri, I have been lecherous. As Saul, I have been disobedient. As Jeroboam, I have worshipped idols. As Joab, I have been a hypocrite. As Nebuchadnez-zar, I have been arrogant. As Balaam, I have been envious. As Nabal, I have been a drunkard. As Sannacherib, I have been a braggart. As Rabshakeh, I have been a blasphemer. As Herod, I have been blood-thirsty. As Ananias, I have been a liar. I can say with King Manasseh,

my sins are more numerous than the sands of the sea and the stars in the heavens. They haunt me day and night and nothing good dwells in my flesh. What I seek and bring forth is all unrighteousness and sin. I do not do that which I will, but that which I do not want to do. Miserable man that I am, I do not know where to turn. In myself, I find nothing but failings, impure desires and a vat of sinfulness. If I go to my neighbor, he has nothing which can help me, neither herb nor dressing. Your word alone can heal all things. As Paul said, the reward for sin is death, but your grace is eternal life. I seek and desire this grace, for it alone is the medicament which can heal my sick soul. The sinful woman sought this grace, for she recognized that she was in need of healing (Luke 7). David sought this grace when he had put the innocent Uriah to death and slept with Bathsheba. His sickness was great when he saw his evil deed and he said, "I have sinned against the Lord." He desired healing and said, "Have mercy on me, O God, according to your unfailing love; according to your great compassion blot out my transgressions. Wash away all my iniquity and cleanse me from my sin" (Psalm 51:1–2). From that moment on, the word of the prophet was full of grace to his ears, "Your sins have been taken away." His heart was at peace and he praised your name. Your mercies were proclaimed far and wide and he praised your grace above all of your works. Lord! Beloved Lord! I am a miserable sinner, suffering from the same sickness. I need the same medicine. Do not close to me the pharmacy of your mercifulness. I seek no comfort but from you alone. Lord, help me for your holy name's sake, so that I may give you thanks and praise eternally. Wash away all of my sins and be merciful toward my misdeeds, for they are many.

12. *Who, then, is the man that fears the Lord? He will instruct him in the way chosen for him.* Sovereign Lord! Your way is the way of peace, and blessed is the person who walks there. For mercy, love, justice, humility, obedience and patience are found along this way. Such a person clothes the naked, feeds the hungry, satisfies the thirsty, comforts the needy, and reproves, warns, consoles and admonishes. Such a person is sober, honest, modest, upright and just. Such a person gives no reason for offense and walks toward eternal life. But there are very few who find this way. I fear, beloved Lord, that hardly ten in a thousand find this way, and of those, hardly five really walk it. So it has been since the beginning. For when there were only four people on earth, the scripture says that three were disobedient and the fourth

was killed by his brother. There were only eight righteous ones who were saved from the flood, and one of those was disrespectful to his father. In Sodom and Gomorrah and the surrounding area, there were only four righteous ones, and one of those turned back to look and was turned into a pillar of salt. More than six hundred thousand fighting men came out of Egypt, among whom only two were able to enter into the promised land. Not, beloved Lord, that all who died along the way were damned. But it was due to their unbelief that their way into the promised land of Canaan was delayed.

Loving Lord, it is the same today concerning that eternal promised land, if only we would walk in that path which you have chosen for us. But instead we walk along that crooked way of death and just like those who did not inherit the temporal land of Canaan, so we refuse to inherit the eternal land. Lord, I sigh as I say it, who is there who truly fears the Lord? Who is there who truly understands? Who is there who truly quests after God? "All have turned away, they have together become worthless; there is no one who does good, not even one. Their throats are open graves; their tongues practice deceit. The poison of vipers is on their lips. Their mouths are full of cursing and bitterness. Their feet are swift to shed blood; ruin and misery mark their ways, and the way of peace they do not know. There is no fear of God before their eyes" (Romans 3:12–18). All that is found among them is mistrust and lies. They disavow and mock your justice, all the while singing and saying much about your truth and praising your holy name. Yet there is not to be found even one ripened grape in their vineyard or even one suitable fruit on their trees. But those who fear you, Lord, withdraw from all evil. As Sirach said, fear of you allays sin and is the beginning of wisdom. Your eyes are upon those who fear you. Your Holy Spirit leads them and your gracious hand protects them. They will neither fear nor tremble, for you are their protection and shield against the mid-day sun. You have freed them from the guilt of sin and have rescued them from the consequences of their transgression. You enlighten them and make their souls rejoice. You give them grace, salvation and abundant peace. The person who fears you walks honorably in all ways, for you lead that person in the ways you have chosen.

13. *He will spend his days in prosperity, and his descendants will inherit the land.* Lord of hosts! The final fruit for those who know you is that their souls shall dwell among the good and in the paradise of their

God. They shall dwell on Mount Zion, in the heavenly Jerusalem, in the community of the living God, in the company of the righteous whose names are written in heaven above. They are redeemed from hell, sin, death and the devil and they serve you their lives long with peace and joy in their hearts. They slumber without fear, for you are their strength and shield. They rest under the shelter of your wing, for they belong to you. They do not suffer the cold, for you warm them with the fiery rays of your love. They do not hunger, for you feed them with the bread of life. They do not thirst, for you give them the waters of the Holy Spirit. They are not in need, for you are their treasure and riches and they live in the house of peace, in confident rest under the cover of your righteousness. As the prophet said, their enjoyment is in your law, of which they speak day and night among all of the people. They wash the feet of their souls in the clear and sparkling waters of your truth. They study their consciences in the clear mirror of your wisdom. Their thoughts are just and true and their words are words sprinkled with the salt of graciousness. Their works are works of truth and faithfulness. The light of their godliness enlightens their path. They find that for which they seek. They gain that which they desire. Their souls dwell in the fullness of your goodness and the mist of your grace is upon them. The meadows of their consciences bring forth oil and fruit beyond all measure. And even though they must suffer much misery, sorrow and affliction in this body of flesh, they will be assured that the way of the cross is the way of life. They are not ashamed to follow the way of the Lord, with the cross as their weapon.

They patiently go with Christ into the battle and struggle courageously until they have won the prize and gained the promised crown. Nothing can stand in their way, for they are partakers of your Spirit and have tasted its sweetness. They neither waver nor turn away. Their house is built on the solid rock. They are as pillars in your holy temple. They have tasted the secrets of the bread of heaven. Praise to you, Lord! Fear of you remains before their eyes and they walk in your way. Therefore, their souls shall dwell in your fullness and their seed, born of the Holy Spirit and the word, will possess the land of the living where you and your chosen ones will reign in joyous glory in all of eternity.

14. *The Lord confides in those who fear him; he makes his covenant known to them.* Lord, Lord! The thoughts of my heart frighten me.

My whole insides shake! Like Esdra, I realize that many are born for nothing. What can I say, beloved Lord? That you have ordained evil people to do the evil which they do? Far from it! I know that you are eternally good and that nothing evil can be found in you. We are the work of your hand, created through Christ Jesus for good works and we should walk in this. You have put water, fire, life and death under our will. You do not will the death of sinners. You will that they repent and have life. You are the eternal light and you hate all darkness in me. You do not will these ones to be lost, but rather that they repent, come to recognition of your truth and be saved. Beloved Lord, how dismally they have blasphemed your unspeakable goodness, your eternal mercy and your almighty majesty with this view. They have made you, the God of grace and the creator of all things, into some kind of cruel devil by saying that you are the cause of evil. But you are called the father of light. It is obvious that good is not the cause of evil, that light is not the cause of darkness, that life is not the cause of death and that God is not the cause of the devil. Yet they want to blame you for their stubbornness of heart and their carnality of mind. Then they have no reason to leave the broad and easy way, for they have an excuse for their sinfulness. They do this because they acknowledge neither your divine goodness nor their own inherent sinfulness. Lord God, you have loved us with an eternal love. You chose us even before the beginning of the world to be blameless and holy before you in love. This is without regard to what the faithful Paul wrote concerning Esau, the Pharaoh and Israel. He wrote this for our edification, that we might give honor to your name, not to ourselves. What have we, miserable sinners, ever done to gloat about? What do we have that we have not received from you? All that we have comes from your fullness and thanks for this is given by all who know your word. Beloved Lord, the secret of your holy word was not given to the rich, the aristocrats or to the wise. It was given to the poor, the simple people and to little children. Yes Father, as Christ said, this was your pleasant will. Isaiah said that you consider the disconsolate, those of broken spirit, who fear your word. Beloved Lord, we disconsolate ones pray that you lead us into your truth, that you teach us your mysteries, that you help us truly to know the power of your covenant, that you are ours and we are yours. You made this covenant with us through Christ because of your perfect kindness and grace, without any worthiness on our part. Your mysteries will be found among those who fear you, and to these you will make your covenant known.

15. *My eyes are ever on the Lord, for only he will release my feet from the snare.* Sovereign Lord! With the prophets, I ask, "If you, O Lord, kept a record of sins, O Lord, who could stand?" (Psalm 130:3). Miserable and grievous sinner that I am, I had turned with all the desires of my heart toward foolishness, toward gold and silver, toward pomp and pride, toward alien and forbidden flesh. I have turned my eyes toward obvious idols of wood and stone and played the whore with them for many years on every mountain and under every green tree. As the prophet says it, my idols were as many as the number of my days. I bent my knee to carved and molten images and asked them to save me and be my God. I looked for sight among the blind, for life among the dead and for aid among those who could not save themselves from dust and rust, from thieves and the creatures of the night. To a mere mouthful of bread—something feeble and wane, something which grew out of the ground and was broken in the mill, baked in fire, chewed by my own teeth and digested in my own stomach—I have said, "You are my salvation." This is just like Israel saying to the Golden Calf, "These are your gods, O Israel, who brought you up out of Egypt" (Exodus 32:4). My God, miserable sinner that I am, I have likewise dallied with the Babylonian whore for many years. For I insisted that she was an honorable, honest and chaste woman, a queen of righteousness, glorious, holy and acceptable in your eyes. For I saw her dressed in purple and scarlet, with gold, gemstones and pearls, a golden chalice in her hand, ruling over all the kings of this earth. I did not see that she was covered with pox and boils, that her beautiful chalice was full of gross filth. I did not see that she was a shameless whore and murderess who had beguiled the whole earth, who persecuted the elect and drank the blood of the saints. But now I have seen her disgraces with my own eyes and touched them with my own hands. And I tremble before you, Living Fountain, that I forsook you for so long and placed my trust in useless puddles which can give no water. I gave honor to idols and images instead of to you. I worshipped the creature instead of the creator, who is hallowed in eternity. This occurred, in part, because of the deception of my eyes. My heart was charmed by the glorious appearance of that woman. But now, beloved Lord, my eyes are fastened on you until you hear me. My eyes are fastened on the throne of your grace with complete trust until I receive your mercy and grace. For you alone can aid me in times of temptation and rescue my feet from being stuck in the net of sinfulness.

16. *Turn to me and be gracious to me, for I am lonely and afflicted.* Lord of hosts! I do not conceal from you my sin, guilt and transgressions. I confess with open mouth that my past years were consumed with the will of the heathen and that I walked according to their godless appetites, in pride and ostentation, in excessive eating and drinking, and in unrestrained, blind idolatry. I did anything that my sinful flesh desired. I was a child of scorn, just like the others. I scoffed at your holy name. I considered your word to be a folk tale. I carried on in all manner of evil, all the while depending on your grace. I was like a beautifully whitewashed crypt. On the outside, before others, I looked moral, chaste and serene. Nobody found fault with my conduct. But on the inside I was nothing but dead bones, stinking flesh and gnawing worms. On the outside, my cup was clean, but on the inside it was full of plunder and indulgence. I am simply ashamed to say what went on with me in private. All of my thoughts were impure, idle, prideful, greedy and ungodly. In my heart was division, hatred, envy, revenge and hostility. My longings inclined toward all kinds of evil and I sinned without restraint. I did not fear God or the devil, law or gospel, hell or heaven. Nothing at all could shock me. I respected neither you nor your word. My direction was toward all that is evil. I wanted nothing other than the friendship and love of this world. The only reason I did not commit such abominations as adultery, whoremongering and the like was not because of my fear of you, but because I desired people's favor and did not want to lose my good reputation. So all of my conceit, short temper, drunkenness, revelry, impure lusts, loves, public sins, defectiveness, pride, distinction and idolatry were called true service to God. Yet all of my actions, both private and public, were never hidden from your eyes. That is how I, grievous sinner that I am, led my life. God of grace, I did not acknowledge you as my God, creator and redeemer until your Holy Spirit taught me through your word. This opened your will to me and brought me to some understanding of your mysteries. Now I recognize how dishonorably I walked before you. It is as if I had spit in your face, pulled your hair, hit you with my fists, tread on you with my feet and mocked you as a fool.

Lord, beloved Lord, I am lonely and afflicted. My sins are great and numerous. My conscience accuses me and my thoughts frighten me. My heart grieves and sighs because of my grievous sins before you. My sinfulness has separated me from you, hidden your face from me and brought your wrath upon me. Indeed, I have become food and fuel for hell. Yet the deeper and deeper I am troubled, the higher and higher I am consoled by your word, for it teaches me of your mercy, grace and kindness and the redemption of my sin through Christ, your beloved son and our Lord, despite the fact that I neither knew nor feared you. This promise gives me peace. This promise gives me joy. Like the sinful woman, this promise compels me to your blessed feet in sure confidence and with a clear conscience. For I know you will never pitilessly spurn a returning son, even though I spent my fatherly inheritance and property disgracefully with whores and scoundrels in foreign lands, squandering it in my unrighteousness. My God, turn the loving visage of your peace toward me. I have sinned against heaven and against you. Lay your hand of grace upon me, for I am lonely and afflicted.

17. *The troubles of my heart have multiplied; free me from my anguish.* Lord, Lord! My heart cries out and laments. My conscience shakes and trembles. My soul feels like the sorrow of a mother who has lost her only child and cannot be consoled. Poor and reckless sinner that I am, many years I did not truly seek, recognize, understand or respond to your divine love and fatherly goodness. I lived in a way more shameful than the dumb animals. At least these animals, in eating, drinking and other natural pursuits, do not go beyond their natural instincts and desires. They do not transgress the natural law which is within them. But I have lived more uselessly and unspiritually, transgressing more against the inborn law of nature, than even the greed of my ungodly flesh desired. I certainly knew that the desires of my flesh would lead to death. Your Spirit warned me often enough to refrain from evil, but this warning was repressed by my flesh. In every sense I had become a slave to sin and sworn to unrighteousness. I drank in sin like water. My desire was for all manner of foolishness. I could not see your hand, graciously extending to me, nor hear your voice calling me, nor want your inviting love. In other words, I hated knowledge of you and threw fear of you from me. And as if this were not enough, beloved Lord, that in my ignorance I acted this way; but I find daily now that even my righteousness is like dirty clothing. When I think I am walking, I fall down. When I think I am standing, I am lying down. And when I think I am something special, I am really nothing at all. Loving Lord, protect me, for the anxiety of my heart is immeasurably great, greater than I can say or write. I feel sometimes like a woman in childbirth. My face pales from fear of you, my hands are on my

groin because of the pain in my heart, the perils of hell are all around me, the marrow in my bones has gone dry. This involves not just money and possessions, or flesh and blood alone. It concerns the eternal life or eternal death of my miserable, naked soul. I pray, therefore, that you not forsake me, loving Lord. Open the eyes of your mercy and see my heavy burden and anxiety. Stand by me and redeem me from all my anguish.

18. *Look upon my affliction and my distress and take away all my sins.* Sovereign Lord! When the righteous call out to you, you hear them. When they begin to draw close to you, you are with them. You are near to those whose hearts are broken. You comfort those whose minds repent. The offerings of those broken in spirit are acceptable to you. You do not scorn those with repentant hearts. You have sent your beloved son, anointed with your Holy Spirit, to preach the good news to the poor, to bind up those whose hearts are broken, to proclaim deliverance to those in prison, freedom for those in bondage, to proclaim the acceptable year of the Lord, to comfort those who mourn, to care for those who grieve in Zion, to bring fine raiment for their sack clothing, the oil of joy for their tears, and beautiful clothing for their troubled spirit. He proclaims redemption to all who are burdened and heavy laden, who come to him with trusting hearts. He invites those who thirst to living waters. He bore all our sins on his own body on the cross. He washed away our guilt with his own blood, just as Moses before him did in shadow and symbol when he sprinkled the impurities of Israel with the blood of oxen, rams and the ashes of the young red heifer. For under the law, purification of all things takes place by the pouring out of blood. Now if the figurative blood had such power as to make the flesh pure and holy, how much more will the pure blood of your beloved son, offering himself without blemish through your eternal Spirit, purify our consciences from dead works for your service. Living God, through the service of your blood we have received forgiveness for our sins in accord with the riches of your grace. Through this blood of the cross he has reconciled all who dwell on earth and in heaven. I confess before you therefore, beloved Lord, that I have or know of no healing for my sins other than the precious blood of your son alone which you have given to me. Not works nor service, not baptism or the Lord's supper (though all upright Christians will use these as symbols of your word and hold them in highest reverence.) This blood alone, out of pure grace and love, has mercifully

delivered me, a miserable sinner, from my former way of living. Therefore, God of truth in whom no deceit can be found, think upon the words of your prophets who spoke in your name, saying, "But if a wicked man turns away from all the sins he has committed and keeps all my decrees and does what is just and right, he will surely live; he will not die. None of the offenses he has committed will be remembered against him" (Ezekiel 18:21–22). My God, do not look upon me but upon Jesus Christ, the eternal Melchizedek, whom you raised up as high priest over your house. Look upon this king of peace of your righteousness who has no beginning or end. He remains the high priest in eternity. He took no honor for himself, but like Aaron, was called and anointed by you. With loud voice and tears he prayed to you and you heard him because he honored you. Hear me now, for his sake. Accept me now, for his sake. Be merciful to me now, for his sake. Comfort your troubled servant. I have no source of comfort on earth or in heaven than you alone. Be merciful to me in my great anguish and misery. My unclean and sinful flesh afflicts me. I am attacked by my own evil nature. Furthermore, for the sake of your word, all people now regard me as spittle, as scum and as a liar. Those who listen to me just shake their heads. Externally and internally, I find no respite. Again I say it, my sins attack me, my soul is troubled and in pain. I do not pray, beloved Lord, for gold or silver. These will be useless to me on the day of your wrath. Neither do I pray for a long life, for my life always heads in the wrong direction. Only this I pray for and desire with all of my heart, that you look upon me, a miserable sinner, with the eyes of your grace and mercy, that you have mercy on me in my great need and comfort me with your Holy Spirit, and take away my sins.

19. *See how my enemies have increased and how fiercely they hate me!* Lord of hosts! When I was one of the world, I spoke and acted as the world did. And I was not hated by the world. But then I ate of the book which you showed me. And although it was sweet as honey in my mouth, it has made my belly very bitter. For in it is written woe, lamenting and grief. When I served the world, the world rewarded me. I was praised by all, even as our forefathers praised the false prophets. But now I regard the world with divine love and from my heart I seek its happiness and welfare. I admonish, reprove and teach it with your holy word, pointing her toward the crucified Christ Jesus. And it has become for me a heavy cross and a bitter gall. I am so

viciously hated by the world that not only I myself, but all those who love me and show me mercy and hospitality, must in some places expect banishment and death. Beloved Lord, I am regarded in their eyes as a manifest thief and murderer. Am I not like a lost lamb in the wilderness of this world, set upon and pursued to the death by ravaging wolves? Am I not like a desperate ship in the deepest seas, without a mast, sail or rudder, tossed about by strong winds and waves? In my flesh I want to say that I have been deceived, for I see that the unjust, restless people live happily, in riches and good fortune, in ease and peace while those who fear God must suffer all manner of hunger, thirst, adversity and grief. Their houses are unprotected and they must work hard for their bread. They are cursed, mocked and hated as garbage and stench by all people. Beloved Lord, my enemies are great and numerous, with hearts like roaring lions. Their words are like deadly arrows and their tongues are set against me. One calls me a false defiler, while another calls me a cursed heretic, although I have nothing but the firm truth, through your grace. So now I have become their deadly enemy, all because I try to lead them in the right way. Lord, I am not ashamed before you or your angels for what I teach, and certainly not before this rebellious world. For I know without doubt that I teach your word. I teach nothing other than sincere repentance, dying to the sinfulness of our flesh and a new way of living which comes from God. I teach a true and authentic faith in you and your beloved son which must be empowered and active through love. I teach Christ Jesus; that he was crucified for us; that he was true God and true human being; that he was born of you before the beginning of time in an unfathomable, miraculous and indescribable way; that he is your eternal word and wisdom; that he is the mirror of your glory and the direct image of you; that in the fullness of time, through the power of the Holy Spirit, he became real flesh and blood, a visible, concrete and mortal human being, like all the Adamic race except without sin, in the unblemished virgin Mary; that he was born of the seed of Abraham and David; that he died and was buried, was resurrected and ascended into heaven and is now our one eternal counselor, mediator, advocate and redeemer before you. If this is not what was clearly taught from the beginning by all of the prophets, apostles and evangelists, then I will gladly accept my shame and punishment. I have taught no other baptism, supper or doctrine than that given to us from the unfailing mouth of the Lord Jesus Christ and the clear example and practice of his holy apostles. I will not even speak here of the

266

ample evidence for this given by the historians and scholars of the early and present church. Now, since I defend my teaching with the extraordinarily clear word and statutes of your Son, who can reprimand me and truthfully declare that I am a seducer? Do not the entire scriptures teach that Christ is the eternal truth? Is not the apostolic church the true Christian Church? We know that all human teaching is spume and chaff and that the Antichrist has polluted and falsified the teachings of Christ. So why do they hate me when I preach the true and pure teachings of Christ and his apostles in a plain and unsullied way? Only those who are themselves members of his party hate one opposing the Antichrist. If I did not have the word of Christ I would gladly have it taught to me, for that is what I seek in fear and trembling. But in this I can no more be deceived, for through your grace I have believed in your holy truth and accepted it through your Holy Spirit as your certain word. In all eternity I will no more be deceived. Let them all cry and shriek, threaten and dispute. Let them vex, boast and rave, persecute and murder all they want. Your word will be triumphant and the Lamb will have the victory. Of this I am sure and certain, that what I teach is your word. On that day of Christ's judgment, not only the world but even the angels will be judged according to this teaching. Even if I and my fellow believers were to rot in the ground or be completely taken away from the earth, your word remains the truth in eternity.

We are no better than those fellow believers who have gone on before us. Yet the world will again cause your hand to be raised. It is perhaps already too late for them to see whom they have so tyrannically speared. Lord, their hatred for me is unjust. Whom have I dishonored with even a single word? Whom have I cheated even a penny? Whose gold, silver, cow or calf, ox or ass have I ever coveted? I have loved them with pure love, even unto death. I have taught your word and will and the way of salvation with great steadfastness through your grace. That is why I have so many enemies and they so unjustly hate me.

20. *Guard my life and rescue me; let me not be put to shame, for I take refuge in you.* Lord, Lord! These words of Paul frighten me, for he said, "So, if you think you are standing firm, be careful that you don't fall!" (1 Corinthians 10:12). If one thinks he is something, he is really nothing and deceives himself. For all flesh which is forsaken by your Spirit is blind in all things of spiritual understanding. It has

fallen into falsehood and unrighteousness, into sin and death, as I have explicitly seen in David and Peter. For when your Spirit left David, even though he was a great prophet and a man after your own heart, true in all of your ways, what happened to his virtue, his love, his humility and his fear of God? Did he not become a public adulterer and assassin, boasting of his own glory? That is, until by your Spirit, through the word of the prophet, he was once again enlightened. Then he recognized how grievously he had sinned and how foolishly he had acted before you. The same happened to Peter. He truly confessed your beloved son Christ, not through flesh and blood but through your Spirit of grace. He was called by Christ a rock and was ready to go with Christ to prison and to death. But when the trial came and your Spirit left even a little from him, he could not even stand up to the accusing word of a servant girl. He denied Christ and swore that he did not know him. But as soon as Christ looked upon him and your Spirit returned to him, he recognized his error and wept bitterly. Then he preached the name of Christ openly among all people without any fear though it was forbidden on pain of prison and whipping. He bravely answered that one must obey God rather than men. I pray therefore, beloved Lord, that you protect my poor soul, which was purchased at such a great price, from ever turning from your truth. For just as with Peter, I may be thinking that I have given my life to you, and with Paul that neither oppression nor anxiety, nor persecution, nor hunger, nor nakedness, nor dangers, nor sword, nor life and death, nor any other thing could separate me from your love. Yet even so I do not fully know myself. I must place all my trust in you. For I have not yet resisted up to the shedding of my blood. Although I have tasted the cup of your suffering, I have not tasted the worst of it. When prison and chains must be suffered, when life and death are laid before us, when we are threatened with fire and sword, that is when the gold is truly separated from the wood, silver from the straw and pearls from the chaff. Do not forsake me, beloved Lord, for it is certain that even a tree with the deepest roots can be uprooted from the earth by the winds of a storm. And the highest mountain can be split by an earthquake. Did not even those most beloved men of patience, Job and Jeremiah, stumble into temptation and murmur against your will? Beloved Lord, do not allow me to be tested beyond my abilities and powers. You are trustworthy and good. Do not allow my soul to be put to shame. I do not pray for my flesh. I know that it must suffer and die. I pray only that you strengthen me in my struggle, that you come to my aid and protect me. Show me the way through my trials. Deliver me and do not let me come to shame, for I trust in you alone.

21. *May integrity and uprightness protect me, because my hope is in you.* Sovereign Lord! When the farmer sowed good seed in his field, his enemy sowed weeds there among the seeds while he slept. Now when the children of God come before the Lord, Satan also is there among them. Wherever Christ is present, there also the devil will be found, as I have certainly seen in the past few years. Your healing word, your gospel of grace, is the true food of my soul, from which it gains eternal life. For many years it was trampled on by the Antichrist as a fable and useless lie. Now it is again in all its power accepted, believed and confessed by some through your merciful grace. Now the hellish lion roars in furious rage and goes around seeking to devour them. He has neither holiday or rest, for he knows that his kingdom and rule are about to fall and be destroyed. He uses all his cunning and cleverness, disguising himself as an angel of light. Those whom he lost through your word he has now again caught in his net and trapped through polluted teachings. He has altered the pure and healing sense of the scriptures into a carnal and seductive perception through false prophets and teachers who lack understanding. He has licensed the sword and weapons and called forth a spirit of revenge against the whole world. He has covered over open adultery by invoking the customs of the ancient patriarchs. He has erected a literal kingdom, complete with a king and other such offenses which cause a true Christian shame and vexation. But all that you have not planted will be put to shame. Lord, protect me plainly and simply in your truth, so that I neither believe nor teach anything that does not conform to your holy will and word. That is, true faith, genuine love, true baptism and supper, a blameless life, and a scriptural separation from all those who cause indignation through doctrine and their way of living. Protect me, beloved Lord, from all heresy and error. Protect me, as you, in your grace, have done until now. Grant that I and my fellow believers may seek, love and fear you with all our hearts. Grant that we obey the governing authorities in all cases where it does not conflict with God's word, for as Paul said, this is good and right before you. Protect us from the deceptions of the devil, who would teach us that there is another spiritual king than Jesus Christ, the king of Zion, who rules from your holy mountain with the iron scepter of your word. He is the king of kings and the lord of lords. He sits at your right hand in

heaven, above all principalities, powers, authorities and lordships and all that can be named, not only in this world but in the world to come. All things are placed at his feet. To him is given all power in heaven above and on earth below. Every knee will bend and every tongue confess that he is the Lord, to the praise of your great name. Beloved Lord, protect me, plainly and simply, under your cross, that I do not forsake you and your holy word in the tribulation, nor cloak your divine truth and will with hypocrisy, with lies or with dark and doubtful words. May I receive with all of the saints that promised kingdom, inheritance and reward at the appearance of your beloved son and my Lord, Jesus Christ, whom we daily await and in whom we hope with assured hearts and full trust in the promise of your grace.

22. *Redeem Israel, O God, from all its troubles!* Lord of hosts! I have confessed my own sins to you and prayed for my transgressions, praising your mercy and desiring your grace. Like David, I must now pray to you concerning my fellow believers. For I see Israel scattered and drifting like sheep without a shepherd. I see the refreshing vineyard of the Lord being wasted and tread upon by all people. The chosen seed of Abraham, the house of Jacob, has once again become a captive slave in the hard service of the Pharaoh of Egypt. I see that the glorious race of Judah and the holy vessels have been carried away as into Babylon, to be misused and mishandled by Belshazzar and his consorts. I see Jerusalem, that lovely image of peace, which is likened to a dove, changed into a roaring lioness, thirsty for the blood of the innocent. She who was a princess among the nations, the city of the great king, now has no king, no citizens, no walls. She has become a barren wasteland. I see that the temple of the Lord, the house of prayer in which sincere worship of God is to take place, has become a place of thieves, a den of lions, bears, wolves, vipers, dragons and serpents, a house of idolatry. Indeed, she has become the whoring bed of the adulterous Jezebel. I see that the bride of Christ, the glorious spouse who was once bedecked by the king with many gifts of honor, has become head to toe a shameless whore. I see that the ark of the Lord, the grandeur of Israel, has been captured by the Philistines and carried away to the temple of Dagon. Why do I lament so? Judah has become Babylon. Canaan has become Egypt. Palestine has become Sodom. And the king of all honor, the eternally blessed Christ Jesus, is daily called a fool and mocked as a jester. The teachings of his holy apostles, the beloved witnesses to your truth, are given back to all people as

lies. His seamless robe, which the scriptures said should not be divided, is torn into four and five pieces. In every land, the Antichrist has dominion through the preaching of lies, and your word is silenced with violence. Whether I go east or west, south or north, I find nothing other than arrogant obstinacy, corruption, blindness, greediness, pride, gluttonous eating and drinking, pomposity, hatred, envy and godlessness on all sides. I find violence, false teaching and a polluted and misleading use of your sacraments. I find over all the world tyrants ruling, forceful and triumphant, in the courts of all the princes. I find that the educated speak as beasts, that they are ambitious, greedy, voracious, earthly and carnally minded, teaching anything that appeases the lusts and desires of the people. There is practically nobody who seeks after truth. And he who does must carry the cross. That is why my cheeks are covered with tears day and night. That is why my soul cannot be comforted. That is why my mouth wants neither bread nor drink. I feel like running naked, like the prophet Micah, roaring like a dragon, or crying like a young ostrich. There is no remedy for the plagues of Israel. With Esdras, I feel like mournfully lamenting, saying, "You see how our sanctuary has been laid waste, our altar demolished, and our temple destroyed. Our harps are unstrung, our hymns silenced, our shouts of joy cut short; the light of the sacred lamp is out, and the ark of the covenant has been taken as spoil; the holy vessels are defiled, and the name which God has conferred on us is disgraced; our leading men have been treated shamefully, our priests burnt alive, and the Levites taken off into captivity; our virgins have been raped and our wives ravished, our godfearing men carried off, and our children abandoned; our youth have been enslaved, and our strong warriors reduced to weakness. Worst of all, Zion, once sealed with God's own seal, has forfeited its glory and is in the hands of our enemies" (2 Esdras 10:21ff.). God, God! Redeem Israel from all its troubles! Look upon our heavy affliction and misery with eyes of mercy. Free us from the iron furnaces of Egypt. Lead us out of the land of the Chaldees. Let the Holy City, with her walls and gates, be rebuilt in her old place. Let the fallen temple, whose stones lay scattered on the streets, be repaired and rebuilt. Gather your drifting sheep together. Receive your returning bride, who consorted so wickedly with foreign lovers. God of Israel! Create in us a chaste heart whose only desire is for your blessed word and will. Send us sincere workers for your harvest, who will reap and gather the grain at the right time. Send us faithful builders, who will lay a sure foundation so that in these final days your house will be glorious, shining above all the mountains. Then many people may come to her and say, "Come, let us go up to the mountain of the Lord, to the house of the God of Jacob. He will teach us his ways, so that we may walk in his paths" (Isaiah 2:3). Then we may walk our whole life long before you in peace and in good conscience, under godfearing authorities and blameless teachers, with a Christian baptism, a true supper, godly living and true separation. Then we might be eternally honored and praised by you as your loving children, through your beloved son Jesus Christ. To him and to you, our Lord and Father, with your Holy Spirit, praise and eternal authority is given. Amen.

Appendix

Dutch Mennonite artist Jan Luyken (1649–1712) devoted much of his career to etchings intended for book illustrations. He contributed more than 100 etchings for the 1685 edition of the Anabaptist martyrology, The Martyrs Mirror. This book was translated into German and subsequently into English. The English translation is presently published by Herald Press of Scottsdale, Pennsylvania, a subsidiary of the Mennonite Publishing House, Inc., who graciously granted permission for the use of these reproductions of the original illustrations.

Because of their insistence on the freedom of conscience in religious beliefs, Anabaptists were considered to be both religious heretics and political revolutionaries. The Martyrs Mirror, an hagiographical narrative, is treasured to this day as a history and teaching tool among those who consider themselves to be a continuation of the Anabaptist tradition.

Figures 1 and 2 are representations of the persecution of Hutterian Anabaptists in Austria who were arrested and either deported as galley slaves or burned for their religious beliefs.

Figures 3 through 7 depict the persecutions of various Anabaptist women. Anabaptist women were usually drowned. In some locations, however, even those of adolescent years were burned at the stake. Although women were not represented among those Anabaptists who left behind theological writings, they were well represented among those Anabaptists who died as martyrs.

Figure 8 shows a young child at the place of the execution of his mother.

Figure 9 depicts a small Dutch Anabaptist congregation which held services in a boat so that others would not be able to report on their teachings.

Figure 10 depicts an incident in the life of Dutch Anabaptist Dirk

273

APPENDIX

Willems which took place in 1569. As the story goes, Willems was being pursued by the authorities. Although he was able to cross the frozen river, the constable fell through the ice. Willems turned and rescued the constable, though he knew this action meant his own arrest and execution.

Figure 1.

Figure 2.

Figure 3.

Figure 4.

Figure 5.

Figure 6.

Figure 7.

Figure 8.

Figure 9.

Figure 10.

Notes

Foreword

1) The foundational work for thirty years has been George H. Williams, *The Radical Reformation* (Philadelphia: The Westminster Press, 1962). Before this time, the Reformation radicals were only perceived as peripheral, as "stepchildren" of the Reformation. One of the enduring results of Williams's work was to bring investigation of the Radical Reformation trends into conversation with Reformation history as a whole. That is to say, after Williams, no Reformation historian could continue to write his or her history as if the radicals never had been. The result of this, however, was a veritable explosion of writing, revision and reinterpretation on the Radical Reformation during these thirty years. Williams remained abreast of these developments and has just published a third edition (second English edition) of his tome, which tracks these developments. Cf. George Huntston Williams, *The Radical Reformation* (Kirksville: Sixteenth Century Journal Publishers, 3d rev. ed. 1992).

2) Cf. Paul Johnson, *A History of Christianity* (New York: Athenaeum, 1979), pp. 267–331.

3) So long as a majority of church leaders, not to mention lay people, were of the belief that the church was under attack by a literal Satan and his demons, it was understandably impossible to conceive of religious differences as anything other than a clear struggle between good and evil, the children of light versus the children of darkness, all or nothing. A spirit of tolerance would have to wait until serious questioning of medieval demonology had saturated the European mind. This only began in the very late sixteenth century and was not brought into the public mind until the eighteenth century. Cf. Alan C. Kors and Edward Peters, eds., *Witchcraft in Europe 1100–1700* (Philadelphia: University of Pennsylvania Press, 1972).

NOTES

4) This has been most thoroughly elucidated by John Howard Yoder in *The Priestly Kingdom: Social Ethics as Gospel* (Notre Dame: University of Notre Dame Press, 1984).

5) I want to caution the reader against any immediate and naive appropriation of the words of these texts. Our time is not the sixteenth century. In the translation process, I was constantly confronted with the dilemma of whether to render something as Spirit or spirit. While the upper or lower case may seem insignificant, as a translator I could not be facile about it. The upper case, Spirit, was used only when it was unavoidable that the intention of the writer referred to the Holy Spirit—the third person in the divine Trinity. Otherwise, I preferred the lower case, spirit, to indicate the spiritual nature of *human* being.

6) Cf. note 1 above.

7) These designations were first presented in the introductory section of *Spiritual and Anabaptist Writers,* ed. George H. Williams and Angel M. Mergal (Philadelphia: The Westminster Press, 1957), pp. 19–38.

8) Very recently a translation of the old Hutterite Chronicles has appeared, *Chronicle of the Hutterian Brethren 1525–1665* (Ulster Park: Plough Publishing House, 1989).

9) The signal essay, which has had an enormous impact on current research, is James Stayer, Werner O. Packull and Klaus Deppermann, "From Monogenesis to Polygenesis: The Historical Discussion of Anabaptist Origins," *Mennonite Quarterly Review* 49 (1975), pp. 83–121. More recently, George Williams and a few others have protested that this view of Anabaptist origins is too narrowly focused on the "Germanic" movement, with no attention paid to Anabaptism among the Italian, Polish, Szekler and other nationalities. I have not ignored this criticism, but chose my texts from among the Germans and Dutch for other reasons.

10) Although written before the impact of the polygenesis thesis (cf. note 9 above), Robert Friedmann's synopsis of Anabaptist theology is of continuing value. Cf. Robert Friedmann, *The Theology of Anabaptism: An Interpretation* (Scottdale: Herald Press, 1973).

11) Not all vestiges of misogyny could be removed, particularly in the selection from Balthasar Hubmaier. This is dealt with in the endnotes connected with that selection.

NOTES

12) On the whole, the Radical Reformation was less prone to anti-judaism than other sixteenth-century options. This is partially so because the Anabaptists were, sociologically speaking, in a similar position to Jews in their society. Any justification on their part for the persecution of Jews would surely backfire on themselves. Therefore, they tended to support a *general* freedom of conscience against state power, extending not only to radical Christians and Jews, but even to Moslems and "heathens." Ironically, the selection in this collection which demanded the most creativity in translation so as to avoid passages which would strike modern ears as overtly antijudaic were the selections from Hans Denck. The irony in this is that, of all people among the sixteenth century, Denck was, both intellectually and socially, the closest to concrete Jewish people and was arguably the least antijudaic of all contemporary interlocutors. He took the rabbinic objections to the Christian gospel seriously and answered these objections as a true "brother." Yet, his dichotomies between spirit/flesh, law/gospel, outer/inner meaning, etc., must strike the modern reader, on this side of Auschwitz, as anti-Jewish. My translations of the selections from Denck reflect the modern sensitivities.

Introduction

1) Hans-Jürgen Goertz, *Die Täufer: Geschichte und Deutung* (Munich: Verlag C.H.Beck, 1980) brought attention to this general anticlerical mood and its effects on the rise of Anabaptism. While relatively new, this interpretation appears to have found solid and enduring support in scholarly investigation.

2) The current understanding of the multiple origins of Anabaptism is outlined in James Stayer, Werner O. Packull and Klaus Deppermann, "From Monogenesis to Polygenesis: The Historical Discussion of Anabaptist Origins," *Mennonite Quarterly Review* 49 (1975), pp. 83–121.

3) The biases of the Anabaptists themselves were that Zwingli believed the same way they did but was cowardly concerning the implementation of their common vision, more concerned for political expediency than for faithfulness to the gospel. In modern scholarship, this view was best expressed by John Howard Yoder, "The Turning Point in the Zwinglian Reformation," *Mennonite Quarterly Review* 32 (1958), pp. 128–40. However, scholars more in sympathy with Zwingli have

questioned this interpretation. In their view, Zwingli was consistently faithful to his vision of a Reformed Christian society, a vision originally shared by the radicals, especially Conrad Grebel. It was the radicals, then, drawn away by their impatience and lack of political sophistication, who "defected" from the original program of reform. This view has been best argued by Robert Walton, "Was There a Turning Point of the Zwinglian Reformation?" *Mennonite Quarterly Review* 42 (1968), pp. 45–56; and in his *Zwingli's Theocracy* (Toronto: University of Toronto Press, 1967).

4) There are several editions of the Hutterite chronicle available. I followed for this translation the 1923 edition, *Geschicht-Buch der Hutterischen Brüder*, R. Wolkan, ed. (Vienna: Carl Fromme Ges. m. b. H., 1923), pp. 34–35.

5) *Quellen zur Geschichte der Täufer in der Schweiz*, ed. L. von Muralt and W. Schmid (Zürich: S. Hirzel Verlag, 1952), p. 39. This tendency has been analyzed in Heinold Fast, "Reformation durch Provokation. Predigstörungen in den ersten Jahren der Reformation in der Schweiz," in *Umstrittenes Täufertum 1525–1975; Neue Forschungen*, ed. H.-J. Goertz (Gottingen: Vandenhoeck & Ruprecht, 1975), pp. 79–110.

6) The full text is given in *The Legacy of Michael Sattler*, ed. and trans. John H. Yoder (Scottdale: Herald Press, 1973), pp. 28–44.

7) Some sources place Denck's expulsion from Nuremberg on the very day, January 21, 1525, when the meeting in the house of Felix Mantz took place in which George Blaurock requested adult baptism.

8) Cf. Mark S. Burrows, "Devotio Moderna: Reforming Piety in the Later Middle Ages," in *Spiritual Traditions for the Contemporary Church*, ed. R. Maas and G. O'Donnell (Nashville: Abingdon Press, 1990), pp. 109–32.

9) A useful essay on the Anabaptist interpretation of Christian living is Robert Friedmann, "The Essence of Anabaptist Faith," *Mennonite Quarterly Review* 41 (1967), pp. 5–24.

10) Quoted in C. M. Dent, "The Anabaptists," in *The Study of Spirituality*, ed. C. Jones, G. Wainwright and E. Yarnold (New York: Oxford University Press, 1986), pp. 50–54.

11) Based on his investigation of one Anabaptist, Hans Schlaffer, Ste-

phen B. Boyd recognized this same dynamic of community, suggesting that for Schlaffer, the community could become the replacement or substitute for the entire sacramental system. Cf. Stephen B. Boyd, "Community as Sacrament in the Theology of Hans Schlaffer," in *Anabaptism Revisited*, ed. W. Klaassen (Scottdale: Herald Press, 1992), pp. 50–64.

12) Much of this final paragraph is informed by various sections in Michael Lerner, *Surplus Powerlessness: The Psychodynamics of Everyday Life and the Psychology of Individual and Social Transformation* (Atlantic Highlands: Humanities Press International, 1991).

Part I: Swiss Anabaptism

1) In these statements it is clear that Mantz and other Swiss Anabaptists no longer saw themselves as part of the larger Protestant movement. They considered the Reformed preachers and scholars to be wolves in sheep's clothing.

2) Felix's view of justification is that of a synergism between human and divine will. When too strong an emphasis is placed on the divine agency and will alone, the picture which emerges is one of Christ "forcing" one to his glory. This picture of divine coercion was rejected by the Swiss Anabaptists.

3) This is a clear and simple statement of the theme of "following Christ," absolutely central to the spiritual life of the Swiss Anabaptists.

4) Hans Denck also wrote a pamphlet which outlined a number of contradictions, or "*paradoxa*," in the Bible, texts which appeared directly to contradict each other. Like Hubmaier, Denck saw in the method of harmonizing these contradictions a pathway into deeper understanding of divine truth.

5) Hubmaier accepted the tripartite anthropology of body/soul/spirit and rejected the dualistic model of body/soul or body/spirit. As will be seen in this writing, Hubmaier understanding of the function of these three aspects of human personality is very similar to the functioning of id, ego and superego outlined by Sigmund Freud and the subsequent analytic tradition of psychology.

6) The mechanism of synergism between human and divine will is

spiritual. God's Spirit aids the human spirit in recognition of divine truth.

7) Hubmaier had a low view of the bodily nature. Although it can be forced to holiness "against its will," so to speak, by the combined efforts of the soul and spirit, it is finally unredeemable until the general resurrection, in which it is transformed into a spiritual nature. The human spirit, which Hubmaier equates with the conscience, while slightly tainted by the fall of Adam, is not pulled fully into sin by that fall. The original sin which the entire race inherits does not extinguish the divine spark, mediated to the individual through the conscience. The drama of the human spiritual struggle is that between the body and the spirit for control of the human soul.

8) Hubmaier was here reflecting a long theological tradition which places the blame for human sin on Eve, and through Eve, on all women. Although I do not think that misogyny was at the center of Hubmaier's theology, I found no way to mute this in the text. This kind of symbolism is, of course, unacceptable to the modern reader and the traces of this misogyny need to be encountered with a critical eye. A good place to begin is with Elaine H. Pagels, *Adam, Eve, and the Serpent* (New York: Random House, 1988). A second valuable book is William Beers, *Women and Sacrifice: Male Narcissism and the Psychology of Religion* (Detroit: Wayne State University Press, 1992).

9) Medical wisdom of that time held that cold beverages were unhealthy, causing a disequilibrium in body temperature.

10) If there is in Hubmaier a doctrine of "total depravity," where the person is fallen into sin in body, soul and spirit, it is in the case of one who has sinned "against the Holy Spirit." It should be noted, however, that one enters such a state only after prolonged and repeated denial of the prodding of the conscience. It is not an inherited state passed on from Adam. Therefore, for Hubmaier, the pangs of conscience are also a sign of hope for salvation.

11) Hubmaier saw the tripartite anthropology as the Hebrew/Christian alternative to the dualism of Greek philosophy, which, especially through Aristotle, was very influential on the church's systematic theology.

12) Hubmaier rejects the idea that the benefits of Christ's work are "limited" to the elect only. Rather, humanity as a whole gained an

awakening of the soul to knowledge of good and evil because of the restoration which is worked through Christ. However, the person must, soul and spirit united, act on this knowledge of good and evil to follow what is right.

13) Hubmaier wanted to emphasize as strongly as he could that although human beings do have free will and can choose good or evil, this is no cause for pride or boasting. Humans only have this free will because God gave it to them in the first place. There would be no knowledge of good and evil apart from the redemptive work of Christ. And this "power" is really more a weakness than a strength.

14) Hubmaier strongly believed that coercion in matters of faith was improper to the nature of God. And if it is improper for God, it is certainly improper for human beings. This was the spiritual basis for Hubmaier's teaching on religious liberty.

15) In Hubmaier's view, only a spiritual reconstruction of the body or flesh could restore it to its rightful place in the economy of salvation.

Part II: South German and Austrian Anabaptism

1) Although Hut shared in a pervasive and general anticlerical prejudice, this particular wording was taken directly from Thomas Müntzer's pamphlet against Luther, "The most amply called-for defence and answer to the unspiritual soft-living flesh at Wittenberg."

2) A very primary motivation in Hut's thinking was that of apocalyptic upheaval which would soon occur. As such, his writings can be read as part of the heritage of apocalyptic spiritual literature, written to comfort those who are in the midst of crisis, especially persecution for their beliefs.

3) Hut believed that God's mercy and the gospel itself were especially for the common people, the poor.

4) As will be seen, Hut consciously used the genitive form, the gospel "of" all creatures.

5) Hut interpreted the metaphor of the church as the body of Christ very physically and literally.

6) For Hut, the gospel takes on the explicit character of a secret, revolutionary doctrine. This can also be seen in his preferred mode of

baptism. The leader dipped a finger in water and made the sign of the Taw on the forehead of the baptisand.

7) Hut here meant that his contemporaries could learn the will of God from these biblical rituals. There is no evidence that Hut encouraged his followers to keep the Levitical rituals in actual practice. However, one group of Anabaptists in Silesia, whose leaders, Oswald Glaidt and Andreas Fischer, were immediate disciples of Hut, did develop a practice of Sabbath (Saturday) worship and in other ways demonstrated clear affection for Jewish and Hebrew customs.

8) That the creatures and our daily work are "scripture" meant for Hut that even those who cannot read, the common people, could learn and know the will of God as easily and clearly as the biblical scholar. The common people are therefore spiritually elevated and their dependence on the "soft-living scholars" is broken. At times Hut seems to imply, in fact, that the written Bible itself is unnecessary.

9) Hut taught that the justification received by belief (Luther's *Sola Fide*) was only a temporary justification. It endured only until a person was called upon to suffer. Water baptism was for Hut, in fact, mainly seen as a symbol of acceptance of the coming "baptism" of suffering. Once the suffering begins, the person is then justified by accepting the suffering. It is clear that, for Hut, this suffering included the internal anguish of anxiety, the mystical "dark night of the soul." But in his context, talk about suffering primarily meant a literal suffering "unto death," to be drowned or burned at the stake.

10) In this passage Hut describes his own experience of spiritual struggle, giving voice to the element of "mystical agony" typical of South German Anabaptist spirituality.

11) It was not for lack of learning, as was perhaps at least partially the case with Hans Hut, that Leonard Schiemer rejected the scholastic theology of his time. He saw that theological argument brought people no closer to a true knowledge of God, which is found in a disciplined life of following Christ.

12) Schiemer, like Hut, saw true Christian teaching as a secret which has been revealed to a small group. This is an interesting counterpoint to another theme in their writings, that the gospel is intended for the common people, for the masses. When they write of the secret nature of the gospel, they usually have in mind that it is being kept secret

287

from the rulers, the educated and the wealthy of society. The common person, on the other hand, can easily grasp it.

13) It was Schiemer's intention here to argue as strongly as possible against the Reformation doctrine of bondage of the will and the corollary doctrine of limited grace and predestination. Christian living was, in Schiemer's view, a volitional matter open to all people, perhaps not even limited to those within Christendom.

14) This willful striving against the Holy Spirit is what Balthasar Hubmaier called "sinning against the Holy Spirit." It is the only sin which cannot be forgiven, because if it happens time and again, the prompting of conscience will cease.

15) Schiemer here was probably speaking of such people as Ludwig Hätzer and Hans Bünderlin. These were inquiring young men, very interested in religious reform. They showed promise as leaders and for a time were both close associates of Hans Denck. But their inquiries took them in directions which Schiemer would have seen as error. Hätzer did die a martyr, but more for his Unitarian views than for his Anabaptist affiliations. Bünderlin left the Anabaptists altogether.

16) This typifies the element of spiritual agony present in the spiritual counsel of South German and Austrian Anabaptism.

17) Schiemer's play on the word *lord*, juxtaposing the lordship of Christ with that of secular authority, is a clear indication that Schiemer conceived of the gospel as oppositional in relation to secular authority.

18) This writing shows an obvious dependence on Hans Hut's writing and teaching on baptism.

19) Although the term *Anabaptist*, which means "re-baptized," has now come into common usage, many early Anabaptists strenuously resisted this as a self-designation for various reasons. Schiemer here said that it gives too much credence to infant baptism to call adult believer's baptism "a second baptism."

20) Although Schlaffer repeats much of Hans Hut's teaching on the gospel of all creatures, and even calls the creatures "a scripture," he did not use this to denigrate the importance of the written Bible, as Hut did.

21) For Schlaffer, the vision of life in the kingdom of Christ gives vent to a strong egalitarian urge.

22) While Schlaffer's understanding of the gospel and its egalitarian consequences was certainly anathema to a hierarchically constructed society, it is clear that he harbored no intentions of violent, revolutionary actions, as might have been in the mind of Hans Hut.

23) The concern for purity among the community of believers was a spiritual desire to create a "bride worthy of Christ." But it also was a practical desire to exclude from among them all who would give them a bad name and create popular assent for their continued persecution.

24) Denck began his treatise on love with an explication of courtly love. This was very unusual among Anabaptist writers, who would be more likely to spurn any intrusion of worldly understanding into the spiritual arena.

25) More than any other Anabaptist, Denck remained in direct contact and conversation with Jewish rabbis. He probably initiated such contact to learn better the fine points of Hebrew language for a translation of the prophets on which he was working. But the conversations continued, and this had a direct effect on this writing, in which Denck repeatedly answers for his teachings not to the criticisms of other Christian reformers but to rabbinical criticism.

26) Like Balthasar Hubmaier, Denck insisted that coercion in matters of faith was contrary not only to God's will, but to God's very nature.

27) In Denck's view, it was in the bringing together of seeming spiritual contradictions, of "*paradoxa*," that a person gained deeper understanding of spiritual truth.

28) As a defense of the Trinity, this is a rather meager section. At best, Denck seemed to imply that "*paradoxa*" exist within the Godhead and this is dealt with by reference to God's triune nature. It must be said, however, that the idea of the Trinity did not hold much fascination for Denck. It is possible that, had he not died of the plague, Denck would have moved in the same Unitarian direction as did his associate and fellow translator of the Hebrew prophets, Ludwig Hätzer (see note 15 above).

NOTES

Part III: Hutterian Anabaptism

1) A foundational urge toward communism among the Hutterians was the elimination of poverty. In many respects, the Hutterian Bruderhof must be seen as the most developed social consequence of that which was set in motion during the German peasants' revolts in the early Reformation years.

2) This rejection of the distinction between "mine" and "thine" has a long history in European religious radicalism, dating back at least to Joachim of Fiore and his vision of the Third Age of the Spirit.

3) Walpot saw many of the prophecies and commandment of Israel as pertaining directly to his own group.

4) Capital accumulation was seen by Walpot as directly contrary to Christian economics. Wealth was to be used by everyone in meeting immediate needs. It was not to be hoarded or saved up.

5) Like all communal movements, the Hutterians had to deal with those who were attracted to them by the prospect of economic gain or a "free lunch," but who were unwilling to work hard for the communal good. Walpot wasted little sympathy on such people.

6) Walpot's writing made many covert or veiled references to other Anabaptists who did not follow the Hutterians in the way of communistic economic practices. Walpot interpreted this as due to lack of true faith.

7) This passage typifies the egalitarian concern in Hutterian spiritual understanding.

8) This was directed at least partially toward the practices of various Mendicant orders who went begging through the countryside and to whom, as a spiritual good deed, people gave gifts of various sorts.

9) As with Hans Hut, the metaphor of the church as a body took on a very physical and literal meaning in Hutterian society. Another favorite metaphor was that of the loaf of bread which, although made up of individual grains, is a new thing, a new creation, different from the simple aggregate of its ingredients.

10) Walpot repeatedly insisted that Hutterian communistic economic

practices were not at all a deviation, but were the logical conclusion of Christian doctrine as a whole.

11) Wealth as excrement has surfaced in contemporary psychoanalytical literature as well.

12) Especially when Walpot spoke of "false brothers," he was referring to Anabaptists who rejected Hutterian communism. For Walpot, economic communism was clearly a watershed issue. Whether or not one could endure it was for him a very crystalline spiritual indicator.

13) The Hutterians positively discouraged seekers from becoming members. They did this not for elitist reasons but to avoid conflict if a member wanted to leave. Once members turned their goods over to the communal use, they were gone. Such persons were given very little in return if they later decided to leave the community. Discouraging converts during the initiation process was a way of testing them and making it very clear that they surrendered their possessions of their own free will.

14) The largest majority of those joining the Hutterians did not bring any wealth with them at all. They were refugees who had to leave almost all they owned behind. Nevertheless, Walpot and other leaders were often accused in such matters and asked to give account for what happened to the wealth of those few converts who did bring something with them.

15) Walpot maintained that communal existence was the highest point of true human existence and what separated humans from animals. This may have been in reply to those who commonly likened the Bruderhof to a beehive or an ant hill.

16) The reference is to a mystical theological treatise of medieval origin which was very influential on Martin Luther as well as on various spiritualist writers of Walpot's time.

Part IV: Dutch Anabaptism

1) Dirk Philips was writing here particularly against "spiritualizing" tendencies within the Anabaptist movement. Certain leaders, such as Adam Pastor and David Joris, had begun to make extreme distinctions between "externals" and "internal essence" in their teachings, placing even such things as baptism and the Lord's Supper in the category

of externals. The claim was that a true and spiritual Christian, who understood the spiritual essence of the externals, could easily neglect or even reject these outward ceremonial observances. Dirk Philips discerned in this, and not without some measure of hard evidence, an antinomian tendency. Thus he set himself against it.

2) Even a stern man like Peter Walpot only referred to his Anabaptist opponents as "false brothers." The severe rhetoric of Dirk Philips was a result of his time and place, but is an indicator of his personality and character as well.

3) Dirk Philips was emphasizing here the volitional, cooperative synergism through which human beings come to salvation—an implicit rejection of bondage of the will and predestination.

4) The reference this early in the writing to the biblical book of Revelation shows how closely apocalyptic materials were studied among the Dutch Anabaptists. To be noted, however, is the fact that Dirk Philips used this passage in a manner totally divested of apocalyptic or chiliastic intent.

5) Dirk Philips agreed with the spiritualizers that the internal essence or meaning of the sacraments was most important. But he disagreed that the internal essence gave license to neglect the outward observance of these symbols. This is very significant, because it was the practice of these externals, particularly adult baptism, which placed Anabaptists outside of the secular law and was the basis for the secular law to hunt and punish them. Therefore, when Dirk Philips referred to the spiritualizers as those who "hate the cross of Christ," he was referring to the fact that they were able to escape persecution by their abjuring of these rites.

6) In various debates in which Dirk Philips took part with the spiritualizers, who were often well-educated and skillful opponents, they made him out to be a kind of dense and thick-headed literalist. This was the mocking to which he referred in this passage.

7) Because of their insistence on holy living as integral to the Christian faith, the Anabaptists were often accused of seeking salvation through their works.

8) One justification for infant baptism was that it washed away original sin. Therefore, Anabaptists, who rejected infant baptism, were often

accused of rejecting the doctrine of original sin. Dirk Philips was here stating in very certain terms that he did not reject the doctrine of original sin.

9) As this passage illustrates, for the Anabaptists discipleship, the following of Christ or imitation of Christ in daily living, was a very central focus of their spirituality. It was not the basis of their salvation, nor was it simply a slavish kind of obedience of a master/servant relationship. It was, rather, the very vehicle through which the human being became a participant in the divine nature.

10) The concept of restitution was much discussed in Dutch Anabaptist circles. The urgency of this issue was a result of the chiliastic and apocalyptic strain running through their religious thinking. The idea that a literal kingdom of Christ would be instituted on earth led naturally into speculation as to what this kingdom would be like. From there it was a short step, once convinced that it is God's will, to attempting to establish this kingdom, by force if necessary. Thus, the fanatical Münsterite Anabaptists, led by John of Leiden, consciously tried to model their "kingdom" after their vision of a restored kingdom of David. The result was a tragic/comic pageant which, after many months of the city being placed under siege and embargo, ended in terrible excesses, including cannibalism. Yet despite this, the theme of an expected restitution or restoration remained strong.

In this writing, Dirk Philips was attempting to prove that all that is to be restored has already been restored, spiritually speaking, in Jesus Christ. Therefore, no restitution of a social or political nature is to be expected. While his sometimes belabored efforts to wring symbols and types of Christ out of the literature of the Hebrew Bible will strike many modern readers as strange, it was a common form of exegesis in his time and was a necessary step in directing the religious life of Dutch Anabaptists toward a more spiritual understanding of these prophecies and biblical, archetypal images.

11) To note here is Dirk Philips's emphasis on the passive element of waiting.

12) The Christian life was here elevated to the highest spiritual level possible, that of direct participation in the divine nature.

13) One of the excesses that occurred in Münsterite and other circles which focused on the Davidic restoration was the acceptance of polygamy or plural marriages.

14) Dirk Philips was here expressing his wider view of human history, which is a drama of 1) God electing, 2) a period of faithfulness, 3) a falling away into idolatry, and 4) a renewal of the Spirit among a remnant.

15) The reference here is to one of Dirk Philips's previous writings, "A Beautiful and True Explanation and Interpretation of the Tabernacle of Moses."

16) One reaction to the disillusionment of failed chiliasm is to fall prey to all manner of strange activities which, by denial of the disappointment, perpetuate the hope. In German Anabaptism, this is perhaps best illustrated by Augustine Bader and his circle in Ulm after the failure of Hans Hut's prophecies. They received some sort of "oracle," a vision of Moses, which instructed them to manufacture a golden scepter, crown and other royal objects in preparation for the coming of the Messiah (who, further revelations told them, was Bader's own infant son). Poor as mice, they still managed to do this, and to engage in rather weird and obscure rituals in honor of the child. Whether in writing this passage Dirk Philips had these activities in mind or other such activities closer to home, his warning here against such lunacies was certain.

17) Legitimation of the right to leadership among the Anabaptists was an ongoing problem. Although they very quickly developed a system of recognized leaders, and even a bishopric, the mechanism in the first generation was that of charismatic authority. In times of uncertainty and persecution, this would lead to a proliferation of divisions and splinter groups. That which the historian, working with an interpretive theory and hindsight, might view as a short-lived and inconsequential deviation, might seem as a considerably more chaotic situation to those directly involved. The burden of holding this chaos together fell directly on the shoulders of leaders such as Dirk Philips, which helps to account for his heightened rhetoric at that point.

18) The immediate reference here was to the papal office. But there is an obvious subtextual reference to the pomp of the Münsterite "kingdom" as well.

19) It is significant to note in this passage the use of Ezra as a legitimation for enforcing the notion of Anabaptist separatism. Dirk Philips saw himself in a similar position, attempting to gather the "true"

remnant, those who would rebuild God's own temple, from among those who claimed legitimacy, yet were, in his view, unfaithful and unworthy of the task.

20) This passage gives us precious insight into the way in which Dirk Philips saw himself and his followers perceived by the wider society.

21) Some religious radicals, Anabaptists and others, resorted to armed defense against secular authorities seeking their arrest. Dirk Philips definitely thought that these people were wrong in such action. Yet the passage contains an undercurrent of sympathy, even as it rejects their position.

Select Bibliography

Sources Used for Translation

Ausbund, das ist: Etliche schöne Christliche Lieder (Lancaster: Verlag von den Amischen Gemeinden, 1984).

Glaubenszeugnisse oberdeutscher Taufgesinnter, Band I. L. Müller. ed. (Leipzig: M. Heinsius Nachfolger, 1938).

Glaubenszeugnisse oberdeutscher Taufgesinnter, Band II. R. Friedmann, ed. (Gütersloh: Güterloher Verlaghaus Gerd Mohn, 1967).

Philips, Dirk, *Enchiridion oft Hantboecxken van de Christelijke Leere ende Religion*. (n.p., 1564).

Quellen zur Geschichte der Täufer in der Schweiz, Band I. Muralt/Schmid, eds. (Zürich: S. Hirzel Verlag, 1952).

Quellen zur Geschichte der Täufer VI: Hans Denck Schriften. Baring/ Fellmann, eds. (Gütersloh: C. Bertelsmann Verlag, 1959).

Quellen zur Geschichte der Täufer IX: Balthasar Hubmaier Schriften. Westin/Bergsten, eds. (Gütersloh: Güterloher Verlaghaus Gerd Mohn, 1962).

Simons, Menno *Opera omnia theologica, of alle de godtgeleerde wercken*. (Amsterdam, 1681).

Related Readings in English

Introduction

Armour, Rollin, *Anabaptist Baptism* (Scottdale: Herald Press, 1966).

Beachy, Alvin J., *The Concept of Grace in the Radical Reformation* (Nieuwkoop: De Graaf, 1977).

SELECT BIBLIOGRAPHY

Cohn, Norman, *The Pursuit of the Millennium* (New York: Harper and Row, 1961).

Davis, Kenneth R., "Anabaptism and Ascetic Holiness," in Stayer/Packull, eds., *The Anabaptists and Thomas Müntzer* (Dubuque/Toronto: Kendall/Hunt Publishing Company, 1980), pp. 54–60.

Davis, Kenneth R., "Anabaptism as a Charismatic Movement," *Mennonite Quarterly Review* 53 (1979), pp. 219–34.

Dyck, Cornelius J., "Life of the Spirit in Anabaptism," *Mennonite Quarterly Review* 47 (1973), pp. 309–26.

Erb, Paul C., "Anabaptist Spiritualist," in Frank C. Senn, ed., *Protestant Spiritual Traditions* (New York: Paulist Press, 1986), pp. 80–124.

Friedmann, Robert, "The Doctrine of the Two Worlds," in Stayer/Packull, eds., *The Anabaptists and Thomas Müntzer* (Dubuque/Toronto: Kendall/Hunt Publishing Company, 1980), pp. 23–27.

_____ , *Mennonite Piety Through the Centuries* (Goshen: Mennonite Historical Society, 1949).

_____ , *The Theology of Anabaptism* (Scottdale: Herald Press, 1973).

George, Timothy, "Early Anabaptist Spirituality in the Low Countries," *Mennonite Quarterly Review* 62 (1988), pp. 257–75.

Jones, Rufus M., *Spiritual Reformers in the 16th and 17th Centuries* (New York: Macmillan, 1914).

Klaassen, Walter, *Anabaptism: Neither Catholic Nor Protestant* (Waterloo: Conrad Press, 1973).

Littell, Franklin H., *The Anabaptist View of the Church* (Boston: Beacon Press, 1958).

Martin, Dennis D., "Catholic Spirituality and Anabaptist and Mennonite Discipleship," *Mennonite Quarterly Review* 62 (1988), pp. 5–25.

Stayer, James M., *Anabaptists and the Sword* (Lawrence: Coronado Press, 2d ed., 1976).

Van Braght, Thieleman J., *The Bloody Theater or Martyrs Mirror of the Defenseless Christians* (Scottdale: Herald Press, 1950).

SELECT BIBLIOGRAPHY

Williams, George Huntston, *The Radical Reformation* (Kirksville: Six-teenth Century Journal Publishers, 3d rev. ed., 1992).

Part I: Swiss Anabaptism

Blanke, Fritz, *Brothers in Christ* (Scottdale: Herald Press, 1961).

Haas, Martin, "Michael Sattler: On the Way to Anabaptist Separa-tion," in Goertz, ed., *Profiles of Radical Reformers* (Scottdale: Herald Press, 1982), pp. 132–43.

————, "The Path of the Anabaptists into Separation: The Interde-pendence of Theology and Social Behavior," in Stayer/Packull, eds., *The Anabaptists and Thomas Müntzer* (Dubuque/Toronto: Kendall/Hunt Publishing Company, 1980), pp. 72–84.

Stayer, James M., "Wilhelm Reublin: A Picaresque Journey Through Early Anabaptism," in Goertz, ed., *Profiles of Radical Reformers* (Scott-dale: Herald Press, 1982), pp. 107–17.

————, "The Swiss Brethren: An Exercise in Historical Reflection," *Church History* 47 (1978), pp. 174–95.

Part II: South German and Austrian Anabaptism

Boyd, Stephen B., "Community as Sacrament in the Theology of Hans Schlaffer," in Walter Klaassen, ed., *Anabaptism Revisited* (Scottdale: Herald Press, 1992), pp. 50–64.

Goertz, Hans-Jürgen, "The Mystic with the Hammer: Thomas Müntz-er's Theological Basis for Revolution," in Stayer/Packull, eds., *The Anabaptists and Thomas Müntzer* (Dubuque/Toronto: Kendall/Hunt Publishing Company, 1980), pp. 118–32.

Gritsch, Eric, "Thomas Müntzer and the Origins of Protestant Spiri-tualism," *Mennonite Quarterly Review* 37 (1963), pp. 172–94.

Liechty, Daniel, *Andreas Fischer and the Sabbatarian Anabaptists* (Scott-dale: Herald Press, 1988).

Mecenseffy, Grete, "The Origins of Upper Austrian Anabaptism," in Stayer/Packull, eds., *The Anabaptists and Thomas Müntzer* (Dubuque/Toronto: Kendall/Hunt Publishing Company, 1980), pp. 152–53.

Ozment, Steven E., *Mysticism and Dissent* (New Haven: Yale University Press, 1973).

Packull, Werner O., *Mysticism and the Early South German-Austrian Anabaptist Movement 1525–1531* (Scottdale: Herald Press, 1977).

Seebass, Gottfried, "Hans Hut: The Suffering Avenger," in Goertz, ed., *Profiles of Radical Reformers* (Scottdale: Herald Press, 1982), pp. 54–61.

Windhorst, Christof, "Balthasar Hubmaier: Professor, Preacher, Politician," in Goertz, ed., *Profiles of Radical Reformers* (Scottdale: Herald Press, 1982), pp. 144–57.

Part III: Hutterian Anabaptism

Friedmann, Robert, *Hutterite Studies* (Goshen: Mennonite Historical Society, 1961).

Gross, Leonard, "Jakob Hutter: A Christian Communist," in Goertz, ed., *Profiles of Radical Reformers* (Scottdale: Herald Press, 1982), pp. 158–67.

―――――, *The Golden Years of the Hutterites* (Scottdale: Herald Press, 1980).

Hostetler, John A., *Hutterite Society* (Baltimore: Johns Hopkins University Press, 1974).

Klassen, Peter J., *The Economics of Anabaptism* (London: Mouton, 1964).

Williams, George H., "Popularized German Mysticism as a Factor in the Rise of Anabaptist Communism," in Müller/Zeller, eds., *Glaube, Geist, Geschichte* (Leiden: E.J.Brill, 1967), pp. 290–312.

Part IV: Dutch Anabaptism

Deppermann, Klaus, "Melchior Hoffman: Contradictions Between Lutheran Loyalty to Government and Apocalyptic Dreams," in Goertz, ed., *Profiles of Radical Reformers* (Scottdale: Herald Press, 1982), pp. 178–90.

Hillerbrand, Hans J., "Menno Simons: Sixteenth Century Reformer," *Church History* 31 (1962), pp. 387–99.

Horst, Irvin B., "Menno Simons: The New Man in Community," in

SELECT BIBLIOGRAPHY

Goertz, ed., *Profiles of Radical Reformers* (Scottdale: Herald Press, 1982), pp. 203–13.

Keeney, William E., *The Development of Dutch Anabaptist Thought and Practice from 1539–1564* (Nieuwkoop: De Graaf, 1968).

Krahn, Cornelius, *Dutch Anabaptism* (Scottdale: Herald Press, 1981).

Kuhler, W. J., "Anabaptism in the Netherlands," in Stayer/Packull, eds., *The Anabaptists and Thomas Müntzer* (Dubuque/Toronto: Kendall/Hunt Publishing Company, 1980), pp. 92–104.

Index

Aaron, 237

Abraham, 103, 181, 209, 216, 222–28 *passim*

Adam, 24–28, 32, 34, 36, 37, 152, 221, 222, 223

Anabaptism: Austrian Anabaptism, 5; Dutch Anabaptism, 7; historical origins, 1–8; life of discipleship, 9–10; South German Anabaptism, 5; spirituality of, 8–14; Swiss Anabaptism, 2, 4, 5; *see also* specific topics, e.g.: Baptism; Community

Annelein of Freiberg, 56; hymn by, 56–58

Antichrist, 121, 223, 224, 226, 241

Anticlericalism, 1, 9

Aristotle, 30, 83

Asceticism, 4–5

Augustine, 195

Ausbund, 41; selections from, 41–59

Baptism, 2, 17, 116, 117; of blood, 63, 96, 108; of Christ, 78, 206; community and, 169–70; Hut on, 64–81; infant baptism, 2, 4, 5, 17, 81, 96, 118–19; obedience to father as, 95; salvation and, 108; Schiemer on, 95–97; of the Spirit, 63, 95, 108; Walpot on, 169; of water, 63, 95–96, 107–08

Beatitudes, 126–27

Blaurock, George, 2–3, 5, 45; hymns by, 46–53

Brethren of the Common Life, 7

"Bruderhof" system of economic community, 137–38

Bucer, Martin, 7

Bünderlin, Hans, 6, 7

Calvin, John, 2

Capito, Wolfgang, 7

Christ, 35–37; as act of grace, 85, 90–93; baptism of, 78, 206; community, 144–96 *passim*; love and, 113–14; on marriage, 222–23; mystical union of believer with, 11, 12–13; new birth through, 201–18 *passim*; spiritual restitution through, 218–46 *passim*; as witness, 104–09

Circumcision, 116, 211–12, 229

Clement, 194–95

Clergy, 1, 9

Communism, 13, 138

301

INDEX

Community, 12–14; baptism and, 169–70; Walpot on, 138–96
Contemplative Life (Philo), 194
Cross: as grace, 92–93; mysticism of the, 5, 63

David, 235–36
Denck, Hans, 5–6, 7, 8, 63, 98, 111–12; "Concerning True Love," 112–21; "Divine Order and the Work of His Creatures," 121–34

Eck, Johannes, 20
Erasmus, 4
Esau, 227
Eucharist, 207, 247; community and, 170

Franck, Sebastian, 12
Free will, 4, 8, 10–11; Denck on, 129–31; Hubmaier on, 21–28

German Theology, 5, 6, 191, 195–96
Glaidt, Oswaldt, 6, 82
God: guiltlessness of God against false accusers, 131–32; immediacy of human relationship with, 9; Trinity, 132; *see also* Christ
Grace, 4, 8, 213; cross as, 92–93; Schiemer on, 83–95
Grebel, Conrad, 2, 3, 4, 17

Hell, 125–26
Hetzer, Ludwig, 3
Hofmann, Melchior, 7–8, 199

Hubmaier, Balthasar, 4, 5, 20–21, 82, 111; "Concerning Freedom of the Will," 21–38; "A Short Meditation on the Lord's Prayer," 38–40
Hut, Hans, 5, 6, 63–64, 82, 98, 111; gospel of all creatures, 6, 63–64, 67–72; "On the Mystery of Baptism," 64–81; "seven judgments of God," 63
Hutter, Jacob, 137
Hutterians, 6, 13, 63, 273

Idolatry, 133–34
Isaac, 103, 216, 224, 226, 228

Jacob, 103, 216, 224, 227–28
James, 94–95, 203
Jereboam, 240–41
Jesus Christ. *See* Christ
John, 93–94, 177–78, 183, 202–03, 217–18
John Chrysostomus, 195
John the Baptist, 78, 85, 117, 120, 143, 206, 226
Joseph, 228
Justification, 11, 111, 115

Karlstadt, Andreas Bodenstein von, 7

Life of Prayer (Philo), 194
Lord's Prayer: community and, 146–47; Hubmaier, 38–40
Lord's Supper. *See* Eucharist
Love: Denck on, 112–21; Walpot on, 159–60, 175–84
Luther, Martin, 2, 5, 6, 7, 98

INDEX

Lutheranism, 7
Luyken, Jan, 272

Mantz, Felix, 2, 3, 4, 17–18;
"Letter from Prison," 18–19;
poetic rendering of letter of,
41–45
Marpeck, Pilgram, 7
Marriage, 222–23, 242
Martyrdom, 11, 12
Martyrs Mirror, The, 273
Melchizedek, 224–25
Melchiorites, 8
Modern Devotion, 7
Moses, 23, 100, 182, 214, 216,
219, 221, 222, 231, 232; as
conduit of grace, 85; love
versus justice, 114;
Tabernacle of, 233
Münster, tragedy of (1534–1535),
8, 247
Müntzer, Thomas, 5, 6, 63, 111;
mysticism of the cross, 5, 63

Noah, 214, 223

Original sin, 10, 11, 24–25, 26,
30, 32, 34, 221

Pacifism, 63
Passover, 237
Paul, 23–31 *passim,* 64, 65, 86, 95,
119, 125, 196, 202, 210–20
passim, 244, 250, 253, 254,
257, 260, 267; baptism, 73,
78; children as symbol, 205;
Christ, 104–05; church as
body of Christ, 12;
circumcision, 211–12;

community, 163–75 *passim,*
184–87 *passim;* gospel of all
creatures, 68, 69, 100–01,
102; greed, 193; schisms, 224;
Scriptures, 103; suffering,
74, 94
Pentecost, 237
Peter, 26, 64, 77, 152, 186, 211,
218; baptism, 95, 210;
community, 164, 176, 187;
new birth, 25, 202; suffering
of Christ, 104
Philips, Dirk, 8, 199; "Concerning
Spiritual Restitution,"
218–46; "Concerning the
New Birth and the New
Creature," 200–18
Philips, Obbe, 8, 199
Philo, 194
Predestination, 123–24; *see also*
Free will
Private property, 13, 137, 145–46,
191; *see also* Community
Psalms: Twenty-fifth Psalm,
Simons on, 248–72

Rebecca, 226
Reformation, 2
Reformed Church, 8
Riedemann, Peter, 137

Sacramentarianism, 247
Salvation, 1, 10, 108, 113–14, 117
Samson, 234–35
Sanctification, 11
Sattler, Michael, 7, 9, 53–54;
hymns by 54–56
Schiemer, Leonhard, 6, 82, 98;
"Three Kinds of Baptism,"

303

INDEX

95–97; "Three Kinds of Grace Found in the Scriptures," 83–95

Schlaffer, Hans, 6, 98; "Instruction on Beginning a True Christian Life," 99–110; "Two Prayers," 109–10

Schleitheim Confession of 1527, 5, 53–54

Schwenckfeld, Caspar, 7

Scriptures, 103–04; three kinds of baptism in, 95–96; three kinds of grace in, 83–95

Simons, Menno, 8, 199, 247–48; "A Meditation on the Twenty-fifth Psalm," 248–72

Sin, 32–34, 125, 127–28, 221; need to sin, 124; original sin, 10, 11, 24–25, 26–30, 32, 34, 221

Sodom and Gomorrah, 225, 258

Solomon, 236, 239, 241, 242

Spiritualists, 7

Swiss Confederation, 4

Tabernacles, 237–38

Theologia Deutsch, 5, 6

Trinity, 132

Vadian, 4

Walpot, Peter, 137–38; "True Yieldedness and the Christian Community of Goods," 138–96

Will: free will, 4, 8, 10–11, 21–28, 129–31; reuniting of God's will and human will, 128–29; separation of God's will from human will, 127–28

Willems, Dirk, 273–74

Zwingli, Ulrich, 2, 3, 4, 17

Other Volumes in this Series

Julian of Norwich • SHOWINGS

Jacob Boehme • THE WAY TO CHRIST

Nahman of Bratslav • THE TALES

Gregory of Nyssa • THE LIFE OF MOSES

Bonaventure • THE SOUL'S JOURNEY INTO GOD, THE TREE OF LIFE, AND THE
LIFE OF ST. FRANCIS

William Law • A SERIOUS CALL TO DEVOUT AND HOLY LIFE, AND THE SPIRIT
OF LOVE

Abraham Isaac Kook • THE LIGHTS OF PENITENCE, LIGHTS OF HOLINESS, THE
MORAL PRINCIPLES, ESSAYS, AND POEMS

Ibn 'Ata' Illah • THE BOOK OF WISDOM and Kwaja Abdullah

Ansari • INTIMATE CONVERSATIONS

Johann Arndt • TRUE CHRISTIANITY

Richard of St. Victor • THE TWELVE PATRIARCHS, THE MYSTICAL ARK, AND
BOOK THREE OF THE TRINITY

Origen • AN EXHORTATION TO MARTYRDOM, PRAYER, AND SELECTED WORKS

Catherine of Genoa • PURGATION AND PURGATORY, THE SPIRITUAL DIALOGUE

Native North American Spirituality of the Eastern Woodlands • SACRED
MYTHS, DREAMS, VISIONS, SPEECHES, HEALING FORMULAS, RITUALS AND
CEREMONIALS

Teresa of Avila • THE INTERIOR CASTLE

Apocalyptic Spirituality • TREATISES AND LETTERS OF LACTANTIUS, ADSO OF
MONTIER-EN-DER, JOACHIM OF FIORE, THE FRANCISCAN SPIRITUALS,
SAVONAROLA

Athanasius • THE LIFE OF ANTONY, A LETTER TO MARCELLINUS

Catherine of Siena • THE DIALOGUE

Sharafuddin Maneri • THE HUNDRED LETTERS

Martin Luther • THEOLOGIA GERMANICA

Native Mesoamerican Spirituality • ANCIENT MYTHS, DISCOURSES, STORIES,
DOCTRINES, HYMNS, POEMS FROM THE AZTEC, YUCATEC, QUICHE-MAYA AND
OTHER SACRED TRADITIONS

Symeon the New Theologian • THE DISCOURSES

Ibn Al'-Arabi • THE BEZELS OF WISDOM

Hadewijch • THE COMPLETE WORKS

Philo of Alexandria • THE CONTEMPLATIVE LIFE, THE GIANTS, AND SELECTIONS

George Herbert • THE COUNTRY PARSON, THE TEMPLE

Unknown • THE CLOUD OF UNKNOWING

John and Charles Wesley • SELECTED WRITINGS AND HYMNS

Meister Eckhart • THE ESSENTIAL SERMONS, COMMENTARIES, TREATISES AND
DEFENSE

Francisco de Osuna • THE THIRD SPIRITUAL ALPHABET

Jacopone da Todi • THE LAUDS

Fakhruddin 'Iraqi • DIVINE FLASHES

Menahem Nahum of Chernobyl • THE LIGHT OF THE EYES
Early Dominicans • SELECTED WRITINGS
John Climacus • THE LADDER OF DIVINE ASCENT
Francis and Clare • THE COMPLETE WORKS
Gregory Palamas • THE TRIADS
Pietists • SELECTED WRITINGS
The Shakers • TWO CENTURIES OF SPIRITUAL REFLECTION
Zohar • THE BOOK OF ENLIGHTENMENT
Luis de León • THE NAMES OF CHRIST
Quaker Spirituality • SELECTED WRITINGS
Emanuel Swedenborg • THE UNIVERSAL HUMAN AND SOUL-BODY
    INTERACTION
Augustine of Hippo • SELECTED WRITINGS
Safed Spirituality • RULES OF MYSTICAL PIETY, THE BEGINNING OF WISDOM
Maximus Confessor • SELECTED WRITINGS
John Cassian • CONFERENCES
Johannes Tauler • SERMONS
John Ruusbroec • THE SPIRITUAL ESPOUSALS AND OTHER WORKS
Ibn 'Abbād of Ronda • LETTERS ON THE SŪFĪ PATH
Angelus Silesius • THE CHERUBINIC WANDERER
The Early Kabbalah •
Meister Eckhart • TEACHER AND PREACHER
John of the Cross • SELECTED WRITINGS
Pseudo-Dionysius • THE COMPLETE WORKS
Bernard of Clairvaux • SELECTED WORKS
Devotio Moderna • BASIC WRITINGS
The Pursuit of Wisdom • AND OTHER WORKS BY THE AUTHOR OF THE CLOUD
    OF UNKNOWING
Richard Rolle • THE ENGLISH WRITINGS
Francis de Sales, Jane de Chantal • LETTERS OF SPIRITUAL DIRECTION
Albert and Thomas • SELECTED WRITINGS
Robert Bellarmine • SPIRITUAL WRITINGS
Nicodemos of the Holy Mountain • A HANDBOOK OF SPIRITUAL COUNSEL
Henry Suso • THE EXEMPLAR, WITH TWO GERMAN SERMONS
Bérulle and the French School • SELECTED WRITINGS
The Talmud • SELECTED WRITINGS
Ephrem the Syrian • HYMNS
Hildegard of Bingen • SCIVIAS
Birgitta of Sweden • LIFE AND SELECTED REVELATIONS
John Donne • SELECTIONS FROM *DIVINE POEMS*, SERMONS, *DEVOTIONS AND
    PRAYERS*
Jeremy Taylor • SELECTED WORKS
Walter Hilton • *SCALE OF PERFECTION*
Ignatius of Loyola • *SPIRITUAL EXERCISES* AND SELECTED WORKS
Anchoritic Spirituality • *ANCRENE WISSE* AND ASSOCIATED WORKS
Nizam ad-din Awliya • MORALS FOR THE HEART

Pseudo-Macarius • THE FIFTY SPIRITUAL HOMILIES AND THE *GREAT LETTER*
Gertrude of Helfta • *THE HERALD OF DIVINE LOVE*
Angela of Foligno • COMPLETE WORKS
Margaret Ebner • MAJOR WORKS
Marguerite Porete • THE MIRROR OF SIMPLE SOULS
John Henry Newman • SELECTED WRITINGS